VICTORY
365

OTHER BOOKS FROM
FELLOWSHIP OF CHRISTIAN ATHLETES

FELLOWSHIP OF CHRISTIAN ATHLETES

VICTORY 365

DAILY
MOTIVATION
FOR A
CHAMPION'S
HEART

Revell

a division of Baker Publishing Group
Grand Rapids, Michigan

© 2016 by Fellowship of Christian Athletes

Published by Revell
a division of Baker Publishing Group
P.O. Box 6287, Grand Rapids, MI 49516-6287
www.revellbooks.com

Some devotions are adapted from *Heart of a Coach, Heart of a Competitor, Heart of an Athlete, Impact Play,* and *True Competitor.*

Printed in the United States of America

Library of Congress Cataloging-in-Publication Data
Names: Fellowship of Christian Athletes.
Title: Victory 365 : daily motivation for a champion's heart / Fellowship of Christian Athletes.
Description: Grand Rapids : Revell, 2016.
Identifiers: LCCN 2016025334 | ISBN 9780800727420 (pbk.)
Subjects: LCSH: Athletes—Prayers and devotions. | Sports—Religious aspects—Christianity.
Classification: LCC BV4596.A8 V53 2016 | DDC 242/.2—dc23
LC record available at https://lccn.loc.gov/2016025334

Unless otherwise indicated, Scripture quotations are from the Holman Christian Standard Bible®, copyright © 1999, 2000, 2002, 2003, 2009 by Holman Bible Publishers. Used by permission. Holman Christian Standard Bible®, Holman CSB®, and HCSB® are federally registered trademarks of Holman Bible Publishers.

Scripture quotations labeled BSB are from The Holy Bible, Berean Study Bible, BSB. Copyright © 2016 by Bible Hub. Used by permission. All rights reserved worldwide.

Scripture quotations labeled ESV are from The Holy Bible, English Standard Version® (ESV®), copyright © 2001 by Crossway, a publishing ministry of Good News Publishers. Used by permission. All rights reserved. ESV Text Edition: 2011

Scripture quotations labeled Message are from THE MESSAGE. Copyright © by Eugene H. Peterson 1993, 1994, 1995, 1996, 2000, 2001, 2002. Used by permission of NavPress. All rights reserved. Represented by Tyndale House Publishers, Inc.

Scripture quotations labeled NASB are from the New American Standard Bible®, copyright © 1960, 1962, 1963, 1968, 1971, 1972, 1973, 1975, 1977, 1995 by The Lockman Foundation. Used by permission. (www.Lockman.org)

Scripture quotations labeled NIV are from the Holy Bible, New International Version®. NIV®. Copyright © 1973, 1978, 1984, 2011 by Biblica, Inc.™ Used by permission of Zondervan. All rights reserved worldwide. www.zondervan.com

Scripture quotations labeled NKJV are from the New King James Version®. Copyright © 1982 by Thomas Nelson, Inc. Used by permission. All rights reserved.

Scripture quotations labeled NLT are from the Holy Bible, New Living Translation, copyright © 1996, 2004, 2015 by Tyndale House Foundation. Used by permission of Tyndale House Publishers, Inc., Carol Stream, Illinois 60188. All rights reserved.

The devotions for Days 12, 131, 218, 303, and 322 are used by permission of BroadStreet Publishing Group, LLC, 2745 Chicory Rd., Racine, WI 53403.

Notes

1. Charles R. Swindoll, *Fascinating Stories of Forgotten Lives: Rediscovering Some Old Testament Characters* (Nashville: W Pub. Group, 2005), 4.

2. Dana O'Neil, "UConn Never Stopped Believing," ABC News, April 8, 2014, http://abcnews.go.com/Sports/uconn-stopped-believing/story?id=23233300.

3. Alan Goldberg, "Handling Winning & Losing," *Competitive Advantage*, accessed March 7, 2016, https://www.competitivedge.com/handling-winning-losing.

4. Yogi Berra, *The Yogi Book: I Really Didn't Say Everything I Said!* (New York: Workman Pub., 1998), 51.

LETTER FROM THE PRESIDENT

Dear Teammate,

At Fellowship of Christian Athletes, we believe in the power of God's Word to change lives. We have gathered the "best of the best" FCA devotionals to train your heart and mind for the sports journey that lies before you. These 365 devotionals are written from a competitor's mind-set and include Bible verses to help you understand God's perspective on key issues. Our hope is that this book will motivate you to develop a consistent, focused way of spending time with God so you will deepen your understanding of His Word and become a true competitor for Jesus Christ.

Whether you are a coach, athlete, or competitor, you have been given a tremendous platform from which to influence others. We pray that God will use these devotions to transform your life so that you can make an eternal impact for Jesus Christ.

Your Teammate in Christ,

Les Steckel
FCA President/CEO

INTRODUCTION
Training Time

In sports, time-outs give athletes and coaches a chance to strategize for upcoming challenges. Similarly, in life, we need to take time-outs to think about our purpose as members of God's team. FCA is excited to present you with a collection of devotions that will challenge you to play and live for the glory of God. Each devotion is written from an athletic perspective and will encourage you to be more like Christ both on and off the field.

Every morning, set aside a special quiet time to be with God. During this spiritual training time, talk to God and let Him speak to you through the Bible. There are many effective methods that can be used for your daily time with God. One method that we recommend is the PRESS method.

The PRESS Method

Pray

Begin your quiet time by thanking God for the new day, and then ask Him to help you learn from what you're about to read. Prepare yourself by

- clearing your mind and being quiet before the Lord
- asking God to settle your heart
- listening to worship music to prepare your spirit
- asking God to give you a teachable heart

Read

Begin with the devotionals provided in this book. Also, try reading a chapter of Proverbs every day (there are thirty-one chapters in the book of Proverbs, which makes it ideal for daily reading), one psalm, and/or a chapter out of the Old or New Testament. You might consider beginning with one of the Gospels (Matthew, Mark, Luke, or John), or one of the shorter letters, such as Ephesians or James.

Examine

Ask yourself the following questions with regard to the passage you read:

- *Teaching:* What do I need to *know* about God, myself, and others?
- *Rebuking:* What do I need to *stop* doing—sins, habits, or selfish patterns?
- *Correcting:* What do I need to *change* in my thoughts, attitudes, or actions?
- *Training:* What do I need to *do* in obedience to God's leading?

Summarize

Do one of the following:

- Discover what the passage reveals about God and His character, what it says or promises about you, and what it says or promises about others (such as your parents, friends, or teammates). Write your thoughts down in a personal journal.
- Rewrite one or two key verses in your own words.
- Outline what each verse is saying.
- Give each verse a one-word title that summarizes what it says.

Share

Talk with God about what you've learned. Also, take time each day to share with another person what you learned during that day's study. Having a daily training time is the key to spiritual development. If you commit to working through these 365 devotionals over the next year, you will establish this as a habit—one that will be vital to your growth in Christ.

If you are committed to establishing this daily training time with God, fill out the box below.

I will commit to establishing a daily habit of spending time with God.

Signed _____

Today's Date _____

Writers

We invited athletes, coaches, team chaplains, and FCA staff to contribute their time, talent, and experience in writing these devotions. These writers come from diverse backgrounds and include representatives from a variety of sports, including baseball, soccer, basketball, football, lacrosse, track and field, and others.

Format

READY   A verse or passage of Scripture that focuses or directs your heart and mind. Turn to the Scripture reference in your Bible and read it within the overall context of the passage.

SET   A teaching point (a story, training point, or thought taken from a sports perspective) that draws a lesson from the passage.

GO   A question that will help you examine your heart and challenge you to apply God's truth to your life—on and off the field.

WORKOUT   Additional Scripture references to help you dig deeper.

OVERTIME   A closing prayer that will help you commit to the Lord what you have learned.

To receive the daily email devotional "FCA's Daily Impact Play," go to www.FCA.org.

DAY 1

Let's Go!

Jimmy Page

READY "Moses gave the men these instructions as he sent them out to explore the land. . . . 'See what the land is like, and find out whether the people living there are strong or weak, few or many.'"—Numbers 13:17–18 (NLT)

SET It's common for coaches to use scouts to help them understand their opponents' strengths and weaknesses. After God set His people free from slavery under the Egyptians, God told Moses to send out twelve men to scout Canaan—the land He had promised to them—and to come back with a report. After forty days, they returned with a full report.

Although the land was bountiful, there were also powerful men described as giants and fortified cities. The opposition looked unbeatable. But the reward for victory would be sweet if the Israelites would go for it. Ten men said, "No way!" Only two said, "Let's go!"

Caleb and Joshua must have entered Canaan with optimism, believing they were gathering intelligence so they could take the land God had promised. Their faith was bigger than their fears. The other ten let their fears overwhelm their faith.

What about us? Will we shrink back when challenges come? Or will we rely on God's presence, remember His promises, and go with power?

GO If you were one of the scouts sent to Canaan, would you have said, "Let's go!"? Why or why not?

WORKOUT Numbers 13; 2 Kings 6:8–17

OVERTIME   Lord, help me to approach every assignment You give me with optimism and enthusiasm. Help me to see the possibilities instead of the problems and say, "Let's go!" Amen.

DAY 2

Worship in Sport

Roger Lipe

READY   "And so, dear brothers and sisters, I plead with you to give your bodies to God because of all he has done for you. Let them be a living and holy sacrifice—the kind he will find acceptable. This is truly the way to worship him."—Romans 12:1 (NLT)

SET   Time, concentration, and the intentional neglect of other pursuits are just a few sacrifices you make to compete in sport. Think of the physical toll your sport takes on your body. Bruises, and sometimes broken bones, are too often part of an athlete's life.

As you experience such sacrifices, how conscious are you that these may be presented to God as holy, pleasing, and spiritual acts of worship? As surely as God is pleased with the service of singing in church, He is pleased with however you express your love for Christ in sport.

Part of presenting our bodies as living sacrifices is shaped by how we do it. Rather than squeezing into the world's way of competition, our minds and hearts are renewed and transformed through study, fellowship, and prayer. In this daily process of sacrifice, our experiences in sport are fashioned into God-honoring worship. This enables us to wisely perceive the good, pleasing, and perfect will of God on and off the field of competition.

GO   What do you sacrifice daily as a part of your life in sport?

WORKOUT   Colossians 3:23–24

OVERTIME   Father, the world of sport is full of Your grace and glory. My life is surrounded by Your merciful power. I revel in moments of quiet communion and in hours of furious activity. I commit this day to You. Amen.

View of the Head Coach

Sarah Roberts

READY "God blesses those whose hearts are pure, for they will see God."—Matthew 5:8 (NLT)

SET There was a little girl in an art class who had a hard time sitting still and listening to the teacher. But one day, the teacher noticed the girl listening intently before she began to draw. As the teacher watched, she asked about her drawing.

"Erica, what are you drawing?" asked the teacher.

"A picture of God," the girl replied.

"But no one knows what God looks like," the teacher replied.

"They will in a minute," she said.

As athletes and coaches, we need to ask: "What does God look like to me?" Is He a God I turn to only when I'm injured? Is He a God that I know will be there for me whether I win or lose?

Often, our views of God are based on worldly experiences:

- If our coach is harsh, so is God.
- If our teammates let us down, so will God.
- When fans love us, so does God.

The problem is that our focus is on the world instead of its Creator. As Christian athletes, we play for the One who loved us so much that He sent His Son to die for us. Our views of God shouldn't be based on our performances or worldly praises, but on God's perfection.

GO As a Christian athlete, what words would you use to describe God?

WORKOUT Psalm 16:8; Psalm 103

OVERTIME Lord, I trust You with my talents, my team, and my heart because You are good, loving, and faithful. Help me not to see You through worldly eyes, but through the eyes of Jesus. Amen.

DAY 4

Quick Word of Prayer

Dan Britton

READY   "Never stop praying."—1 Thessalonians 5:17 (NLT)

SET   We say it all the time: "Let's have a quick word of prayer." The underlying message here is, "Before we get to the important stuff, let's rush through the God stuff." But prayer isn't something to hurry through to get to the work. Prayer *is* the work!

Prayer was never intended to be confined to a pre-game blessing or the start of a meal. It's a nonstop conversation. It needs to be the driving force in our lives because it's our greatest weapon against the enemy and our greatest connection to the Father.

In 1 Thessalonians 5:17, Paul encourages us to pray without ceasing. He tells us to keep the lines of communication with God open at all times and to live a life of prayer. Jesus modeled and encouraged that by frequently getting away to pray, telling us to stay connected to the Father and to ask for things in His name.

If we want to live and compete at our potential, we must learn to pray. Prayer is what makes us, molds us, and matures us. It helps us handle every situation, on the field and off, with spiritual maturity and grace.

Instead of praying really quickly, let's be quick to pray and watch Him work in and through us.

GO   How can you be quick to pray without praying quickly?

WORKOUT   Ephesians 6:18; Philippians 4:6–7

OVERTIME   Father, forgive me for praying quickly when I should be praying constantly. Help me to be quick to pray without hurrying through prayer. Teach me to pray, Lord. Amen.

Living On Purpose

Amanda Tewksbury

READY "My goal is to know Him and the power of His resurrection and the fellowship of His sufferings."—Philippians 3:10

SET I'll never forget my middle school coach, Coach Harris. Our team of girls would huddle eagerly around him, eyes filled with excitement and readiness. What in the world could get a group of middle school girls so focused for a midweek practice at 3 p.m.? Purpose. Coach Harris consistently filled our minds with goals and purpose. We never lost a game that season, but most importantly, we never lost the important purposes Coach instilled in us.

In *The Purpose Driven Life,* Rick Warren states, "Everyone's life is driven by something." Warren explains that drive can be defined as "to control, to guide and to direct." As athletes and coaches, we have endless pressures driving us: the desire for approval, wanting to be remembered, the hope of being perfect, etc. If we're not careful, the purposes we focus on can be self-centered and temporal.

In Philippians 3, the apostle Paul looks to a more eternal purpose: "to know Him." What if we competed and coached with the purpose of growing in our knowledge of Jesus and focused on leaving a lasting impact through our relationship with Him? Sport can be a limitless way to create a lasting legacy for Jesus if we live, coach, and compete with His purposes.

GO What drives you in athletics? In life?

WORKOUT Philippians 3:13–15; 2 Peter 1:3–11

OVERTIME Lord, I know You created me for a life of significance: to love You and love others through You. Give me the grace to live this life focused on Your purposes. Amen.

Correct, Don't Criticize

Tony Dungy

READY   "For the Lord corrects those he loves, just as a father corrects a child in whom he delights."—Proverbs 3:12 (NLT)

SET   When I first worked toward becoming a head coach, people wondered if I could do it. I wasn't the type to yell. I wasn't the type to get in people's faces. They didn't know if I could control the players. How would they respond to my coaching style? My style relies on motivation, encouragement, and teaching. I want to help people get better. Correction is not about tearing people down. It's about helping them improve.

Certain things need to be done a certain way and aren't negotiable. The punishment is already set. But if a rule is a broken and you have to correct, it's best to avoid sharp criticisms and instead discipline with love. Jesus corrected by telling stories. He showed examples. He didn't just say, "This is wrong and this is right." When He corrected His disciples, they walked away understanding that it was for their benefit.

As a society, we need to develop young people that are correctable. Youth are sometimes difficult to correct because of the way they've received correction in the past. Building relationships takes time and patience.

But when we follow Jesus's model of correction and avoid the temptation to criticize, we are better able to build long-lasting relationships and increase our influence over those within our care.

GO   What are some things that you can do to become less critical and more encouraging as a coach?

WORKOUT   Hebrews 12:11; 2 Timothy 3:16–17

OVERTIME   Father, thank You for loving me and helping me grow through correction. Help me to model Jesus's style of correction to those I teach and influence. Amen.

Attitude

Donna Noonan

READY   "Whenever the king consulted [Daniel, Hananiah, Mishael, and Azariah] in any matter requiring wisdom and balanced judgment, he found them ten times more capable than any of the magicians and enchanters in his entire kingdom."—Daniel 1:20 (NLT)

SET   Daniel is one of my favorite people in the Bible. He kept a great attitude in spite of his circumstances. He was moved to a strange land against his will, kept in captivity for most of his life, and had his life threatened. He was loyal to his boss and worked for some difficult people. If we think our coaches are tough sometimes, look at Daniel's life. Nebuchadnezzar laid siege on Jerusalem, tried to kill Daniel's friends, and eventually lost his mind. Belshazzar was a heavy drinker, had several wives, and stole sacred items from the temple. Darius had Daniel thrown into the lions' den for being obedient to God. Yet, Daniel never complained.

Daniel never forgot where his talent came from or whom he really served. As athletes, there are many things out of our control—the starting lineup, the quality of the officials, and the schedule. The two things we can control are our attitude and effort. Daniel did a great job in both of these areas, making him an outstanding worker, teammate, and leader.

GO   How would you evaluate your attitude and effort in school? In your sport?

WORKOUT   Ephesians 6:7–8; Colossians 3:23–24

OVERTIME   Father, thank You for never leaving my side. Help me be strong and obedient like Daniel. Give me the courage to live up to Your standards with my eyes focused on You. Amen.

Making a Contribution

Les Steckel

READY   "He said to them all, 'If anyone wants to come with Me, he must deny himself, take up his cross daily, and follow Me.'"—Luke 9:23

SET   In a survey, managers and employees were once asked what aspects of their job were most important to them. The results uncovered that while the managers focused on things such as job security and benefits, the employees simply wanted to know that what they were doing made a difference.

What is the first thing that we as athletes or coaches look for when we see the new team photograph? Ourselves, right? We are naturally selfish beings. Coaches might say, "There's no 'I' in 'team,'" but no matter how many times we repeat it, the "I" is always a problem. We fight a daily battle with selfishness, which affects how we contribute to our teams, businesses, families, and even our relationship with Christ.

Jesus was the only human who did not yield to selfish tendencies. He offered the greatest contribution humanity has ever known: the sacrifice of His life for our sins! In order to make a powerful impact for Christ and contribute our gifts to building His kingdom, we are called to follow His selfless example. Through His power in us, we can live out Jesus's words in Luke 9:23, denying ourselves in following Him. When we do, it will undoubtedly lead to the most significant contribution we'll ever make!

GO   Are your contributions for your sake, or for Christ and His kingdom?

WORKOUT   Philippians 2:1–4; 1 Peter 5:1–7

OVERTIME   Lord, I pray that You would increase in me as I decrease! Amen.

DAY 9

Devotion: A Way of Life

Al Schierbaum

READY   "The one who has My commands and keeps them is the one who loves Me. And the one who loves Me will be loved by My Father. I also will love him and will reveal Myself to him."—John 14:21

SET   In the ancient Middle East, there were three main ways to obtain water. The first two were by digging a well or carving out a cistern. But the third way came naturally—through the earth! A spring of water sometimes bubbled to the surface. Often in Scripture, that spring became a picture of God's grace and provision. Jesus said, "Whoever believes in me, as Scripture has said, rivers of living water will flow from within them" (John 7:38 NIV).

When we devote ourselves to something—our families, our sport, or our church—we often find ourselves giving out of the spring within us. Sometimes that spring runs dry as if we're drawing water from our own broken cisterns, or from the wrong place. But when we allow God to be our source, His Spirit flows from within us.

From the well of Christ's living water flows a sense of deep respect for others. Due to our respect for them, we want to please them. We enjoy being around them. Imagine what happens when we devote ourselves to Jesus, who emptied Himself for our sake! Devotion to God means spending time with Him, drinking from His eternal well and loving Him by obeying His Word. When we do, our thirst will be satisfied!

GO   What motivates you?

WORKOUT   Isaiah 40:12–31; John 14:21–23

OVERTIME   Living Water, You alone satisfy all my longings! Forgive me for trying to draw water from my own abilities. Turn me back to Your well today so that others, too, may drink of You! Amen.

Identity

Roger Lipe

READY "For God wanted them to know that the riches and glory of Christ are for you Gentiles, too. And this is the secret: Christ lives in you. This gives you assurance of sharing his glory."—Colossians 1:27 (NLT)

SET People in sport often find their identities in their sports, successes, and failures. Too often they determine their worth by their most recent performance. To define ourselves entirely by our performances is not wise, but it is common. Most of us would confess that we feel the sting of grief after losing a competition. For many of us, that feeling is more intense if we find our identities in our sport, instead of in Christ Jesus.

It is God's plan to reveal His glory to our world through the profound mystery of Jesus, who lives in us, gives us hope, and leads us to life everlasting. He is in us, and we are in Him. His powerful and loving hands hold our identities secure.

On our best and worst days in sport, we are secure. He is in us, and we are full of hope and glory—win or lose, championship or last place.

GO When are you most aware of Christ's indwelling presence in your life?

WORKOUT Ephesians 2:4–10; Colossians 1:21–23

OVERTIME Jesus, thank You for my life in sport. I confess that my flesh wants to find my identity in performance, but my heart is committed to You. My identity is found only in my relationship with You. On my best days and on my worst days, I will rest in the love of God. Amen.

Steadfast

Sean McNamara

READY "Create in me a clean heart, O God. Renew a loyal spirit within me . . . Restore to me the joy of your salvation, and make me willing to obey you."—Psalm 51:10, 12 (NLT)

SET The locker room is a dark, smelly, unenviable place. On game day, though, it's a place filled with music, excitement, and an enthusiasm that grows as game time draws closer. In those pre-game moments, you never question that you are going to play your best and win.

A coaching friend once told me: If you can win the first five minutes of the game, it greatly increases the likelihood that you'll win overall. When our faith first became real, our appreciation for Jesus's sacrifice never faltered and changed the way we saw everything. But, over time, just as a game progresses, the initial enthusiasm can be hindered by unexpected or disappointing events.

As athletes, our goal is to carry the same passion and enthusiasm we had in the game's first minutes throughout the entire competition. And sometimes we need to stop, call a time-out, and refocus. If you've noticed things aren't the way you hoped they would be in your faith, I encourage you to pray Psalm 51 and ask God to cleanse your heart and renew your spirit. Jesus has already won the victory; we are just called to live that victory out each day.

GO At times when your faith seems to waver, do you stop to pray for renewed, steadfast faith? Why or why not?

WORKOUT 1 Corinthians 15:58; Isaiah 26:3

OVERTIME Lord, help me to renew a steadfast spirit in my heart so I never lose sight of Your victory over my sin, the abundant life I can experience today, and my hope for eternity with You. Amen.

DAY 12

What's Your Go-To?

Dan Britton

READY "Before daybreak the next morning, Jesus got up and went out to an isolated place to pray."—Mark 1:35 (NLT)

SET When the lacrosse game was on the line and a goal was needed for the team, I went to my go-to move: the inside roll dodge. This go-to move allowed me to excel, perform my best, and contribute to the team.

Every athlete has their go-to move, and every coach has their go-to play. I believe it is especially true for the spiritual world. What is your go-to move that allows you to be your best for Christ? Dan Webster recently shared with me three spiritual go-to moves that can help you maximize your impact for Christ.

1. **Go-To Place**
   Where do you go every day to connect with God? Where and when we engage God is essential to a vibrant Christian walk. Where is your go-to place? Find one and get there every day.

2. **Go-To Passage**
   What passage gives you the greatest comfort and hope, direction and guidance? What verses are reviving your soul? A go-to passage can be the same for a week, a month, or a year.

3. **Go-To Person**
   Who is your go-to person? Everybody needs at least one go-to person. Isolation is the Christian's silent enemy; however, key relationships can stop the sin of isolation.

When we have a go-to place, passage, and person, we are putting ourselves in the best possible position to be used by God in a powerful way.

GO What is your go-to place, passage, and person?

WORKOUT Matthew 6:6–8; Colossians 3:12–17

OVERTIME   Father, I desire to have these three spiritual go-to moves in place. I ask for You to show me the right place, passage, and person. Amen.

DAY 13

What's at Your Center?

Joe Matera

READY   "I am the resurrection and the life. The one who believes in Me, even if he dies, will live. Everyone who lives and believes in Me will never die—ever."—John 11:25–26

SET   As athletes and coaches, we are motivated to think, "I can handle any challenge!" We are used to having challenges, but on my 52nd birthday I was faced with news I couldn't handle. I was diagnosed with stage IV cancer and given six months to live. I was a surfer with an active lifestyle and no obvious health issues. The "c" word was the furthest thing from my mind, and the news was like a tsunami washing over my family.

Eventually, my family and I discovered that my diagnosis was taking a toll on us. The problem was that our focus was now cancer. Imagine the nucleus of an atom—cancer was now the center, and we were revolving around an unknown entity that was trying to destroy us. We decided to pray and ask the Lord to be our center, that He and our family together would be the nucleus. With God's power we pushed cancer to the outer rim of the atom, making it seem smaller, having less influence on our lives.

Have you been living your life on your own strength, thinking you can handle it alone? Do you put your faith and trust in God more than your own abilities? Let Him be your center and push everything—sports, success, challenges, sickness—to the outer rim.

GO   Is God at the center of your life?

WORKOUT   John 11:4; Romans 5:2–5

OVERTIME   Lord Jesus, thank You for being my hope and strength. Help me push aside anything that is distracting me from focusing on Your love and promises. Amen.

DAY 14

Ambassadors

Kerry O'Neill

READY   "So we are Christ's ambassadors; God is making his appeal through us. We speak for Christ when we plead, 'Come back to God!'"—2 Corinthians 5:20 (NLT)

SET   Coaches often emphasize to athletes the privilege of wearing their team's jersey. As athletes, we represent something bigger than ourselves. We represent our team, school, and community. We play for the name on the front of the jersey (our team) instead of the back (ourselves).

As Christians, we are called ambassadors for Christ. Ambassadors are high-ranking officials sent by governments or rulers to represent them in the country to which they've been sent to live. Ambassadors' words and actions are not seen as their own, but rather those of the rulers or nations they represent.

So it is with Christian coaches and competitors. While we represent our families and teams, our primary identities are as God's children, and our words and actions are perceived to be reflections of Him. Ambassadors do not have their own agendas or plans. Likewise, Christ's ambassadors surrender their own agendas, words, and actions to do what the Lord has called them to do.

We may be the only Bible some people ever read and the only Jesus some will ever see. We must speak words of life and put our faith into action. Jesus chose us to represent Him on and off the field. People should see glimpses of Him as we live our lives and do His will "on earth as it is in heaven."

GO   How can you be more aware that you represent Jesus?

WORKOUT   2 Corinthians 5:17–21; Ephesians 5:1–2

OVERTIME   Lord, help me to remember that I represent You as Your ambassador, and help me to represent You well so that others are drawn to You. Amen.

DAY 15

You Matter

Rex Stump

READY   "Jashobeam the Hacmonite . . . was leader of the Three—the three mightiest warriors among David's men. He once used his spear to kill 800 enemy warriors in a single battle."—2 Samuel 23:8 (NLT)

SET   Once, President Teddy Roosevelt was standing in a presidential receiving line. An aide on his left whispered the name of each person ahead of time so he could greet people by name. The president looked down the line, turned to his aide, and asked, "Who's that fella?" The aide replied, "Oh, you know him, Mr. President, he made your pants." As the man reached the front, the president greeted him, "Why, hello, Major Pants, we're so glad you're here this evening. Welcome to the White House."[1]

I'm not sure whether that story is completely true, but I am completely sure that all of us have felt unimportant at some point. Someone forgets our name. We get overlooked for a promotion. Something makes us feel insignificant.

The Bible contains many incredible characters who we quickly recognize by name. But what about the faithful servants with unfamiliar names? The warrior Jashobeam the Hacmonite took out 800 armed, skilled men with his spear.

Jashobeam's name is recorded because he mattered to David. To many he may have been a "nobody," but to David he was a "somebody."

God says *you* are a "somebody." You matter! For God so loved you (somebody), that He gave His One and Only Son, Jesus Christ (John 3:16).

GO   Knowing that God values you, how can you compete differently regardless of the outcome?

WORKOUT   Matthew 10:29–30; Luke 15

OVERTIME   Father, thank You for loving and valuing me. In Your eyes I'm somebody. Forgive me when I've thought less of myself and when I've treated others with less value. Amen.

DAY 16

Lasting Integrity

Ward Kinne

READY   "So let's not get tired of doing what is good. At just the right time we will reap a harvest of blessing if we don't give up."—Galatians 6:9 (NLT)

SET   Our integrity is revealed when we're faced with a decision to do what is right, even if it conflicts with what we want. We are called to act according to God's will instead of our own.

On a beautiful spring day in 1980 in northwestern New York State, the Watertown Cyclones, a powerhouse lacrosse team, were visiting their rivals, the General Brown Lions. Though underdogs, the Lions were a gritty blue-collar team with home field advantage. If all their starters played at 100 percent, they had a chance to win.

Sadly, the Lions' hopes crashed before the game started. Three of their starters were caught smoking pot in the parking lot before the game. The coach was near tears with anger and hurt, yet he didn't hesitate to kick the players off the team, no matter how much he wanted to beat the Cyclones. The players begged to play but, as a man of integrity, the coach stood his ground.

This coach's integrity cost him in the short term. The Lions were defeated and people questioned his "harsh" discipline. But in the long run he helped shape one of those kids into a responsible Christian man—me.

I never got that varsity letter, but I gained something more valuable—a lesson in integrity.

GO   What is a daily discipline you can follow to remain firm in your faith?

WORKOUT   Psalm 55:22

OVERTIME   Jesus, thank You for the opportunity today to live according to Your will and to do what is right and good in Your eyes. I trust that You will give me the strength I need to stand firm in my faith. Amen.

DAY 17

Fight the Good Fight

Sherri Coale

READY   "I have fought the good fight, I have finished the race, and I have remained faithful."—2 Timothy 4:7 (NLT)

SET   When recruiting players, one of the most important qualities I look for is fight. Fight serves as the axis for our team—it's the one thing we can control. Some things come and go, but you can always control how much effort you give and how hard you fight. It gives you the chance to be your best, and it gives you a chance to compete even when you aren't as talented as your opponent.

No matter the struggle that comes your way, fight is a way of life. That is also very true when it comes to our existence as Christians. In athletics, we coach our players to fight through adversity on the playing field. But in the spiritual realm, we coach those within our influence to fight the good fight. We help prepare them to fight through adversities on this journey to our eternal life in heaven.

When you talk about standing your ground, maybe nowhere is it more important than in your daily Christian walk and in moment-by-moment decisions. That means doing things that aren't always easy. That requires fight. That requires perseverance. And eventually, we'll finish the race and be able to say, as the apostle Paul did, we have kept the faith.

GO   How can you incorporate "fight" into the daily spiritual challenges and decisions you face?

WORKOUT   1 Corinthians 9:24–25; 1 Timothy 6:12

OVERTIME   Father, thank You for giving me the strength to fight the good fight. Help me to stand against daily temptations and challenges, and to stand up for my faith. Help me to have fight in my spiritual life. Amen.

DAY 18

Hold On to Hope

Rebekah Trittipoe

READY   "But I will keep on hoping for your help; I will praise you more and more."—Psalm 71:14 (NLT)

SET   I was happy in my convertible, cruising down the highway with the roof down, my hair whipping in the wind. My destination? The Mohican 100-Mile Race, a footrace held in hilly, north central Ohio. I was meeting my brother, and together we would make our way from start to finish. As I waited for him to arrive at the host campground, excited to be running together since my brother had yet to complete a 100-mile event, I started preparing for the race. Then my phone rang and everything changed.

I received word from my husband that both our sons had suffered devastating, life-changing setbacks. I felt sick. I couldn't be encouraged by my brother. I could barely eat or drink. Sleep wouldn't come. Hope for anything good coming from this race faded.

The gun went off in the wee hours. By mile 13, I was cramping, and by mile 25, I began throwing up. I had no energy. The heat was overpowering. I was distraught, having failed at being the rock my brother needed. Hope was nowhere to be found—I lost it somewhere on the course. Somewhere after mile 60 I quit and watched my brother head out into the darkness—alone.

In order to continue, I needed hope. No matter how bad it seems, we must hold on to hope in Jesus. Hope allows us to endure. And when we endure, we are made stronger.

GO   Think of a time you lost hope. Would the result have been different had hope remained?

WORKOUT   Romans 15:5–6; Hebrews 10:23

OVERTIME   You are an awesome God who gives endurance and encouragement, and with that, hope. Please, help me to remember. Amen.

DAY 19

Our Identity in Christ

Cheryl Baird

READY   "Since, then, you have been raised with Christ, set your hearts on things above, where Christ is, seated at the right hand of God. Set your mind on things above, not on earthly things."—Colossians 3:1–2 (NIV)

SET   As competitors, whenever we are asked, "How are you?" we often reply in terms of our team: "We struggled early but regrouped late in the season." Unfortunately, it's far too easy for us as competitors to become consumed with our team's performance. Learning to separate athletic expectations from our true identity in Christ is an ongoing challenge. As followers of Christ, we can't lose sight of what matters most in life.

In Paul's letter to the Christians in the city of Colossae, he warned about the distractions of the time and their inherent dangers. Paul knew that this world's temporary rewards beckon with a fierce and determined strength. And just as the false teachings were attractive to the misguided Colossians, so can a winning record be equally alluring to a coach!

If we become ensnared by the rewards and attention inherent in success, we make ourselves vulnerable to the idolatrous practices that Paul warned against. We will continually be disappointed and feel a loss of hope and will look to the next season or next recruit to fulfill us. Anything that stands in the way of our relationship with Christ keeps us from fully surrendering our hearts and minds to Him. Only He can satisfy our longings!

GO   Can you separate who you are in Christ from your team's performance?

WORKOUT   Philippians 3:7–20; Colossians 2:8

OVERTIME   God, I want to find my whole identity in You! Please help me release the desire to replace You with any worldly thing. Amen.

DAY 20

Vision Eyes

Dan Britton

READY   "'For I know the plans I have for you,' says the LORD. 'They are plans for good and not for disaster, to give you a future and a hope.'" —Jeremiah 29:11 (NLT)

SET   At age two, Craig MacFarlane was blinded in a tragic accident. But he turned his defeat into victory by becoming a world-class athlete with more than one hundred gold medals in wrestling, track and field, and downhill skiing. Craig can't physically see, but he has a powerful vision that fuels his drive to overcome.

While we can't see or predict the future, we need to face tomorrow with confidence because God will take care of us and give us hope. The key is to have a "God vision." God vision is putting what's on God's heart onto our own and seeing things the way He sees them. When we have a God vision, we shall *rise up tomorrow*!

Answer these questions to clarify your God vision:

Is your God vision too small? If your vision doesn't terrify you, it's too small. A God vision should be so huge that you understand that you are bound to fail without God's interference.

Is your God vision too narrow? If your vision doesn't include others, it's too narrow. God vision includes others like friends and teammates.

Is your God vision just a daydream? If your vision doesn't get accomplished, it's just a daydream. A God vision must always produce results.

Discover God's vision for your life and rise up tomorrow!

GO   As a competitor, do you have a God vision? In two or three sentences, write it down.

WORKOUT   Amos 3:7; Proverbs 29:18

OVERTIME   God, help me to *rise up tomorrow*. The future is unknown, but I trust You with it. Help me to see things the way You see them. Amen.

No "I" in Team

Josh Carter

READY   Then Abram said to Lot, ". . . Isn't the whole land before you? Separate from me: if [you go] to the left, I will go to the right; if [you go] to the right, I will go to the left."—Genesis 13:8–9

SET   In his sixteen years as coach of the Boston Celtics, Red Auerbach guided his team to nine NBA Championships. He retired after the 1966 season as the winningest coach in NBA history with 938 wins. While his teams had some great players, they were characterized more by their team play, which included a new concept of using role players. "That's a player who willingly undertakes the thankless job that [must] be done in order to make the whole package fly," Auerbach said.

In the Bible, Abraham and his nephew Lot were a team. But as they traveled together with their flocks, herds, and households, they realized that the land could not support them both. The result was strife among their people. Rather than flaunt his role as the leader, Abraham gave Lot his choice of land. Abraham could have been selfish, but instead he sacrificed his desires for the good of his people and trusted God to provide what they needed.

In the same way, Christ gave up His authority by going to the cross, and we, too, can reflect such sacrifice as we serve others. Christian competitors have a great opportunity to serve their teams by being willing to give up their place.

GO   What's one thing you can do today to reflect a selfless attitude toward other players?

WORKOUT   1 Corinthians 10:24; Philippians 2:3–4

OVERTIME   Jesus, thank You for Your life of sacrifice. I pray that You would increase that I may decrease as I serve others for Your glory! Amen.

DAY 22

Rules

Donna Noonan

READY   "Be careful to obey all my commands, so that all will go well with you and your children after you, because you will be doing what is good and pleasing to the LORD your God."—Deuteronomy 12:28 (NLT)

SET   Often, we view rules as restrictive—things that are made to be broken or bent. But rules in sports are often seen differently. They define purpose, outline the scoring system, provide a sense of fairness, and determine penalties.

Our culture tells us that God's Word is restrictive, and not relevant to today's world. It's just a list of don'ts. But in reading the Bible, you will discover that God's commands (His rules) exist because of His love for us and His desire for us to flourish.

Rules are like guardrails on a highway. They protect us from danger. If you crash into them, you may not get hurt, but your car will need repairs. When you break God's commands, you may not see the consequences immediately, but there will be damages needing repair. He gives us commands because He loves us, and we obey them because we love Him.

Playing a game in which players constantly break rules or make them up as they go would not be fun or worth playing. Similarly, living a life contrary to God's Word might seem like fun, but it's not the life we are called to live.

GO　What does it mean that you may prosper forever if you obey all these things God commanded?

WORKOUT　Proverbs 3:1–2; John 15:10

OVERTIME　Lord, I know that Your commands are for my good, and You give them because You love me. Help me to deepen my love for You so that my "have to" becomes a "want to." Amen.

DAY 23

The Calling

Roger Lipe

READY　"He who calls you is faithful, who also will do it."—1 Thessalonians 5:24

SET　Many times on the Christian journey, we sense God calling us to do something. Sometimes, though, the task seems too great or our resources too small. Other times, God's call can feel overwhelming and cause us to doubt whether we really heard Him at all. Thankfully, He has given us His Scriptures to speak directly to our fears and doubts related to His call.

The apostle Paul knew that his friends in Thessalonica sometimes struggled with whether they had heard God's call. So he wrote to them about why they could trust God when He asked them to do something, reminding them that God had never stopped being faithful to provide for them, lead them, or be with them.

Paul's words in 1 Thessalonians 5:24 are a promise for those who hear God's call to coach. The verse says nothing about the abilities of the hearer, but it speaks volumes about the One who does the calling. He is called faithful—fully reliable to fulfill His promises. But He does not stop there: He says that He will bring it to pass.

This powerful verse causes me to trust in the Lord through this marvelous process of pursuing His will. He both calls us and carries out His will in us. Our part is to answer, to make ourselves available for His service and to look to Jesus who is proof of His faithfulness!

GO Do you see being an athlete or a coach as a calling?

WORKOUT Exodus 3:1–10; 1 Samuel 3:1–9

OVERTIME Gracious God, please give me ears to hear Your voice calling me to Yourself, and the confidence to respond for the sake of Your glory. Amen.

DAY 24

What's Your Purpose?

Brian Roberts

READY "The Lord will fulfill His purpose for me. Lord, Your love is eternal; do not abandon the work of Your hands."—Psalm 138:8

SET I've been in the Major Leagues for over ten years with the Baltimore Orioles. Looking back I can think of specific men who were crucial to my development and maturity. Now, as a veteran player, I want to share what I've learned with others.

As David says in Psalm 138, I know the Lord has a purpose for me, and He will fulfill it. As a Christian competitor, I try to use every opportunity I can to share the gospel along with my struggles and the lessons God has taught me along the way. I've realized that my purpose goes far beyond playing baseball. God purposed this sport as my mission field.

We've all been put here by God to be lights for Him, and we've each been given our unique gifts. It is up to us to recognize those gifts and use them in our sport for God's glory. It should be our ultimate goal to have our teammates, coaches, and fans see Christ in our performance.

Even though we'll make mistakes, God's grace is sufficient enough to pick us up and continue to use us for His purposes. His plans are larger than our faults, and He will always fulfill the purpose He has set for us.

GO What do you feel is your God-given purpose? How does that apply to your athletic or coaching career?

WORKOUT Psalm 19; Hosea 14:9

OVERTIME Father, You've given us each a specific purpose in this life. Let it be my passion to find that purpose and share Your message through it. Amen.

DAY 25

LOVE = U B4 Me

Rex Stump

READY "So now I am giving you a new commandment: Love each other. Just as I have loved you, you should love each other."—John 13:34 (NLT)

SET Coaches often search for that new strategy or that new look— something that will give them the edge over their opponents. So they attend clinics, read books, and watch other successful programs to discover something new. Here's the secret: Before Jesus left this earth, He sat down with His team, looked them in the eyes, and told them, "Love each other" (John 13:34 NLT).

Jesus showed the fullness of His love as He took on the role of a servant and washed His disciples' feet. One of the disciples could have washed everyone's feet, but none of them did. Their focus was on themselves, not on serving and loving. So Jesus washed their feet. Then, He sat down with them and shared the Passover meal, all before sacrificing His own life at the cross.

Jesus gave us a simple equation: Love = U B4 Me.

All teams and coaches are faced with choosing selfishness over selflessness. So we must apply the equation. I will coach my team to be their best, sharpen their skills, and accept their faults. I will not allow my agenda, pride, or desire to win to diminish my love for others.

Love is selflessness. Love = U B4 Me!

GO　How can you apply "U B4 Me" at practice or work today?

WORKOUT　1 John 3:16; 1 John 4:11–12

OVERTIME　Father, forgive me for the times I have not loved others as You have loved me. Give me the focus, desire, and strength to obey Your commands to love others! Amen.

DAY 26

In It Together

Jill Lee

READY　"If one part suffers, all the parts suffer with it, and if one part is honored, all the parts are glad. All of you together are Christ's body, and each of you is a part of it."—1 Corinthians 12:26–27 (NLT)

SET　Legendary University of Tennessee Lady Volunteers basketball coach Pat Summitt was diagnosed with early onset dementia. The 59-year-old, winningest college basketball coach of all time made the shocking announcement and said she would attempt to continue coaching as long as she could.

To UT fans and sports fans in general, Summitt had seemed indestructible. But even the strongest of people still face challenges in life. As the news unfolded, Summitt received major support from others—including her players, both past and present. One of her athletes made this statement: "As players and coaching staff, we're in this; we're all together. This is something we're going to come together as a group on."

In life, we are parts of various "teams." Whether those are athletic teams, families, circles of friends, churches, or offices, these teams all operate on the same concept of working together and offering mutual support. As Christians, it is our responsibility and honor to bring the love of Christ to our teammates who are hurting or in need and to be His hands and feet for them as they face their battle.

Think about your "team." Is one of your teammates struggling? If so, put your faith into action and rally around them. Through your actions, they will see and experience God's love and will be encouraged to trust Him through the challenge.

GO   How does supporting others and working as a team demonstrate God's love?

WORKOUT   Acts 2:42–47; James 2:14–17

OVERTIME   Lord, help me to demonstrate Your love by encouraging and serving those I influence. Amen.

DAY 27

In Tandem

Clay Elliott

READY   "Then Joshua told the people, 'Purify yourselves, for tomorrow the LORD will do great wonders among you.'"—Joshua 3:5 (NLT)

SET   God does amazing things all the time. He separated the waters of the Jordan River so His people could walk to the other side. He chose a virgin to deliver His Son to the world. He inspired more than forty authors to create His Holy Book that still guides our lives thousands of years later.

Consecrating yourself is an act of full surrender to God—a declaration of giving yourself to God for His purposes. You can do this in a multitude of ways—including prayer, music, poetry, or our own routines.

Andre Mercurio played four years of baseball at San Jose State University. He was the starting center fielder and the leadoff hitter. Before each at bat, Andre stepped in front of the batter's box, turned his bat upside down, made a cross with it in the dirt, and tapped it twice before he was ready. That was his act of consecration, and God did many amazing things through Andre because his heart was fully surrendered to God's will.

We must fully consecrate ourselves to God. God's gift to us is that He does amazing things in our lives. And when we give ourselves to God for His work to be done through us, the potential impact is unlimited.

GO Do you have an act of consecration before you compete to remind yourself and others that God can work through you? If not, consider what it would look like if you did.

WORKOUT Leviticus 20:7–8; Matthew 5:13–16

OVERTIME Father, I consecrate myself to You. I willingly submit to You and ask that You would do amazing things for You through me. Amen.

DAY 28

Overcome Adversity

Tamika Catchings

READY "In all these things we are more than victorious through Him who loved us."—Romans 8:37

SET As a child, I dealt with the embarrassment of having to wear glasses and braces. And to make matters worse, I had hearing problems, which required me to wear a hearing aid and affected my speech. You can imagine the name-calling that ensued. I remember one day on the way home from school, I was so frustrated that I took off my hearing aid and threw it into a ditch. My parents weren't too happy about that.

By the time I was in middle school, my parents divorced. I used sports as an escape from my problems. But even there, I faced my share of difficulties. Throughout my career I've torn my ACL, my meniscus, and my Achilles tendon. When I faced tough times, it would have been easy to give up. But I represent God in everything I do, and I knew He had a plan for my life. And through those injuries and struggles, I've drawn closer to the Lord.

God has a plan for everyone, and no one but you can stop it from coming to pass. I've personally experienced what it means to be "victorious through Him who loved us." By His grace, those adversities made me stronger and helped me inspire others and become who I am today.

GO   Read Romans 8:28. Are you able to see how God has used difficult situations in your life for the greater good? Explain.

WORKOUT   Romans 8:28; 2 Corinthians 12:9–10

OVERTIME   Lord, help me to see Your purpose for my life. Give me the strength to overcome adversity that seeks to discourage me from fulfilling Your ultimate plan. Amen.

DAY 29

Free to Be Our Best

Phil Jones

READY   "Whatever you do, do it enthusiastically, as something done for the Lord and not for men, knowing that you will receive the reward of an inheritance from the Lord. You serve the Lord Christ."—Colossians 3:23–24

SET   As coaches and athletes, we put all our hearts, bodies, and emotions into our endeavors. As we give it all we've got, we begin to understand what Paul was saying to the Colossian Christians. Paul communicates what could happen if our efforts were fully focused on honoring God, rather than man. But that's not easy in today's self-centered society, in which we attach our personal value, worth, and dignity to our performance. The more we work to gain notoriety or impress others, the more we find that we are not free to be the people we were created by God to be.

The good news is something that Paul experienced firsthand: that what we do is *not* who we are! He wanted us to understand that our value is based solely on Christ's sacrifice, not on what we can do through our own effort.

Knowing that our ability comes from God and that He loves us regardless of our performance eliminates the need we have to perform for others. When we understand and accept the reality of Christ's offering, we are *free* to be who we were intended to be.

GO   How can you be free to compete with enthusiasm for the Lord, not for others?

WORKOUT   Psalm 37:1–6; Matthew 6:5–8, 26–34

OVERTIME   Lord, help me to work enthusiastically today for You and with You so that others might know the riches of Your love! Amen.

DAY 30

Community

Roger Lipe

READY   "How wonderful and pleasant it is when brothers live together in harmony! . . . Harmony is as refreshing as the dew from Mount Hermon that falls on the mountains of Zion. And there the LORD has pronounced his blessing, even life everlasting."—Psalm 133 (NLT)

SET   Think for a moment about the best teams with whom you have ever competed. Recall the rich community you had as you traveled together, laughed, cried, won, and lost. Consider how much you would have missed had you not been involved in the life of that team.

Life on a sports team and in a church is much the same. It is meant to be good and pleasant. We are meant to live together in harmony. It makes our experiences as fresh and clean as morning dew on bare feet. When we experience God's presence in the life of our team or church, we are living in the Lord's blessing. We get a foretaste of eternity, life forevermore.

Let's make it our goal and our daily mission to build our team in a way that is good and pleasant because we live together in harmony. In doing so, we will experience the best the Lord has to offer in sport and in life off the field of competition.

GO   What have been some of your good and pleasant experiences with team unity?

WORKOUT   Ephesians 4:1–6; Colossians 3:14

OVERTIME   Father, thank You for my teammates. May we all honor You and respect one another. May we experience the best this sport has to offer as we compete today for Your glory. Amen.

DAY 31

Training Camp

Kerry O'Neill

READY   "He chose his servant David . . . He took David from tending the ewes and lambs and made him the shepherd of Jacob's descendants—God's own people, Israel."—Psalm 78:70–71 (NLT)

SET   Often, when an athlete has an amazing performance, the media will interview the athlete's coaches and teammates with questions or comments like, "Did you know Joe was capable of playing like that?" "You must be shocked to see Abigail have such a breakout performance."

The responses are fairly typical: "Everyone on this team knows Joe is capable of playing like that because we see it in practice every day." "None of her teammates are shocked with Abigail's performance because we see her work ethic day in and day out."

Every successful competitor chooses the path of hard work even when no one is watching. Many famous coaches and athletes can point to humble beginnings when they anonymously, but faithfully, trained and sacrificed to improve.

David was one of those guys. Before he was King David, he was shepherd boy David. Before he was famous, he was forgotten. But he wasn't forgotten by God. The Lord had David in training camp—serving daily, faithfully, and anonymously in ways that many would find "beneath them." Yet, through doing the everyday—and sometimes mundane—tasks, David developed the character and skills he utilized when he served as king.

GO   Do you focus more on being faithful now or on future opportunities?

WORKOUT   Matthew 25:23; Colossians 3:23–24

OVERTIME   Lord, help me focus on being faithful to You where You have me now instead of looking ahead for future promotions and successes. Teach me Your ways so I am fully ready for anything You ask of me. Amen.

DAY 32

Be Courageous

Matt Cullen

READY   "Haven't I commanded you: be strong and courageous? Do not be afraid or discouraged, for the LORD your God is with you wherever you go."—Joshua 1:9

SET   As an NHL player, I've never been quick to admit my fears. But when facing Edmonton in Game 7 of the 2006 Stanley Cup Finals, I was more nervous than I'd ever been in my athletic career. Leaning on God during that game helped me find strength to face my fears head on. We ended up winning the game and the Stanley Cup, a first for the Carolina Hurricanes.

When my third son, Joey, was born, I dealt with a different kind of fear. I was in Pittsburgh for the playoffs when my wife went into labor, and I couldn't get home in time for the delivery. When I got word that Joey was having problems with his lungs, I had to rely heavily on my relationship with the Lord to keep fear from taking over. He gave me peace to trust that He was taking care of my son and everything would be okay.

Fear is a natural reaction and something we all have to face sometimes. But the Bible clearly tells us that we *don't* have to be afraid when troublesome circumstances come our way. To conquer fear, we need to remember that God is always with us. He will faithfully give us the courage to walk through any challenge we face in all aspects of our lives.

GO   How is fear related to a lack of trust in God?

WORKOUT   Isaiah 41:10; Philippians 4:6

OVERTIME   Lord, give me courage when life's troubles come my way. Remind me of who You are so that I can be courageous and capable of facing any situation. Amen.

DAY 33

Breaking Free

Lauren Holiday

READY   "Now the Lord is the Spirit, and where the Spirit of the Lord is, there is freedom."—2 Corinthians 3:17

SET   In 2008, I made my first US Olympic Soccer Team. I was still in college and one of the youngest players on the roster. In 2012, I was chosen for the Olympic squad again, but this time I was considered a veteran, with the 2008 Olympic gold-medal game and the 2010 FIFA World Cup under my belt. There was a great deal of pressure that came with the job.

The pressure of high expectations in sport can be difficult to manage. The hardest part is playing freely and not allowing the pressure to negatively impact your performance and steal your joy in the process.

In order to break free of the pressure that comes with expectations, there are some important steps to follow. First, make sure that your confidence is in Christ—not in yourself. Second, understand that your identity is in Him. And third, always keep in mind that your sport should be your spiritual act of worship. Whatever talent Christ has blessed you with ultimately belongs to Him. These steps will help relieve the pressure from high expectations. They will also bring you true joy and allow you to give God the glory in everything you do.

GO   Read 2 Corinthians 3:17. How might inviting His Spirit into your athletic life bring freedom and help you deal better with pressure?

WORKOUT   Romans 12:1–2; John 8:32

OVERTIME   Lord, I want to break free from worldly expectations and pressures. Transform my thoughts and fill my heart with the kind of joy that only You can bring. Amen.

DAY 34

Sweat Equity

Harry Flaherty

READY   "You intended to harm me, but God intended it for good to accomplish what is now being done, the saving of many lives."—Genesis 50:20 (NIV)

SET   A mutual respect exists among athletes. To some degree, all athletes have a single-minded, committed lifestyle that is laced with adversity. This is the price we pay to excel. An athlete's identity and purpose hinges on his or her performance.

What we see as adversity, God sees as opportunity. In Genesis 38–39, we read the story of how Joseph was sold into slavery by his own family and then imprisoned for thirteen years for a crime he did not commit. But Joseph stood firm. He knew that what men meant for evil, God used for good (Gen. 50:20). Joseph was right: Years after being sold into slavery, he became second in command over all of Egypt!

Playing ball meant the world to me as a young man. God blessed me with natural ability and I excelled at every level. Then adversity struck. I was cut by the first NFL team that signed me. Down and out, I begrudgingly headed to Tampa Bay to play for the Bandits of the USFL. It was there that I met Jesus through the Bandits' chapel program. God then called me to youth ministry.

I am living proof that God can do great things in adverse situations. Whether we have been deceived, beaten, jailed, surrounded by lions, or cut from a team, we are being prepped through adversities for divine opportunity!

GO   What adversities and challenges are you currently facing in your life?

WORKOUT   Genesis 50:15–21; Psalm 23

OVERTIME   Father, help me today to draw upon Your strength when facing adversity. Use these situations for Your glory and Your purpose. Amen.

DAY 35

Who Am I?

Wade Hopkins

READY   "Everything was created through him and for him."—Colossians 1:16b (NLT)

SET   If you've coached or played for any significant period of time, you have most likely gotten your name in the newspaper. And that may be a good thing *or* a bad thing.

I remember one headline read "Hopkins Phenom." I thought that was pretty cool, and I framed the article. Well, it wasn't long afterwards that I got invited to the head coach's office, and it wasn't so I could autograph his copy of the newspaper. I was let go—cut. Didn't he know I was a *phenom*? That's when I asked myself, "Who am I? Am I the phenom the paper said I was, or do I not measure up and fit into the team's plans, like coach said? Whose opinion counts, anyway?"

That's when it hit me: It doesn't matter what anyone thinks or says. The Head Coach's opinion is the only one that matters. The Bible says we are remarkably and wonderfully made—and for a purpose. We must trust what God says. He has declared who He is and who we are in His Word: "I am the way, the truth, and the life. No one can come to the Father except through me" (John 14:6, NLT).

God's opinion is the only one that matters.
God wants us on His team.
God created us for a purpose.

GO   What would be different if you lived and played for an audience of One?

WORKOUT   Psalm 139:14; 1 Corinthians 15:58

OVERTIME   Lord, please help me live in the powerful truth of who You are and who You say I am. Amen.

DAY 36

What Are Your Expectations?

Amanda Tewksbury

READY   "But when the young man heard this, he went away sad, for he had many possessions."—Matthew 19:22 (NLT)

SET   Coaching to inspire is hard. I find it challenging to work with players who won't fully invest in the team because their playing time isn't what they expected. Their unmet expectations hold them back from being the best teammate they can be.

In Matthew 19, a rich young ruler asks Jesus to clarify what he must do to have eternal life. Jesus tells him to "keep the commandments" and lists off a few of them. Jesus finishes by telling him to love his neighbors as himself. The young ruler tells Jesus that he's kept all of the commandments mentioned, then asks what else he must do. Jesus responds, "Go and sell all your possessions and give the money to the poor, and you will have treasure in heaven. Then come, follow me" (Matt. 19:21, NLT). The young man ended up walking away grieving because he had many possessions. Sadly, the expectations the young man had for his life—one centered on his possessions—controlled the way he responded in his life with Christ.

Do you have expectations that might be hindering you from a deeper relationship with God? Ask God to help you recognize such expectations. As you let go of them, you will find a deeper life of following Christ and serving others.

GO What two or three expectations do you have that hinder or control you?

WORKOUT Matthew 13:45–46; Romans 6:17–23

OVERTIME Lord, help me to be humble enough to see the things in my life I need to let go of and trust You. Forgive me and give me wisdom and more love for You and others. Amen.

DAY 37

Surprising Strength

Jean Driscoll

READY "I have great confidence in you; I have great pride in you. I am filled with encouragement; I am overcome with joy in all our afflictions."—2 Corinthians 7:4

SET Have you ever been nervous before a big game? Have you ever felt like quitting an event before you even started? The first time I competed in the Boston Marathon, I didn't think I belonged in the race. As I sat on the starting line, in my mind I was yelling at my coach, *I don't belong here! I'm not strong enough!* However, one of the most amazing things happened. Although on the starting line I doubted my ability to even finish the famous Boston Marathon, 26 miles later I won the race and broke the world record by almost seven minutes!

When the Israelites prepared to enter the land of Canaan, they were most likely also a bit nervous. Moses had died and they were now under the leadership of Joshua. However, God told them to be strong and courageous, for He was about to give the land that He had promised to them. He said to Joshua, "I will be with you, just as I was with Moses. I will not leave you or forsake you" (Josh. 1:5).

Being nervous before an event is normal. It tells us that what we're about to do is important. But God encourages us to be brave and courageous by performing for Him, the audience of One.

GO Off the track, do you seek the Lord's strength to help you overcome little worries that plague your day?

WORKOUT Joshua 1:9; Philippians 4:13

OVERTIME God, help me to be calm and courageous during competition. Help me to focus on You, my audience of One. Amen.

DAY 38

Consumed by a Desire to Serve

Dan Britton

READY "Based on the gift each one has received, use it to serve others, as good managers of the varied grace of God."—1 Peter 4:10

SET As Christian competitors, we realize that God has called us to serve. But do we understand that we should be *consumed* to serve? Is there a consuming fire that burns in us to serve others around us who are hurting and to help those who need to experience the love of Christ through us?

We serve because the ultimate purpose of serving is to glorify Christ. Rick Warren said, "We serve God by serving others. . . . [but] in our self-serving culture with its me-first mentality, acting like a servant is not a popular concept." In the athletic world, everyone struggles to some degree with the "me first" mentality. We buy into the lie that we are better than others because of our talent in athletics. So are we consumed with self or consumed with serving?

When serving, we need to have intentionality (*plan it!*), intensity (*seize it!*), and intimacy (*feel it!*). Samuel Chadwick said it best: "Spirit filled souls are ablaze for God . . . They serve with a devotion that consumes . . . Love is perfected in the fire of God."

On and off the field of competition, we need to be radical about serving. The revolution can begin with you.

GO   What is one practical way you can serve your team today?

WORKOUT   Jude 24–25

OVERTIME   Jesus, serving is hard. I struggle daily with the "me first" mentality. Help me to see with spiritual eyes the ways I can serve my team. I want to be one who is consumed to serve. Amen.

DAY 39

Replacement Refs

Rex Stump

READY   "Do not have other gods besides Me."—Exodus 20:3

SET   During the first weeks of the 2012 NFL season, the use of replacement referees due to ongoing labor disputes was the hot topic of discussion. Unfortunately, it wasn't for positive reasons. The replacement referees delivered multiple ineffective performances. The inconsistent management of the rules of the game became more obvious as the weeks continued. It was almost as if the players and coaches were treating these referees like substitute teachers—doing all they could to get away with infractions and even intimidate the referees to make calls.

In a similar vein, it seems that our nation is suffering from chaos and infractions because we have chosen replacement gods to keep order in our lives. Instead of living in obedience to God, who gives us life, direction, and purpose, we choose the replacement god of self-sufficiency. Instead of making sacrifices to serve under the order of our Mighty King, we cheapen our choices for the gods of convenience and comfort. There are no worthy replacements for our Lord. It is He alone that provides us the guidance needed for life.

In the end, without God "officiating" our lives, we are left with disappointment and disruption. We must resist the temptation to use the replacement gods of the world and keep focused on God's instructions for our lives. Only then will we experience true peace and order.

GO   Have you given in to a replacement god?

WORKOUT   Exodus 34:14; Deuteronomy 28:14

OVERTIME   Father, forgive me if I have replaced Your authority for convenience. Today I proclaim You are the only God in my life and I will serve You alone. Amen.

DAY 40

Clear Vision

Matt Yeager

READY   "But thank God! He has made us his captives and continues to lead us along in Christ's triumphal procession. Now he uses us to spread the knowledge of Christ everywhere, like a sweet perfume."—2 Corinthians 2:14 (NLT)

SET   As Lindsay took the field for her high school sectional soccer tournament, her coach gave her the assignment to mark the district player of the year—a girl who had scored more than one hundred goals so far in her high school career. Throughout the game, Lindsay happened to strike up a friendship with her opponent. And though Lindsay executed her job well, her team still lost by a large margin.

Lindsay's teammates shed tears after the game as they saw their season come to an end. To Lindsay's surprise, as she began to exit the field her opponent was waiting to talk with her. She had seen the light of Christ shining through Lindsay throughout the game and was drawn to it. As a result, Lindsay was able to invite her to church.

When we compete, it's easy to miss the big picture. Our focus is on winning, and often we forget that God wants to display His character through us. We can compete as driven and determined athletes, but we can also be selfless team players, encouragers, and yes, we can even love our enemies (oops, I mean opponents)!

GO   How can you change your focus so that you compete with the big picture in mind and represent God to the best of your abilities?

WORKOUT   Matthew 6:20–22; Philippians 2:1–8

OVERTIME   Lord, please expand my vision so that I can see what is important to You. Help me to allow Your Spirit to reflect Your character through my actions. Amen.

DAY 41

Pre-Game Speech

Mark Wood

READY   "I am telling you these things now while I am still with you."—John 14:25 (NLT)

SET   One of my favorite parts of sports, as a player and later as a coach, is the pre-game locker room speech, especially before a big championship game. Prior to one of the team's biggest games, Herb Brooks, head coach of the 1980 USA Hockey Team, said, "You were born to be a player. You were meant to be here at this moment. You were meant to be here at this game." That team went on to defeat the Russian hockey team in one of the greatest wins of all time.

The best coaches use pre-game speeches to focus their remarks and advice on what really matters—often delivered in a few carefully chosen words. Their words will have to direct, motivate, and sustain their players as they enter the battle ahead of them.

Jesus, the greatest coach ever, knew that the words He gave the disciples in His last week of life would also be His final message before they entered the battle ahead of them. He must have chosen His words so carefully, knowing that this message would have to sustain them (and those of us who would follow Him later) as they entered the battle against sin.

I urge you to read or reread Jesus's few, carefully chosen words in the book of John, but to read them as the greatest pre-game speech ever given from the greatest "coach" who ever lived.

GO   What message are you drawing on to sustain you in battle on the field? In life?

WORKOUT   John 16:33; Mark 16:15

OVERTIME   Lord, help me to make reading Scripture a priority in my life. Amen.

DAY 42

Training for Godliness

Kristy Makris

READY   "For the training of the body has a limited benefit, but godliness is beneficial in every way, since it holds promise for the present life and also for the life to come."—1 Timothy 4:8

SET   Most professional athletes will train a minimum of six to eight hours a day, seven days a week. In addition to the crunches, curls, and cross training, they eat nutritious food, drink plenty of fluids, and get good rest. There are few things more amazing to watch than a finely tuned athlete at the top of their game.

The Scripture in 1 Timothy reminds us that physical training has value, but of even greater value is training our minds, actions, and attitude for godliness. Just like the athlete, in spiritual training we consider a goal and then calculate what we must do to achieve it. We are training for godliness when we read Scripture and pray *every day*, watch our diet to make sure we take in wholesome nutrients that will keep us energized, and rest so that we can think clearly. None of these are done out of guilt, but out of gratitude for what Christ has done for us.

A strong Christian walk does not happen overnight. It develops over years and years, committing your life to your goal—to know Christ and make Him known.

GO   What type of a person do you want to be this time next year? More disciplined? Merciful? Grateful?

WORKOUT   1 Timothy 4:7; 1 Corinthians 9:25

OVERTIME   Lord, help me to train for godliness, which has value over all things. Amen.

DAY 43

The Competitor's Prayer

Dan Britton

READY   "Pour out your hearts before Him. God is our refuge." —Psalm 62:8

SET   Often, pre-game prayers can be like a "rah-rah" talk or a desperate plea to God for a big win. But as true competitors, we need to ask, "How should we pour out our hearts before God so that we will be spiritually ready for competition?" Here is a great prayer that you can pray before a game, competition, workout, or practice:

"Lord, I compete for You alone. In every victory and every loss, I play for You. Every time I compete, I stand for the cross. I play for You, Lord, when I put on the uniform, lace up the shoes, and walk out of the locker room. I declare my loyalty to You.

"My drive comes from the Holy Spirit. Through the pain and through the cheers, I will not give in or give up. The champion inside of me is Jesus. My only goal is to glorify the name of Christ. To win is to honor Him.

"All of my abilities are from You, Jesus. My heart yearns for Your applause. I will respect and honor my teammates, coaches, and opponents. I will play by the rules. I will submit to You as my ultimate coach.

"I wear Your jersey, Lord. Victory does not lie in winning but in becoming more like You. There is no greater victory. In Your name, I pray. Amen."

GO   How can you develop your prayer life in the arena of competition?

WORKOUT   Mark 11:24–25; John 5:14–15

OVERTIME   Lord, I admit that my prayers before competition are more focused on the scoreboard than on becoming like You. Develop in me a pure heart. Amen.

DAY 44

Play with Purpose
Ruth Riley

READY   "We have different gifts, according to the grace given to each of us . . ."—Romans 12:6 (NIV)

SET   I've been blessed to accomplish amazing feats that few female basketball players have achieved. I've been honored to play on an NCAA National Championship team, a WNBA Championship team, and an Olympic gold medal team. At Notre Dame, I hit the game-winning shot and was voted the 2001 Final Four's Most Outstanding Player. With the Detroit Shock, I was named the 2003 WNBA Finals MVP. At the 2004 Olympics in Greece, however, I had a completely different experience.

I was the 12th and final player chosen for the US team. I knew going into the competition that I would not be a significant contributor, but I was determined to prepare for whatever I was asked to do. Every day in practice I had the opportunity to guard Lisa Leslie, one of the best players in the world. And that was my role.

In Romans 12:6–8, the apostle Paul teaches us that we all have God-given gifts that we are called to use for His purpose. This is true for all aspects of our life. As athletes, it might be the difference between leading the team and providing support from the bench. As Christians, it might be the difference between speaking from a platform and serving others anonymously. But regardless of our role of responsibility, it's important that we remember to play with purpose, live with humility, and desire to make a difference through Christ's love.

GO What do you think it means to "play with purpose"?

WORKOUT 1 Corinthians 12:27–31; Colossians 3:23

OVERTIME Lord, I want to embrace my role and embrace the gifts and abilities You've given me. Help me transfer this principle into every aspect of my life. Amen.

DAY 45

Discipline Is a Good Thing

Kerry O'Neill

READY "No discipline is enjoyable while it is happening—it's painful! But afterward there will be a peaceful harvest of right living for those who are trained in this way."—Hebrews 12:11 (NLT)

SET When did *discipline* become a bad word? If students misbehave at school, they are disciplined. Discipline, often, has become synonymous with punishment. The dictionary offers seven different definitions of discipline, and only one deals with punishment. In fact, all the other definitions describe discipline in such a way that it means to train to develop a skill to act in accordance with the rules. Discipline is much more than the bad stuff that follows bad choices. It is a positive exercise that can prevent negative consequences in the future.

Athletes: Your coaches discipline you and teach you to discipline yourself so that you are prepared for the challenges ahead. Discipline grows you.

Coaches: As you encourage discipline in your athletes' lives, don't forget that the best lessons are often caught, not taught. Model a disciplined life.

Christ-followers: Do you see the similarity in the words *discipline* and *disciple*? Every disciple of Christ must practice discipline as we "train [ourselves] to be godly" (1 Tim. 4:7 NLT). It's interesting to note that the original Greek word used for *discipline* in that verse is the word from which we get the English word *gymnasium*. Training, practice, discipline, and work—God's gym for success in sports and in life.

GO   Do you welcome discipline as training or avoid it like it is punishment?

WORKOUT   Hebrews 12:3–13; Psalm 94:12–13

OVERTIME   Lord, help me to see discipline from You and others as a good thing. Give me courage to embrace the difficult training that will make me more like You. Amen.

DAY 46

Finish the Race

Sarah Roberts

READY   "I have fought the good fight, I have finished the race, I have kept the faith."—2 Timothy 4:7

SET   Less than halfway into the 1968 Mexico City Olympic marathon, Tanzanian runner John Stephen Akhwari's dream of gold was shattered. Unaccustomed to the city's high altitude, he began cramping early in the race, but managed to stick close to the leaders. Then, as runners jockeyed for position near the 11-mile marker, he collided with another athlete. Akhwari fell hard to the pavement, dislocating his knee and hitting his shoulder and head. Badly bleeding, he stood up and continued running.

Akhwari was the last out of the fifty-seven competitors (eighteen dropped out) to finish. Even though there were only a few thousand people left in the stands, he finished to a standing ovation. When asked why he continued to run when he was so badly injured with no chance of winning, he answered, "My country did not send me 5,000 miles to start the race; they sent me 5,000 miles to finish [it]."

Akhwari was a competitor because he knew he wasn't in the Olympics to start a race, but to finish it. Jesus served as our ultimate example of a competitor, knowing His purpose wasn't to just begin His race of redeeming all mankind, but to complete it at the cross by saying, "It is finished" (John 19:30). As Christian athletes, we are also called to finish every "race" we run. No matter how badly we are beaten down, through Christ's strength we can persevere and cross any finish line.

GO   What are some areas in your life that God's calling you to finish strong?

WORKOUT   Philippians 4:13; 2 Corinthians 8:11

OVERTIME   Lord, help me to finish the races that You've set before me. I look to You for guidance in everything I do. Amen.

DAY 47

The Hustle Contract

Rob Potts

READY   "Fathers, do not provoke your children to anger by the way you treat them. Rather, bring them up with the discipline and instruction that comes from the Lord."—Ephesians 6:4 (NLT)

SET   My daughter likely received more scrutiny playing sports than some other children did. I tried to motivate her to be more aggressive and play harder, and I used many tactics to do so. I thought I had tried everything, but then I came up with another great idea—the "Hustle Contract." The purpose of the Hustle Contract was to set some expectations for her effort. When I presented it to her, she first thought it was a joke, but when she discovered that I was serious, she looked defeated. That evening, I prayed about it. I realized that I was putting unreasonable pressure on her. Ultimately, the message in the contract was that my love for her was somehow tied to her soccer performance.

The next morning I sat down with her and confessed, "I was wrong. You don't need to focus on anything other than your relationship with Jesus. If you do that, He will help you with the rest of it." When I asked her to tear up the contract, the biggest grin stretched across her face. It was a privilege to have this conversation with her. I thank God for teaching me about grace.

Though we should compete with excellence, know that our performance doesn't earn God's love. God loves us no matter what we do or don't accomplish on the field.

GO   How can we best deliver the message of high expectations for performance with the underlying theme of grace?

WORKOUT   Matthew 11:28–30; 1 John 1:9

OVERTIME   Father, thank You for loving me for who I am, not what I do. Amen.

DAY 48

God's Game Plan

Jere Johnson

READY   "After Moses came back, he summoned the elders of the people and set before them all these words that the LORD had commanded him."—Exodus 19:7

SET   Head coaches spend a lot of time in preparation for their program's upcoming year. And it's not just the season preparations that need to be done—preseason, postseason and summer workouts are also considered.

Moses had quite a team. After patiently dealing with Pharaoh, the Israelites finally were given the freedom to go with their head coach and leader, Moses. Moses listened to and followed God in order to lead his team. Though his team grumbled, Moses convinced them to stick with the plan. Moses would go and speak with God and then come back and meet with his "assistant coaches" (elders or tribal leaders) and present to them God's game plan for the day or week. The Israelites responded to God's plan through Moses by saying that they would do all the Lord had asked of them. However, Moses's team did not always follow the plan. They relied on their own selfish desires and disobeyed.

As competitors, we need to stick with God's game plan for our lives even in tough times. If we endure, we may reach our ultimate goal one day. Our Coach's (Jesus's) Spirit will lead and guide us, helping us to stick with the plan. He also equips us to assist Him in carrying out His game plan for others. This flawless game plan is the only one that you will ever need!

GO   How can you start to implement God's plan for your life today?

WORKOUT   Exodus 21; Proverbs 3:5–6

OVERTIME   Lord, please show me where I need to adjust my game plan to fit Yours. Amen.

DAY 49

Fearless Perseverance

Sean McNamara

READY   "Even when I walk through the darkest valley, I will not be afraid, for you are close beside me. Your rod and your staff protect and comfort me."—Psalm 23:4 (NLT)

SET   I trained for almost a year for my first ultramarathon. At the beginning of the race, I heard a group of four men discuss how many years they had successfully completed the race we were about to begin.

When I mentioned this was my first race, one of the veteran runners offered me some great advice: Walk the uphills and run the downhills. His advice, which was helpful for me in that particular race, is also good counsel for all believers. There will be great moments in our lives, but there will also be dark times. We know that during those "uphills" we have to put one foot in front of the next and keep moving. We do so because we have a living hope that on the other side of that hill we will have another opportunity to run.

Because of God's presence in us, we can fearlessly persevere during the good times *and* in the most challenging moments of our lives. If we find our comfort in Him, then as competitors and as Christians we will always be able to fearlessly persevere no matter what obstacles we face.

GO   Reflect on a time when you experienced a "downhill run" following an uphill battle.

WORKOUT   Romans 5:3–5; Psalm 91:4

OVERTIME   Thank You, Lord, for the uphills and the downhills of life and for Your promise to never leave me. Amen.

DAY 50

For the Glory

Dan Britton

READY   "No wise man, enchanter, magician or diviner can explain to the king the mystery he has asked about, but there is a God in heaven who reveals mysteries."—Daniel 2:27–28 (NIV)

SET   As competitors, it's often difficult for us to give glory where glory is due. Training, discipline, perseverance, and drive are all characteristics that can propel us to the next level. Often, the praise, honor, and glory are focused on us as individual athletes.

Daniel had the chance to take the glory for himself, but instead he chose to give it to the Lord. "No wise man, enchanter, magician or diviner can explain to the king the mystery he has asked about, but there is a God in heaven who reveals mysteries," he told the king (Dan. 2:27–28 NIV). "The great God has shown the king what will take place in the future. The dream is true and its interpretation is trustworthy" (Dan. 2:45 NIV).

The FCA Competitor's Creed states:

- I do not trust in myself.
- I do not boast in my abilities or believe in my own strength.
- I rely solely on the power of God.
- I compete for the pleasure of my Heavenly Father, the honor of Christ, and the reputation of the Holy Spirit.

The results of our efforts must result in God's glory. To accept glory for ourselves is to rob God of His glory.

GO   What does it mean to compete for the joy of the heavenly Father?

WORKOUT   2 Corinthians 5:1–10

OVERTIME   Lord, please forgive me for often taking the credit when, in reality, my athletic accomplishments should be a fragrant offering to You. Help me to understand that the results of my efforts must result in Your glory. Amen.

DAY 51

Pressure Release

Debbie Haliday

READY   "To the weak I became weak, in order to win the weak. I have become all things to all people, so that I may by every possible means save some."—1 Corinthians 9:22

SET   We entered summer league basketball with a young team. Our inexperienced guards struggled to get our offense working, especially against a high-pressure, man-to-man defense. One day in practice, the coach taught us several pressure-release, back-door plays that changed our focus and took advantage of the defense. He told us that we would invite the pressure so that we could cut and score layups. We were skeptical.

In the next game, when the defense was zealous and our guards wide-eyed, the coach called a time-out to remind the team what we'd learned. Still afraid, we decided to try to execute the play. It worked!

Sometimes, the toughest defenses that teams face are the walls some players put up. Coaches try to love and care for them, but the players are skeptical. They ignore instruction and dare coaches to connect with them. To reach such players, we need to master the back-door play.

Paul understood this and "[became] all things to all people . . . [to] save some." Because God came to Earth as man to reach us, He can help us find ways to release the pressure that players might feel. As we begin to understand how to reach players in creative, back-door ways, the defenses will come down, and we can speak Christ's love to them!

GO   Do you expect players to adjust to you, or do you sometimes adjust to them?

WORKOUT   Isaiah 61; John 15:9–17

OVERTIME   Father, please give me the creativity and energy needed to coach this generation of athletes for Your sake. Amen.

DAY 52

Lean on Me

Jere Johnson

READY   "Send some men to explore the land of Canaan, which I am giving to the Israelites. From each ancestral tribe send one of its leaders."—Numbers 13:2 (NIV)

SET   When you walk onto a court to play a game, do you immediately think that you're going to lose or that you're going to win? Do you see obstacles, or do you see opportunities?

In Numbers 13, the spies were sent into Canaan to check out the land. God had already given them great victories in battle and rescued them from tough situations. During the forty days that they were evaluating the land, they could have seen a great opportunity, but they didn't. Only two guys, Joshua and Caleb, thought that they could succeed in acquiring the land. The rest of the team did what I think many of us would have done: They saw a wall and a formidable opponent and said, "We don't think that we can do this!"

Well, that much is true. We can't, but God can. God has already given us much. We only need to receive what He has promised. We are so much like these Israelites when faced with challenging situations. But I pray that we can be more like Joshua and Caleb, who received and believed in the opportunity that God had given them.

GO   What practical steps can you take to increase your faith in God's plan for your life?

WORKOUT   Deuteronomy 31:8; 2 Corinthians 12:9

OVERTIME   Lord, help me to remember that through my doubt, I can see only obstacles, but through my faith in You, I can see opportunities. Amen.

DAY 53

Everybody Loves a Comeback

Steve Beckerle

READY   "If God is for us, who can ever be against us?"—Romans 8:31 (NLT)

SET   Everybody loves a great comeback. In 2003, the Indianapolis Colts scored 21 points in the final five minutes to beat the Tampa Bay Buccaneers 38–35. Vince Lombardi once said, "It's not whether you get knocked down; it's whether you get up."

The Bible is full of great comebacks. God often chose to use people who, by our standards, didn't seem like the right person for the job or had a losing record. One great example is Peter. Peter was chosen as a disciple by Jesus and spent a lot of time with Jesus. Peter walked on water and saw Jesus perform many miracles. But as the death of Jesus neared, Peter fell asleep while praying and even denied knowing Jesus three times! In Matthew 16:13–20, we see that God redeems Peter, and Peter makes his great comeback. Peter will be the Rock on which Christ builds His Church (Matt. 16:18).

There are countless other stories in the Bible about God using broken people to make great comebacks for His glory. In Christ, we will have victory, no matter how bad the outcome looks when there are only five minutes left on the clock.

GO   In what current situations in your sports life do you feel like you need God's help to make a comeback?

WORKOUT   Acts 9; Matthew 16:13–20

OVERTIME   Lord, please help me remain strong in my faith in You. Help me see where I lack faith. Help me glorify You in times of victory and use me to build Your Kingdom. Amen.

DAY 54

Big Me, Little Team

Eileen F. Sommi

READY   "Everyone should look out not only for his own interests, but also for the interests of others."—Philippians 2:4

SET   I'll never forget standing in the locker room with my Division I field hockey players, listening to their postgame chatter. I was their new assistant coach and we had just lost our first game. To my amazement, I didn't sense the usual sober mood that comes with losing.

The players seemed upbeat, discussing their personal stats and goals as they changed out of their uniforms. None of the "superstars" cared about our injured fullback. I wanted to give some constructive feedback—but no one seemed interested. The players continued highlighting their own efforts. I walked out, bewildered.

As the season progressed, I realized that I wasn't coaching a team, but rather individuals primarily concerned with personal success. They had no idea that they could be better than the sum of all their parts. After their last game, few seemed sad that the season was over. Watching a group of gifted athletes lose game after game showed me how much is lost when we choose ourselves over our team. I can only wonder what the women on the team would have been like if they had decided instead to live like Christ—the one who washed Peter's feet, served lunch to five thousand and, ultimately, took our place on the cross.

His life, death, and resurrection remind us that the call to serve others is the greatest victory we can ever experience!

GO In what ways can you model Christ's service to others on your team?

WORKOUT Romans 12; 1 Corinthians 12

OVERTIME Jesus, fill me with Your Spirit that I might love others more than myself. Amen.

DAY 55

Driven

Chris Klein

READY "And you should imitate me, just as I imitate Christ."
—1 Corinthians 11:1 (NLT)

SET When it comes to excellence, I first have to look at everything through God's eyes. I look at who Jesus was as the ultimate example of excellence, service, and humility, and all of those values. I look at Him, and I obviously fall short in each of those in comparison to Him. His example is the definition of pure excellence.

It all starts with Jesus and looking at Him and His life. You look at the Christian faith and who we are as people, and we all fall short of Christ's example. But that doesn't mean we should stop striving for excellence. When we give up on that, we miss the whole concept that Jesus teaches us. Especially in sports, there may be a misconception that as Christian athletes we get too "nice" or don't want to compete. But for me, it's about competition. It's about competing as hard as I can for His glory.

It's not for my glory but for where He wants to take me in life. That's what drives me to continue.

GO   What is your definition of excellence? What drives you to be competitive and excellent?

WORKOUT   Romans 3:23–28; 1 Peter 2:19–25

OVERTIME   Lord, teach me the true meaning of excellence as displayed through the life of Jesus Christ. Give me the strength and drive to emulate His example in everything I do. Amen.

DAY 56

Contagious Consistency

Amanda Tewksbury

READY   "For his unfailing love for us is powerful; the Lord's faithfulness endures forever. Praise the Lord!"—Psalm 117:2 (NLT)

SET   I remember one teammate in college who was more consistent and faithful to her team than any other teammate I'd ever had. During practice, she was a focused leader who challenged us with her incredible work ethic and consistency. In four years, she missed only one practice because of an injury. Yet, she still worked out on the stationary bike while she watched the team practice. She sweat more than we did that day as we practiced on the court! She inspired me to be a more committed player and teammate.

Her commitment to her team reminds me of God's incredible faithfulness to His people since the beginning of time. From Genesis to Revelation,

God remained faithful to His people even when they turned their backs on Him—even when the crowd of people cried, "Crucify Him!" at Jesus's trial before Pilate. At all times, God is faithful to us through the work of the Holy Spirit in and among us. When we wholeheartedly believe this truth, our gratitude and love for God grows, and we are moved to be more committed and faithful to Him and His kingdom.

It's easy to lose focus on Jesus. We must seek to help one another remember God's faithfulness. Our consistency will be contagious!

GO   Where are you consistent in your competing or coaching? Where could you use more consistency?

WORKOUT   Genesis 32:9–10; 1 Thessalonians 5:23–24

OVERTIME   Thank You, God, for Your faithfulness to Your people in every moment throughout history. Help me to remember Your faithfulness and show me how You can use me today to demonstrate Your faithfulness to others. Amen.

DAY 57

God's Grace

Danny Burns

READY   "My soul, praise the LORD, and do not forget all His benefits. He forgives all your sin; He heals all your diseases. He redeems your life from the Pit; He crowns you with faithful love and compassion. He satisfies you with goodness; your youth is renewed like the eagle."
—Psalm 103:2–5

SET   If we were to count on our hands the number of times someone has let us down or the number of times we've disappointed someone else, we'd definitely run out of fingers! As humans, we fail all the time, whether it's in our relationships, careers, or daily disciplines. So it's a good thing that we have promises like Psalm 103:12: "As far as the east is from the west, so far has He removed our transgressions from us."

But an incredible thing happens when we begin to see ourselves through the eyes of our heavenly Father. No matter what mistakes we make, no matter the pain or regret we might feel, in God's eyes we shine brightly.

With the example of the perfect life of Jesus on Earth, we can move beyond those feelings of inadequacy and shame to partake of His transforming grace! His presence in our daily lives redeems us and rescues us from the pit. God continually invites us to Himself so that He can restore us and use us for His purposes—especially when we see ourselves through His eyes of grace!

GO   Do you fully realize that you are loved and forgiven?

WORKOUT   Micah 7:18–19; Romans 5:1–11

OVERTIME   Lord, change my heart today that I might be confident of Your love, and fill my mind with thoughts of Your grace so that others might also know You! Amen.

DAY 58

Meekness Is Not Weakness

Bill Burnett

READY   "God blesses those who are humble, for they will inherit the whole earth."—Matthew 5:5 (NLT)

SET   In Coach John Wooden's *Pyramid of Success*, he talks about the character quality of fight, which is a determined effort. He calls it "intensity under control." As I read about fight in Coach Wooden's book, I wrote the word *meekness* in the margin. Christ described himself as meek, and He calls on us to follow His example (Matt. 5:5). Meekness is not weakness. The meaning of the word in Greek, which was the original language of most of the New Testament, is "power under control." Another word for meekness is humility.

Picture a talented linebacker who doesn't act like part of the team and does his own thing instead. An unbridled linebacker doesn't listen to the coach and won't carry out his assignments. He merely tries to wreak as much havoc on the offense as possible. While his power is the envy of every coach, his unwillingness to submit makes him worthless to the team, because his power and passion aren't focused.

Christ was meek, and we must be also in order to fulfill God's purpose in our lives. Matthew 5:5 teaches that when we are surrendered to Christ, bridled by Christ, and living under His control, then we are blessed. The closer our lives line up with God's purpose for us, the more blessed we will be.

GO   Why do you think pride is the opposite of meekness?

WORKOUT   Matthew 11:28–30; 2 Timothy 4:7

OVERTIME   Lord, teach me about meekness. I am so prone to pride and self-sufficiency. Help me see the value of being bridled by You, allowing You to be in control of my life. Amen.

DAY 59

Play with Passion

DeLisha Milton-Jones

READY   "Whatever you do, do it enthusiastically, as something done for the Lord and not for men."—Colossians 3:23

SET   Throughout my WNBA career, I've been known as a highly competitive player. I use every inch or margin within the rules of the game to my advantage. It used to really bother me when I was accused of being a dirty player. I sought out wise counsel from people close to me, and ultimately came to the conclusion that if I'm not being competitive then I'm not giving my best to God. So I had to figure how to maintain my edge without losing my godliness. It took me a few years before I got it down pat, but once I was able to harness my passion, that's when I was truly able to glorify Him through basketball.

Playing with passion is all about giving God your best and striving for excellence. This goes beyond the court and into every aspect of my life.

It's about me having a passion for serving others and doing everything "enthusiastically" for the Lord.

As an athlete, it's important to let that passion show up when you train, practice, and play your sport. But it's just as important to strive for the same level of excellence in your relationship with God, your relationship with others, and anything that He calls you to do.

GO   What do you think is the connection between passion and excellence?

WORKOUT   Matthew 5:14–16; Ecclesiastes 9:10; 2 Timothy 4:7

OVERTIME   Lord, light a fire of passion within my heart so that I might strive for excellence in everything I do. I want to passionately pursue You, serve others, and play my sport to Your glory. Amen.

DAY 60

AWEsome Attitude

Rex Stump

READY   "He alone is your God, the only one who is worthy of your praise, the one who has done these mighty miracles that you have seen with your own eyes."—Deuteronomy 10:21 (NLT)

SET   There's a story about a time when Jesus healed a boy possessed by a demon. This boy had been possessed his whole life, causing him pain as well as taking away his freedom, joy, and peace. Jesus approached the scene and the people went crazy! "They were overwhelmed with awe," and "they ran to greet him" (Mark 9:15 NLT). Like a mob of junior high girls chasing down their favorite boy band, the people ran to see Jesus.

I once watched a tremendous high school football playoff. The home team was winning 9–7 with seventeen seconds left on the game clock. The visiting team had the chance to win the game with what seemed to be an inevitable field goal. But as the ball was snapped, the defense gave just enough of a push to get through and block the field goal. The home stands erupted in amazement and joy. The awe displayed at the game was similar to the awe people had for Jesus in this story.

There are times when we humbly and quietly approach our Lord in worship. But there are also times when we need to be in awe, cheering our socks off, and running to Him! Our God's not dead! He is alive, AWEsome, and worth running to!

GO   Do you run to meet Jesus? Why or why not?

WORKOUT   Mark 9:14–29; Psalm 40:16

OVERTIME   Father, You are awesome! Your miracles are outstanding. Give me an attitude change. Let me run freely to you with amazement. Amen.

DAY 61

The War That Rages On

Danny Burns

READY   "Be alert and of sober mind. Your enemy the devil prowls around like a roaring lion looking for someone to devour. Resist him, standing firm in the faith, because you know that the family of believers throughout the world is undergoing the same kind of sufferings."—1 Peter 5:8–9 (NIV)

SET   Watch any of the famous *Rocky* movies and you'll find a prime example of someone who never gave up in battle. With every movie, Sylvester Stallone's character, Rocky Balboa, faced an even bigger challenge. Yet through each 12-round beating, he always managed to get back up on his feet and find victory.

The first line of the FCA Competitor's Creed states: "I am a Christian first and last." As Christians we are faced with a battle that rages all around us. Our souls are up for grabs. We carry a large target on our backs as believers in Christ. For Satan, there's a higher price on our lives because we work for the Kingdom. The more we grow in

Christ and the more people come to know Christ through us, the more Satan loses.

The Competitor's Creed states: "I give my all—all of the time. I do not give up. I do not give in. I do not give out. I am the Lord's warrior—a competitor by conviction and a disciple of determination."

A lifetime of war isn't going to be easy. But if we draw on God's grace and God's power, we too can keep getting up round after round.

GO   What are the weak links in your armor where Satan attacks you the most?

WORKOUT   Colossians 3:1–5; James 4:7

OVERTIME   Lord, I know the battle ahead of me isn't going to be easy. Help me to rely on You alone for the strength and wisdom I need. Amen.

DAY 62

Finding Time

Jere Johnson

READY   "Come to Me, all you who are weary and burdened, and I will give you rest."—Matthew 11:28

SET   The life of an athlete goes something like this: get up early, go to the gym, go to class, go to lunch, go to practice, follow up with coaches and players, and finally, head home. At home, the schedule is just as full. How could anything more possibly fit into the day? But one thing often goes missing—something of vital and eternal importance. This is where "the squeeze" comes in.

The squeeze is the brief amount of time that we spend each day with Jesus. Those five or ten minutes often aren't listed in our day planners. Then out of guilt or obligation, we squeeze in a few minutes with our Master Coach. As the season picks up, though, He gets squeezed out rather than squeezed in.

Life gets busy and overwhelming, and the One who can help us the most often doesn't get the opportunity. But Jesus waits, patiently. In Matthew's Gospel, Jesus says, "Come to me." He knows that we are tired and weary. He knows that we need a break. In fact, He became weak on the cross so that we might be strong and filled with Him. Even when life's demands are pulling you in a million different directions, just remember that squeezing Him in is always better than squeezing Him out. Once He is in, listen, love, and learn from the only Coach who can give us more than we ever imagined.

GO   Are you squeezing the Lord in or out of your life?

WORKOUT   Isaiah 40:27–31; Hebrews 12:2–3

OVERTIME   Father, thank You that You forgive me for the times that I forget You. Help me protect my time with You, Lord. Amen.

DAY 63

Mirror, Mirror

Nate Bliss

READY   "For if you listen to the word and don't obey, it is like glancing at your face in a mirror. You see yourself, walk away, and forget what you look like."—James 1:23–24 (NLT)

SET   Have you ever stood in front of a mirror and really looked yourself in the eyes? According to these verses, reading the Bible is like looking in a mirror and seeing who we really are. There are two problems, however, when competitors try to act like they are who the Bible describes them to be.

The first problem is that we don't look into this "mirror" enough to know what the Bible says about us—truths like:

- You can do all things through Christ who gives you strength. (Phil. 4:13)
- God causes all things to work together for the good of those who love Him, for those who are called according to His purpose. (Rom. 8:28)

- God is able to accomplish things in your life that are exceedingly, abundantly beyond your wildest dreams. (Eph. 3:20)

The second problem arises when we forget what the Bible says about us and choose to listen to the wrong voices that call us losers, failures, and dumb jocks—voices that tell us, "You don't have what it takes." Listening to negativity prevents us from clearly seeing and believing God's Word.

Today, look in the mirror of God's Word and choose to see yourself the way He sees you.

GO What are three changes you would make if you started to act on what the Bible says about you?

WORKOUT Psalm 139:13–18; 2 Corinthians 1:20

OVERTIME Father, help me compete in life by believing what You say about me. Protect my heart and mind from the lies and give me the strength to consistently act upon Your Word. Amen.

DAY 64

Spiritual Muscles

Dan Britton

READY "So then, just as you received Christ Jesus as Lord, continue to live your lives in him, rooted and built up in him, strengthened in the faith as you were taught, and overflowing with thankfulness."—Colossians 2:6–7 (NIV)

SET It seems like only yesterday that I was in my high school weight room pumping the weights with the music cranked up to a deafening level. I have no doubt that the thousands of hours I spent in the weight room as a high school, college, and professional athlete have paid off throughout my athletic career. As a young man, I wanted not only to get big but also to excel in my sport. Lifting weights built me up and strengthened me to be the best athlete I could be. The muscle that I added helped me perform better and kept me from injury.

In Colossians 2:7 (NIV), Paul writes that as followers of Christ, we need to be "strengthened in the faith." The Lord desires for us to develop spiritual muscles by hitting the spiritual weight room. Our faith grows and has an impact on other lives when we develop spiritual muscles.

When I am in the weight room, I have a detailed, specific workout routine. Maybe we also need the same thing for our spiritual workout routines. God desires for you to invest the time to develop those spiritual muscles—not for your gain but for His glory!

GO   What does it mean to work out spiritually? Can you list some specific ways?

WORKOUT   1 Corinthians 9:25–27; 1 Timothy 4:7–8

OVERTIME   Lord, I often feel spiritually weak. I know that You desire for me to be strong. Please help me develop the spiritual muscles I need to serve You well. Amen.

DAY 65

It's Who I Am

Adrienne Sherwood

READY   "And a voice from heaven said, 'This is my dearly loved Son, who brings me great joy.'"—Matthew 3:17 (NLT)

SET   We were sitting on the bench before my varsity high school basketball game when my coach came over to sit by me. It seemed like she knew everything—even about our personal lives. I was fifteen years old and searching for love in all the wrong places. I was emulating my friends' behaviors and looks because I wanted to be accepted by my peers. She said, "Adrienne, I know you are trying to find yourself right now, but you need to understand that you will never really find yourself until you see yourself through Jesus's eyes."

I rolled my eyes and told her I knew who I was. But I was terrified after she walked away. It was as if she'd seen straight through to my heart, exposed for what it was: chasing after everything but Jesus.

When we accept Jesus as our Lord and Savior, He takes away all our sins, and His perfect blood covers us. As humans, we're born into sin. Maybe you feel like you cannot remember a time when you didn't struggle with lying, stealing, lust, addictions, or any number of other things, but our stories do not end how they begin! As a follower of Jesus, your identity in Him is the truest thing about you.

GO   Are you seeking other broken people to define you, or are you seeking the Word of God to tell you who you are?

WORKOUT   Genesis 1:27; Jeremiah 1:5

OVERTIME   God, thank You for loving me as Your child. Please help me find my identity in You. Amen.

DAY 66

Dreams

Roger Lipe

READY   "Now to him who is able to do immeasurably more than all we ask or imagine, according to his power that is at work within us, to him be glory in the church and in Christ Jesus throughout all generations, for ever and ever! Amen."—Ephesians 3:20–21 (NIV)

SET   Every year I look at my team's schedule of games during pre-season and start to calculate wins and losses. Though each season is filled with uncertainty and challenges, most competitors I know still dream about championships and MVP awards. What's exciting to me is that God can do immeasurably more than all of these expectations combined.

In the apostle Paul's letter to his friends in Ephesus, he reminds them that God's ability far surpasses their dreams. According to the power that

He works in those who believe, God is willing to go above and beyond what humans can imagine.

This means that God's plans for each of us are even greater than any we could dream of on our own, and He proves that to us in the person of Jesus Christ. And because of His faithful provision of grace, we can absolutely trust God to make provision for our lives in ways that we can't even conceive. He is able to do immeasurably more than all we even know to ask or imagine. Whatever challenges we as coaches and athletes face today, we can face them with the confidence that comes from God, knowing that His power and plans for us eclipse our wildest dreams!

GO   What are your God-sized dreams?

WORKOUT   John 14:12–14; Ephesians 3:14–20

OVERTIME   Lord, thank You that Your dreams for me are greater than any I could imagine on my own. Amen.

DAY 67

Whatever

Debbie Haliday

READY   "Remind the people to be subject to rulers and authorities, to be obedient, to be ready to do whatever is good, to slander no one, to be peaceable and considerate, and always to be gentle toward everyone." —Titus 3:1–2 (NIV)

SET   "Whatever." How many times a day do you hear that word? How many times do you say it?

"Whatever . . . I don't really care."
"Whatever . . . Coach will never give me playing time."
"Whatever . . . I quit."

The apostle Paul also used the word "whatever" a lot. His use of "whatever" wasn't about frustration or resignation; it was about completeness and wholehearted commitment. Whatever you are doing, do it for God's glory (1 Cor. 10:31). Whatever gifts you have, use them to serve others—be a team player (Rom. 12:6–8). Whatever is excellent or pure or whatever is right, think about those things (Phil. 4:6–8).

Jesus lived a "whatever" lifestyle. Whatever His Father wanted Him to say or do, He did it. Jesus never questioned His Father's will, because He trusted His Father. And trust is the key to the "whatevers."

You can say "whatever" because you don't trust people around you, or you can say "whatever" to Jesus because you trust Him. You can say, "Jesus, I know you want the best for me, so I will say 'whatever' to You and Your will for my life."

GO   What areas of your life need to move from an apathetic "whatever" to a sold-out "whatever"?

WORKOUT   Mark 10:35–45; Philippians 4:8–9

OVERTIME   God, I want to live a "whatever" life that brings You honor and glory—both on and off the field. I trust You and the plan You have for my life. Amen.

DAY 68

You Are What You Think

Kathie Woods

READY   "Whatever is true, whatever is honorable, whatever is just, whatever is pure, whatever is lovely, whatever is commendable . . . dwell on these things."—Philippians 4:8

SET   Almost every Christian team I know wants to have a positive philosophy of coaching. But in the battle of competition, sometimes we lose our focus in the heat of the moment. We may stay positive on the outside, but inside we are feeling the tension that causes us to lose our positive edge.

I have found that what athletes are *told* to think about is exactly what they *will* think about. We may say, "Don't ever miss a serve on game point." What are they thinking when they come to the line? They are thinking about *not* missing the serve. What do they see? Missing the serve is exactly what we told them to think about!

Instead, in the same way Paul instructs us to "dwell on these things," we need to encourage our teammates to focus on the good and right and true ways to compete. This way, they are not thinking about anything else. Jesus is the perfect example of this: He was so single-minded in His purpose on Earth that He never wavered. He completely fulfilled the task that He had been given to do: go to the cross for our sake!

Paul says in Philippians to keep our minds *dwelling* on what is true, pure and excellent. When we do, our athletes will fulfill their goals and develop their gifts—and we will receive God's peace.

GO   Do you spend more time dwelling on the positives or the negatives?

WORKOUT   Psalm 119:97; Romans 12:2

OVERTIME   Thank You, Lord, for renewing my mind in Christ and redirecting my focus to be centered on Your grace! Amen.

DAY 69

Jump In

Fleceia Comeaux

READY   "Therefore the disciple, the one Jesus loved, said to Peter, 'It is the Lord!' When Simon Peter heard that it was the Lord, he tied his outer garment around him . . . and plunged into the sea."—John 21:7

SET   A clear sign marks where you have just crossed the earth's equator. North of the equator, a low-pressure weather system will rotate counter-clockwise; south of the line, it will move clockwise. Whichever direction it comes from, there is a gradual progression of movement that slowly increases its momentum as the storm gets further away from the equator.

The equator is a good illustration of our decisions for God. We are in one of three places:

1. We are moving to the north of the line: progressing toward God's purposes in the right direction.
2. We are moving to the south of the line: progressing away from God's purposes in the wrong direction.

Or

3. We are stuck in the middle without any movement: slowly dying because of our lack of commitment.

Are you like the disciple who recognized the Lord but did not move, or like Peter who threw caution to the wind and jumped in to be with the Lord? Every coach wants a committed, dependable athlete. God is no different. He wants your consistency in love, faith, and obedience on and off the field. Commit today to take the leap and jump in!

GO   How can you jump in to what God wants to do on your team and at your school?

WORKOUT   Mark 12:30; 1 Timothy 4:14–16

OVERTIME   Father, even when I do not consistently choose You, You are always choosing me. Help me to venture toward You with a willing heart and reckless abandonment. Amen.

DAY 70

The Examined Life
Clay Elliott

READY   "Test yourselves. Surely you know that Jesus Christ is among you; if not, you have failed the test of genuine faith."—2 Corinthians 13:5 (NLT)

SET   Professional baseball player Josh Hamilton has suffered much in his life. His propensity for "druggin' and drinkin'" created some incredible hardships for him. The lifestyle he chose resulted in brutal hangovers, regrettable tattoos, severe loneliness, bad company, an inability to play baseball at a high level, injuries, and more. As he examined his life, he realized that the drugs and alcohol were killing him and that he could not, on his own or by his own strength, overcome the grip that these things had on him.

When we examine our lives based on the truth of God's Word, we are reminded that Scripture points us to God's plan. Josh examined himself against God's Word and confessed his need for Jesus. God saved him. He became brand new, and his life became radically different. But the temptations of life never end. Josh has been brought down through relapses and failures multiple times since his conversion to Christianity.

Examining our lives is something we should do all the time. We are told, "Examine yourselves to see if your faith is genuine. Test yourselves" (2 Cor. 13:5 NLT). The Christian life is not a simple statement of "I believe" before continuing on our merry way. The Christian life is one of constant examination.

GO   What areas of your life are unexamined?

WORKOUT   Psalm 26:2; Lamentations 3:40

OVERTIME   Father, the unexamined life can unravel fast. I ask You to use Your Word to test me so that I may be found in the faith. Amen.

DAY 71

Right Place, Right Time

Jere Johnson

READY   "Who knows but that you have come to your royal position for such a time as this?"—Esther 4:14 (NIV)

SET   The gym was packed with screaming fans. Late in the fourth quarter, Luke entered the game—his first as a varsity player. The ball was passed to him, and he dribbled toward the basket. The ball bounced off of his foot and out of bounds. *I am so out of place here*, Luke thought.

With less than a minute left, Luke's team got the ball back. Minutes later, it was a tie game. Luke picked up the ball, risked it all, and made the winning shot.

In the Old Testament, Esther, of Jewish descent, had the great honor of being chosen as King Xerxes's queen. But Esther's uncle Mordecai needed her help—there was a plan to rid the kingdom of all Jews. Esther knew that she had to speak to the king, but in those days to enter the king's presence uninvited was to risk death. So she rallied the people and leaned on the Lord for help.

Sometimes, you may not understand God's plan. But like Esther, when you realize God's purpose for your life, you will feel empowered. Taking a risk is easier when you know God is in control. Esther trusted that God would provide, and He did. Feel out of place in your life? Find God and join Him there.

GO Are you willing to take a risk for God today?

WORKOUT Esther 8; John 14:15

OVERTIME Lord, guide me in Your ways so that I will know how to take a stand for You, just as Esther did. When I start to feel out of place, help me to know You are near. Amen.

DAY 72

The Thankful Competitor

Dan Britton

READY "And whatever you do, in word or in deed, do everything in the name of the Lord Jesus, giving thanks to God the Father through Him."—Colossians 3:17

SET A Christian competitor is a thankful competitor. Every time you step onto the field of competition, your heart explodes with thankfulness, because you are abundantly grateful for God's blessings. You have a deep conviction that your athletic abilities have come from Him alone.

There is no room for pride in a thankful heart. A thankful competitor is a humble competitor.

When you are thankful, you don't try to impress others. You don't put unrealistic expectations on your teammates' shoulders when you realize God's grace in your life. You don't care about the scoreboard when your definition of winning is becoming more like Jesus every time you compete. You don't view competition as crushing your opponent when you desire to play in such a way that elevates all participants to a higher level of competition. You are not consumed with what others think when you are focused on an audience of One.

You don't criticize teammates when you believe the best about them. You don't have to play for others when you already feel God's pleasure. Let the power of thanksgiving change the way you compete. A Christian competitor is a thankful competitor.

GO   When do you struggle to give thanks? When is it easy?

WORKOUT   2 Corinthians 9:10–11; Colossians 3:15

OVERTIME   Father, I want to be a thankful competitor. Whatever I do or say, I will do it all in the name of the Jesus, giving thanks to You. Amen.

DAY 73

The Sweet Spot of Serving

Nancy Hedrick

READY   "Show family affection to one another with brotherly love. Outdo one another in showing honor. Do not lack diligence; be fervent in spirit; serve the Lord."—Romans 12:10–11

SET   When I was a teenager, I played a match I'll never forget. I'd drawn a top seed at a national tennis tournament. My opponent and I battled the purest match I've ever played before or since with points won on effort, not errors. Back and forth were the deuce-ads, neither of us willing to give up. When it was over, I was elated. I had never played that well.

She and I hugged, drenched in perspiration. The score? 6–1, 6–1. (For her!) According to the score I had been crushed. It was strange to feel simultaneously exhilarated and embarrassed.

Yet, God taught me a valuable lesson on serving—not aces, not others, but Him. God showed me that while I played, I respected her and her play (love and honor), and I intensely fought for every point (with diligence and fervency in spirit). Because of that, I served Him in that match. And on His scoreboard, I won.

In serving Him, I was in effect also serving my opponent, my teammates, and the spectators. And just like the exhilarating feel of hitting the "sweet spot" for a blistering ace, perfectly disguised drop shot, or winning point, I had discovered the sweet spot of serving my God. And no win could replace my elation.

GO How does serving Him in your sport serve your opponent, your team, and the spectators?

WORKOUT Romans 12:9–18; Mark 12:28–31

OVERTIME Lord, even in the midst of competition when it can be the most difficult, help me to be in the sweet spot of serving; serving You first by displaying love, honor, diligence, and fervency in spirit.

DAY 74

Pick Me! Pick Me!

Jere Johnson

READY "Accept my instruction instead of silver, and knowledge rather than pure gold. For wisdom is better than jewels, and nothing desirable can compare with it."—Proverbs 8:10–11

SET Coaches often travel the country recruiting future players, selling their programs, and enticing future stars to choose to attend their schools. Blue-chip recruits are in high demand, and every coach is inwardly yelling, "Pick me! Pick me!" In the same way, wisdom calls out to us and pleads her case about why we should pick her. Choosing wisdom is invaluable; it is better than solid gold or pure silver; whoever finds wisdom finds happiness and life and obtains favor from the Lord (Prov. 8:34–35).

We find wisdom in Jesus Christ, who lived a sinless life on Earth yet was with the Father in the beginning of creation when wisdom was formed (Prov. 8:22). In Jesus, we discover the exact representation of God's sustaining wisdom. And when we live in Him, we grow in the knowledge and wisdom that guides our lives. With Him, there is health, peace, and life.

As we act out wise choices and decisions based on our relationship with Christ, we will experience the rich harvest that righteous living brings! Wisdom is calling out to us, "Pick me! Pick me!" When we do, we will never be disappointed!

GO   How can you start living in the wisdom that comes from Christ?

WORKOUT   Proverbs 8; James 1:5

OVERTIME   God, guide me this day with the mind of Christ, and protect my heart with the grace that wisdom brings. Amen.

DAY 75

What's Your Name?

Rick Horton

READY   "You must not misuse the name of the LORD your God."
—Exodus 20:7 (NLT)

SET   Our names are important to us. Perhaps we were named after a favorite relative, a great leader, a biblical character, or maybe a sports legend. Our names are often the way in which we identify ourselves.

As athletes, we will have lifelong struggles to not allow our identities to be wrapped up in our performances and achievements. We are more than just the names and numbers we wear on our backs. We will also struggle to reject certain labels put on us from others. We don't want to be misidentified.

The Bible has powerful things to say about names. In Matthew 16, Jesus asks Peter to tell Him "who he is" according to the people. Peter tells Him that some believe He is John the Baptist, others Elijah, others Jeremiah or one of the prophets. Peter's answer represented just a few of the misunderstandings at the time when it came to Jesus's true identity. Jesus then asks Peter a follow-up question: "Who do you say I am?" Peter confidently and accurately answers that He is the Christ, the Son of the living God.

Who are you? As we desire to have others know who we really are, we should strive to know others accurately without false judgment. We should also seek to know the true character and attributes of God.

GO   What are ways we are tempted to misuse God's name?

WORKOUT   Exodus 20:7; Matthew 16:13–19

OVERTIME   God, please help me to never misuse Your name. Guide my thoughts, actions, and the words that come out of my mouth. May I honor You in everything I say and do. Amen.

DAY 76

Team J. C.

Josh Carter

READY   "Now the large group of those who believed were of one heart and mind, and no one said that any of his possessions was his own, but instead they held everything in common."—Acts 4:32

SET   NASCAR racing isn't often thought of as a team sport. But ask any driver and he will tell you that without a good pit crew, his chances of winning are slim. Jeff Gordon credited his team for putting him in a position to win the 2005 Daytona 500, which he did by holding off Kurt Busch and Dale Earnhardt Jr. over the last two laps. "I knew over 500 miles, with that pit crew, that team—that hopefully some patience would pay off."

The FCA Competitor's Creed states that "I am a member of Team Jesus Christ." So what is it that constitutes membership on Jesus's team? We can learn some valuable insights from the early church in Acts. First, they had at their core the common bond of faith in Jesus and His purposes. Second, they were obedient to Jesus's command to love one another sacrificially as He had loved them.

In sports, it is important that we have faith in our team and that everyone is on the same page regarding the team's goals and objectives. We must also be willing to give sacrificially of ourselves for the good of the team.

GO   Are you a member of Team Jesus Christ? How do you know?

WORKOUT   Luke 9:23; Acts 2:42–45

OVERTIME   Lord, thank You for sacrificing Your Son and inviting me to be a member of Your team. I pray that You will help me have a sacrificial love for others in a way that points people to You. Amen.

DAY 77

Influence with Integrity

Adam Wainwright

READY   "The one who lives with integrity lives securely, but whoever perverts his ways will be found out."—Proverbs 10:9

SET   In today's sports world, it seems that anything done for an advantage is fair game—as long as you don't get caught. As a major league pitcher, I've seen it all. Managers who spend their entire careers stealing the signs of other coaches from the dugouts and down the baselines. The list goes on.

As Christians, however, we are held to a higher standard. Our goal should be to live a life that's pleasing to God and that allows us to have influence on those around us. People seem to gravitate toward those who do things the right way. And on the other hand, if you're not living with integrity, your influence will quickly be torn down.

Daniel was a man who lived with great integrity. When given the chance to turn his back on God's commands, Daniel stood strong and gained influence over an entire kingdom. And there is no greater example of integrity than Jesus. He was who He says He was and lived a sinless life despite many opportunities to succumb to temptation.

Living with integrity in this day and age isn't easy. But with God's Word and the Holy Spirit guiding your steps, it is possible to be the person of integrity that He created you to be.

GO What can you start doing today that will help set you on a path toward godly integrity?

WORKOUT Daniel 1; Proverbs 28:6

OVERTIME Lord, I want to walk upright in Your sight. Give me the determination to live with integrity and help me build trust within my relationships so that I might influence others for Your Kingdom. Amen.

DAY 78

How Would Jesus Compete?

Josh Carter

READY "You have heard that it was said, An eye for an eye and a tooth for a tooth. But I tell you, don't resist an evildoer. On the contrary, if anyone slaps you on your right cheek, turn the other to him also."—Matthew 5:38–39

SET When the 2004 NBA Western Conference semifinal series between the Minnesota Timberwolves and the Sacramento Kings heated up, tempers started flaring. Kings guard Anthony Peeler hit former teammate Kevin Garnett in the face with an elbow during the third quarter of Game 6 and was immediately ejected from the game. "It was retaliation after [Garnett] hit me with an elbow," said Peeler.

Retaliation is a natural response when we feel we have been wronged. If others hurt us, we want to hurt them back so that they know how it feels. However, as Christians our desire is to live as Jesus did, so we must look at how He handled injustice. 1 Peter 2:21, 23 says:

> "For you were called to this, because Christ also suffered for you, leaving you an example, so that you should follow in His steps . . . when He was reviled, He did not revile in return; when He was suffering, He did not threaten but entrusted Himself to the One who judges justly."

Handling inappropriate behavior aimed at you doesn't mean you can't play hard. We should play hard—not to pay back another person, but to honor the Lord and help our team win.

GO Why is it important, in competition, to handle personal assaults the way that Jesus did?

WORKOUT Proverbs 20:22; 1 Thessalonians 5:15

OVERTIME Father, help me compete in a way that reveals Jesus's presence in me. Help me turn the other cheek, even when I don't feel like it. Amen.

DAY 79

The Leadership Secret

Dan Britton

READY "'O Sovereign Lord,' I said, 'I can't speak for you! I'm too young!' The Lord replied, 'Don't say, "I'm too young," for you must go wherever I send you and say whatever I tell you. And don't be afraid of the people, for I will be with you and will protect you.'"—Jeremiah 1:6–8 (NLT)

SET In an age obsessed with leadership, it's hard to find someone who talks about leadership in an authentic, transparent way—especially in the world of sports.

Most leaders are taught to never admit we don't know something be-cause others would consider us inadequate. But I believe all great leaders are aware of their personal limitations and inadequacies. The "Inadequate Leader" recognizes his or her imperfections. Here are my three key characteristics of the Inadequate Leader:

1. **The Inadequate Leader has acute self-awareness.**
   When a leader is self-aware of his or her natural skills, strengths, and spiritual gifts, then the leader understands his or her leadership fingerprint as well as weaknesses.
2. **The Inadequate Leader doesn't hide weaknesses.**
   Lead with your strengths and lean on your weaknesses. Your weakness will be another's strength; when you try to do it all on your own, you prevent others from leading with their strengths.
3. **The Inadequate Leader realizes failure is inevitable without God's intervention.**
   The Inadequate Leader knows that failure is at the doorstep every day unless God steps in.

We are inadequate, but God is not. Trust Him.

GO   What does it look like for God to do the impossible in the world of sports?

WORKOUT   Proverbs 3:5–6

OVERTIME   Father, teach me to depend on You, the Adequate One. I pray that You will use me as an Inadequate Leader. Amen.

DAY 80

Fickle or Positive

Rex Stump

READY   "This means that anyone who belongs to Christ has become a new person. The old life is gone; a new life has begun!"—2 Corinthians 5:17 (NLT)

SET The stadium filled with a crowd ready to see their ranked team bring home another victory. The visiting team came out strong to start and through halftime. With only three minutes left in the game, the home team finally began showing signs of a comeback. Finally the home crowd began making noise! But in spite of a valiant effort, the home team lost.

The home team fans quietly left the stadium with about the same intensity they displayed during the game. I felt like I was watching a bunch of "fickle Christians"!

What is a fickle Christian?

- **Fickle Christians live with no sense of urgency.** As God's children on His victorious, ranked team, we still can't think, "We are the ranked home team; we're supposed to win." We must live with urgency to win and not underestimate our opponent.
- **Fickle Christians sit back and expect others to get the job done.** It appeared the crowd wouldn't participate unless they liked how the team was performing. No matter what, we must engage in cheering on our fellow brothers and sisters in Christ.
- **Fickle Christians complain instead of cheer.** It is so easy to complain and whine when things don't go our way. Instead, let's use words of encouragement.

Don't be caught with a fickle attitude. We are new in Christ, and therefore we live with Him working through us!

GO Evaluate your faith; is it fickle or fantastic?

WORKOUT Philippians 2:14; Colossians 3:1–17

OVERTIME Father, thank You for this new day! Help me to be alert to living in a positive manner. Give me opportunities to serve and encourage others. Amen.

Media Day

Sarah Rennicke

READY   "Instead, you must worship Christ as Lord of your life. And if someone asks about your hope as a believer, always be ready to explain it."—1 Peter 3:15 (NLT)

SET   On Media Day for Super Bowl XLIX, reporters, players, and fans packed University of Phoenix Stadium in preparation for the big game. Players from both teams fielded questions about the season, their team, and the upcoming competition, as well as personal life lessons they'd adhered to along the way.

As I watched the conference, I mused on the fact that this enormous platform was available for players to support teammates, mention a love of the game, and even note God's goodness. Some expressed gratitude for the opportunity to play, and others missed the mark. Athletes are paid to play professional football, but with that task comes other responsibilities, such as press appearances and fulfilling media obligations. They've been placed on a pedestal of influence, and can either make the most of ample opportunity or let it slide by untouched.

What about your Media Day? When the time comes for you to share how Christ has changed your life, what will you say? Everything? Nothing at all? When the chance comes to share your story with others, whether the platform is big or small, may you understand there are willing ears eager to hear about your God, and that you're meant to speak truth and love.

GO   Are you eager or apprehensive to share your faith with others? Why?

WORKOUT   Psalm 145:18; Ephesians 4:29

OVERTIME   Lord, help me to realize that I have a platform that people are watching, waiting to hear what I say. May my mouth be filled with offerings to You, that others can know You and what I believe. Amen.

Linger Longer

Dan Britton

READY "Where can I go to escape Your Spirit? Where can I flee from Your presence?"—Psalm 139:7

SET Unfortunately, as athletes and coaches we often approach devotions as something that needs to get done due to our "conquer it" attitude. It becomes an action item that gets checked off the to-do list, because we love the feeling of accomplishment. Our mind-set toward devotions is like taking medicine or eating spinach, something that we *have to* do instead of *long to* do! Devotions become all about us—what we can get out of it and how much we need it. Yes, we do desperately need it, but we also need to realize that God longs for us to be with Him.

Too many people go through the motions. No spiritual grit. No investment made for the long term. We're running on spiritual fumes instead of having a full tank. Soaking in God's presence daily moves us from spiritually surviving to spiritually thriving.

Sit at the feet of Jesus and wait for Him to speak. Listen to the Holy Spirit instead of filling the time with your words. Linger in His presence and find out what's on God's heart. We need to STOP–DROP–SOAK. STOP daily; DROP before the Lord; and SOAK in His presence. Stopping is our discipline; dropping is our posture; and soaking is our worship. Extend your time with the Savior and enjoy His presence!

GO How can soaking in God help the stress you face as a competitor?

WORKOUT Psalm 62:5; Psalm 27:14

OVERTIME Lord, help me to linger longer in Your presence today. Open my ears and heart to hear from Your Spirit. Amen.

Choosing Sides

Les Steckel

READY "You did not choose Me, but I chose you. I appointed you that you should go out and produce fruit and that your fruit should remain, so that whatever you ask the Father in My name, He will give you."—John 15:16

SET When I was a kid, our neighborhood basketball court—the kind with the chain nets—was the place where everybody went to play the best basketball. One day, I was chosen by a college player to be on his team—something I really didn't want to do. To me, the opposing team looked a lot more capable of winning. The college player said to me, "You don't want to be on our team, do you? I *chose* you, but I can tell that you don't want to be on our team." I hadn't said a word to him about it, but my body language had betrayed my thoughts. He agreed to let me change teams; our team lost.

When God chooses us and invites us to follow Him, thank goodness He doesn't change His mind if one day we don't look like we're much of a Christian! In fact, the Bible says that He will leave the flock of ninety-nine to search the hills for the one lost sheep (Luke 15:4).

Even when we don't make winning decisions, Jesus remains faithful in His devotion to us. And if for some reason we get a little distracted, He stands waiting for our return to His side.

GO How can His devotion *to* you inspire devotion *from* you?

WORKOUT Joshua 24:14–15; 1 Corinthians 15:58

OVERTIME Thank You, God, for seeking me and choosing me to be Your disciple! I ask that You would help me to bear fruit today that reflects Your devotion. Amen.

What God Hates

Roxanne Robbins

READY "The LORD hates six things; in fact, seven are detestable to Him: arrogant eyes, a lying tongue, hands that shed innocent blood, a heart that plots wicked schemes, feet eager to run to evil, a lying witness who gives false testimony, and one who stirs up trouble among brothers."
—Proverbs 6:16–19

SET Can you think of times, perhaps even recently, when you have done something that God abhors? It's interesting (and convicting) that the Lord puts shedding innocent blood and spreading strife among brothers in the same list. To the world, shedding innocent blood is certainly considered much worse than creating conflict. But just what does it mean to stir up "trouble among brothers"?

"Strife" can be defined as "a bitter, sometimes violent conflict or dissension; an act of contention; exertion or contention for superiority." On a sports team, this could take many forms. Even if the argument or hard feelings only exist between you and the other person, everyone on your team feels the tension, and that leads to strife.

Consider how you're treating your teammates and the other people in your life. If you're creating strife, ask the Lord for wisdom. Ask Him to help you behave differently and then act on the guidance He gives you.

GO How can you mend strife on your team based on God's teachings?

WORKOUT Matthew 5:21–24; 1 Thessalonians 4:1–11

OVERTIME Father, I am guilty of manipulating my teammates and friends to get what I want. Please forgive me and show me the way to correct these actions. Cause them to be as detestable to me as they are to You. Amen.

All-In Sacrifice

Hal Hiatt

READY "And so, dear brothers and sisters, I plead with you to give your bodies to God because of all he has done for you. Let them be a living and holy sacrifice—the kind he will find acceptable. This is truly the way to worship him."—Romans 12:1 (NLT)

SET All-in sacrifice is rare in sports and in life. It's the kind of sacrifice that takes a commitment to doing more than you think you can do and to giving more than you think you can give. Sacrifice always costs something, and that's the reason it's rare. Human nature wants to receive more and keep more for self. But sacrifice means putting the needs of self second. All-in sacrifice is even rarer because it costs everything. It involves a total surrender that keeps absolutely nothing in the reserves.

Sacrifice in sports often means giving up other activities for the sake of being on a team. All-in sacrifice in sports means leaving every ounce of energy you have on the field. Whether you're practicing or competing, you give your all for your team.

All-in sacrifice is what God has done for you through His Son, Jesus. Jesus died for our sins because it was the only way for us to be restored to God. Jesus's death on the cross was the ultimate all-in sacrifice.

GO What things will you need to reprioritize in order to be "all in" in your sacrifice for your sport and your life for Christ?

WORKOUT Romans 2:1–2; 1 John 4:19

OVERTIME Lord, give me the strength and the courage I need to be "all in" with my sacrifice the way that You were "all in" with Your sacrifice for me. Amen.

Attitude Is Everything

Brad Tippins

READY   "You must have the same attitude that Christ Jesus had."
—Philippians 2:5 (NLT)

SET   As a coach and a player it can be a challenge to have the right attitude. Many times we will say of a player, "He needs an attitude adjustment," or "Her attitude stinks," or especially, "If he had the right attitude, he could be a great player."

Sometimes when we are winning, we can have a prideful attitude that is not pleasing to God. Sometimes we need to be humbled, and that humbling can be quite painful.

As a coach at the middle school level, I have found that teaching young athletes to have the right attitude has become one of the most difficult parts of my job. We see too many high-profile athletes on TV who are glorified as they display a prideful attitude. The "me first, I'm great" attitude is a big negative that we all have to battle. But if we demonstrate the "team first" concept, we may just find great success.

GO   How can we find the balance between being confident in our abilities and that of our team, and being too prideful?

WORKOUT   Proverbs 11:2; Philippians 2:5–11

OVERTIME   Lord, thank You for the success You've given us. Help us remember to give the glory to You, because You have blessed us with abilities and talents which we are to use for that purpose. Help us to be walking examples for the young people You've given us to work with. Amen.

DAY 87

It's Not about You

Dan Britton

READY   "They do everything to be observed by others . . . The greatest among you will be your servant. Whoever exalts himself will be humbled, and whoever humbles himself will be exalted."—Matthew 23:5, 11–12

SET   As competitors, we want to be the best in everything. Being good is good, but being best is better. We want to go from *good* to *great* in every aspect of life. We have to be #1—on and off the field. Nobody remembers the loser. Second place? Seriously? We engage in the relentless pursuit of excellence!

Striving to get better in all aspects of our life isn't a bad thing. But if it's a selfish pursuit, it will never satisfy. We get—so we can give to others. We are loved—so we can love others. We are blessed—so we can bless others. NFL players like Tim Tebow and Ray Lewis understand this concept. When they step into the weight room or onto the practice field, everybody gets better; their desire to be their personal best spills over onto their teammates. Tebow and Lewis feel an obligation to give back, serve others, and make others better. These men model the words of Jesus.

When Jesus is the center, we take our eyes off of ourselves and we are willing to invest in others. Serve. Sacrifice. Give. Love. Coaches and athletes, this is what we are called to do: make others better, *today*.

GO   As a competitor, what ways can you intentionally serve, build up, and encourage others?

WORKOUT   Philippians 2:1–11; John 13

OVERTIME   Lord, I desire to make others better. Teach me Your ways so that I can help, bless, and encourage others. Show me how to put others before myself. Amen.

Didn't See It Coming

Jere Johnson

READY   "When the donkey saw the Angel of the LORD, she crouched down under Balaam. So he became furious and beat the donkey with his stick. Then the LORD opened the donkey's mouth."—Numbers 22:27–28

SET   John was a great miler. He always liked to take the lead early in the race and run to victory. His coach, however, was concerned about an upcoming race. John's top opponent was a runner who liked to come from behind to win. When the race started, John raced to the lead. His coach told him to move to the inside of lane one, but John ignored him. During laps two and three, his coach told him the same thing, but John again ignored him—he knew the victory was his. On lap four, John's coach became more insistent, but John stayed firm—and remained right in the middle of the lane.

On the final turn of the race, John's opponent passed him on the inside and took the victory. John's coach had seen what John himself had been blind to.

John had a blind spot and could not see what was coming. Many times, we do not listen to others who want to show us areas in which we can improve because we cannot see the need ourselves. But we need to pay attention to others. God may be using them to show us what we need to change today.

GO   How can you eliminate your spiritual blind spots?

WORKOUT   Proverbs 13:10; 15:22

OVERTIME   Lord, please bring bold friends into my life—true friends who can show me my spiritual blind spots. Allow them to speak to me with truth in love. Amen.

The Eternal Prize

Jill Lee

READY "Do you not know that in a race all the runners run, but only one gets the prize? Run in such a way as to get the prize. Everyone who competes in the games goes into strict training. They do it to get a crown that will not last, but we do it to get a crown that will last forever."—1 Corinthians 9:24–25 (NIV)

SET As a member of the sports media, I hear quite a few stories about athletes who build their entire lives around their sport. They eat, sleep, breathe, and live specifically to achieve their personal athletic goals. But then something unexpected happens. Suddenly, they're stripped of the sport that had occupied so much of their time and energy. And when it's gone, they're left with nothing. Complete emptiness.

It's at this point that many athletes realize they need something more—something that can't be found in trophies or medals—something that is eternal. God has brought them to this point for them to realize their need for Him and to show them that all aspects of this world are temporary. Nothing will last forever except the crown of life that can only be found in a relationship with Jesus.

What is your motivation for competing? Today, make sure that the most important race you are running is the one that offers the prize of eternity. Run to "get a crown that will last forever."

GO How would you react if your sport were taken away from you today?

WORKOUT Matthew 6:19–21; Colossians 3:23–24

OVERTIME God, help me to keep my eyes focused on the eternal prize. I want You to be first in my priorities and I want to compete for Your glory, not mine. Amen.

One-Two Punch

Kerry O'Neill

READY "He cared for them with a true heart and led them with skillful hands."—Psalm 78:72 (NLT)

SET Many competitors are described as either very talented but not very hard-working or not very talented but very hard-working. In a similar manner, people are often described as being good at what they do but lacking in character, or being a really nice person who is not very good at what they do.

However, it really doesn't need to be an either/or situation. The talented athlete should also be a hard worker. The successful coach should also be someone of high character. King David was such a leader. He had the incredible combination that we should all desire in our lives—a pure heart and skillful hands.

Purity of heart with unskillful hands is ineptitude. Impurity of heart with skillful hands is corruption. Purity of heart with skillful hands is beauty and strength. Having skillful hands does not mean that talent came naturally; skillful hands require hard work to become the best you can be.

You don't have to be perfect in character or skill. You need to focus on the two things you can control: your attitude and your effort. Give your best attitude and effort and trust the Lord to make you not only more like Christ in your character but also more skilled at what you do.

GO Which area have you neglected more: your character or your effectiveness?

WORKOUT Proverbs 14:23; 2 Thessalonians 3:10–12

OVERTIME Lord, develop in me a pure heart and skillful hands so I can effectively love and serve You and others. Amen.

Correction

Donna Noonan

READY "All Scripture is inspired by God and is useful to teach us what is true and to make us realize what is wrong in our lives . . . God uses it to prepare and equip his people to do every good work."—2 Timothy 3:16–17 (NLT)

SET I know of a young girl who at six years old had an amazing ability to play golf. Once, she played with her mom, and after three-putting one of the greens, the girl took her putter and slammed it into the green. Her mom immediately told her she was done and would have to sit in the cart for the rest of the round. Afterward, the mom asked her daughter if she knew why she had to sit. The girl responded, "Because I three-putted?" Her mom told her that she loved her and explained that it was not the three-putt, but rather her reaction. It was not the performance; it was the behavior.

How often do we miss the reason the Lord allows correction in our lives? We get so focused on the consequences that we totally miss the lessons the Lord is teaching us. What I see as punishment for failing, Jesus sees as a tool to make me more like Him. As athletes and coaches, we constantly receive and give correction. When correction occurs, we need to stop, think, and listen to learn the true lesson being taught so that we may be complete—equipped for every good work.

GO In what ways do you respond differently to correction if it comes from your coach, your parent, or your friend?

WORKOUT Proverbs 15:32; Hebrews 12:5–6

OVERTIME Lord, I want to be made complete and equipped by You. Create a hunger in me to study Your Word and apply it to my life. Amen.

It's All Good

Clay Elliott

READY "Noah was a righteous man, blameless among his contemporaries; Noah walked with God."—Genesis 6:9b

SET "Dad, it's all good! Everybody is doing it." This was exactly what my oldest daughter told me when she decided it was okay to say, "I swear to G—." Well, I don't really like that statement, and so I declared that it wasn't "all good" in my house! When we are faced with peer pressure it ends up having some kind of huge power over us. Our tendency is to buy in and participate, whether it's good or bad.

Noah lived in a day when everybody was joining in and doing it. It was so corrupt that God decided to wipe everyone on the planet out! Everyone was corrupt . . . except Noah. So, how did Noah not succumb to the pressure? He walked with God. A righteous lifestyle is not about fitting in. It's not about saying, "It's all good." A righteous life includes purging the world and its standards from your walk and embracing God and His standards in your life. So don't be tempted to buy into the world's ways. Instead buy into God's. Walk with Him daily, and keep your focus on what He says is "all good" when making choices in life.

GO What can you add or take away in your daily walk with God to reflect more of His righteousness?

WORKOUT Exodus 15:26; Isaiah 5:21

OVERTIME Father, I desire to hear You say "it's all good" as I walk with You on the field of competition. Give me the strength to not succumb to the pressures of this world. Amen.

Soul Nutrition

Amy Richards

READY "God, You are my God; I eagerly seek You. I thirst for You; my body faints for You in a land that is dry, desolate, and without water."—Psalm 63:1

SET *This year is our year.* A common phrase heard in the sports world. Work hard, train, and study for hours to hopefully achieve perfection. Eat the right foods to sustain a high level of performance on the field. Lift weights to increase strength. Get enough sleep. All in the hopes of having the best year yet.

As competitors, our lives are marked by a voraciously competitive spirit. We want to be the best athlete, the winningest coach, or part of the perfect team. We discipline our minds and bodies to attain the highest level of performance, all in an effort to feed this insatiable appetite for competition.

As believers, we should transfer this same deep desire to satisfy our competitive cravings into a desire to nourish our souls instead. We hunger and thirst for a "win," but what about our relationship with Jesus? In our soul training, do we allow ourselves to snack on God-substitutes or use anything other than Jesus as our primary source of meaning, self-worth, comfort, or fulfillment?

C. S. Lewis said, "We are far too easily pleased." As competitors, we wouldn't eat a diet of unhealthy foods and expect to perform at the highest level. So, in nourishing our souls, let us not be "easily pleased." Let's satisfy our hunger with the richest of foods—the Word of God.

GO Are there any "God-substitutes" in your life?

WORKOUT Psalm 42:1; Psalm 63

OVERTIME Father, give me the same focus and devotion to You and Your will as I have toward my sport. Help me to nourish my soul with Your truths so my soul will continually hunger for more of You. Amen.

Five Minutes

Dan Britton

READY "I also consider everything to be a loss in view of the surpassing value of knowing Christ Jesus my Lord."—Philippians 3:8

SET As the Competitor's Creed states, your desire as an athlete is to "compete for the pleasure of [your] Heavenly Father, the honor of Christ, and the reputation of the Holy Spirit." That is truly competing with a spiritual focus, not a physical focus.

On July 25, 2003, Andrii Serdinov, a Ukrainian swimmer, experienced five brief minutes of glory when he achieved his lifelong goal of setting a world record in the 100-meter butterfly. His joy, however, was short-lived, and his time in the spotlight disappeared just as quickly as it had arrived. Five minutes later, eighteen-year-old US swimmer Michael Phelps broke Serdinov's world record. It happened so fast that Serdinov could not even finish one interview about his incredible accomplishment.

Fame is like the wealth described in Proverbs 23:5 (NIV): "Cast but a glance at riches, and they are gone." The glory that is of this world will never last; it will all be destroyed. The only thing that lasts is God's kingdom. As athletes, we strive to be the best, but we cannot hold on to our accomplishments. We must offer them to the Lord to be used for His glory. Seek first the kingdom of God, and if He blesses you with five minutes of glory, make sure that you offer it back to Him.

GO Why is it so hard to focus on the eternal things and so easy to focus on the things that are temporary?

WORKOUT John 12:25; 2 Corinthians 4:16–18

OVERTIME Lord, please forgive me for getting awards and records for my own gain. I want to be a surrendered athlete, not a selfish one. Amen.

Putting It into Practice

Rachel Pace

READY "Study this Book of Instruction continually. Meditate on it day and night so you will be sure to obey everything written in it. Only then will you prosper and succeed in all you do."—Joshua 1:8 (NLT)

SET Muscle memory is vital for every athlete. The hours dedicated to running the same play are not a waste. Experienced athletes know that once their muscles replay normal moves without a second thought, they can focus on developing more complex skills to be adequately ready for their game.

As Christians, we have to work to make our faith second nature. Although the Holy Spirit is alive in us and guides us in our actions, we still have to battle our sinful human nature when facing tough choices. The only way to be ready for those days of tough choices is by preparing for those days today. In Ephesians, Paul described a Christian's fight as a battlefield against Satan. He told the church in Ephesus to be strong and to put on the full armor of God so that they can "stand firm against all strategies of the devil" (Ephesians 6:11 NLT). The armor of righteousness, truth, and faith equips us to not only defend ourselves from attacks but also fight against them.

Like we practice for an upcoming game, we have to daily read God's Word and pray so that our faith becomes second nature.

GO What are you doing now to strengthen your faith?

WORKOUT James 1:2–4; Ephesians 6:10–18

OVERTIME Lord, it's easy to get comfortable in my faith and not push myself to know You more. Give me the passion to search Your Word daily, and help me to see the opportunities You give me to live out my faith. Amen.

In One Ear

Marc Agnello

READY   "Do not merely listen to the word, and so deceive yourselves. Do what it says."—James 1:22 (NIV)

SET   I read an article once about a professional baseball player who couldn't seem to make the necessary adjustments needed in his approach to hitting. The player contended that his hitting was fine, but many of his current and former coaches disagreed. They pointed to the fact that his batting average had continued to decline and that he was striking out at an alarming rate.

In one game, the player might have three hits, but in the next four games he wouldn't get a hit, striking out nine times. It's not that the player didn't have good coaching—one of his previous coaches was a former batting champion. The problem was that he wasn't doing what the coaches were asking. James 1:22–24 (NKJV) says:

> Be doers of the word, and not hearers only, deceiving yourselves. For if anyone is a hearer of the word and not a doer, he is like a man observing his natural face in a mirror; for he observes himself, goes away, and immediately forgets what kind of man he was.

A man who listens but does not put what he has heard into action immediately forgets what kind of man he is. It is not enough to simply hear about something, know about it, or even talk about it; you must live it.

GO   As a competitor, in what areas of your life do you need to put into action what you have heard?

WORKOUT   Ephesians 6:6; Hebrews 13:16

OVERTIME   Lord, please help me live out Your Word in my daily life. I fall short so often, but I trust that, with Your help, I can be a living witness to the gospel. Amen.

Priorities

Al Schierbaum

READY "Watch out and be on guard against all greed because one's life is not in the abundance of his possessions."—Luke 12:15

SET At the beginning of every football season, Coach Tom Landry would give his players his priorities: God, family, and football, in that order. By keeping these priorities, he avoided the madness and chaos that often consume a coach's life.

These priorities provide great wisdom for us as we seek balance in our lives. When we keep first things first, we honor God and others around us, which helps us avoid relational destruction. Sadly, though, many coaches become "life losers" because they put their sport first and everything else second. They measure their self-worth by what they accomplish on the athletic field and by the wins they attain. In the process, everything else suffers. Their families fall apart, and they feel empty because their soul is not being nourished by a relationship with God.

Jesus warns us against getting caught in this web of deception. In fact, He says that at the heart of this "accomplishment complex" is personal greed. This attitude produces a no-win season in God's eyes because it puts another god before the one true God, Jesus Christ.

Putting Jesus first means keeping Him at the center of all we do. By keeping Him first, we can't help but pursue excellence for His sake and keep our careers in proper perspective.

GO What changes in your life can you make to reflect God's priorities?

WORKOUT Psalm 127:1–5; Galatians 5:16–26

OVERTIME Father, turn my eyes away from the empty ambitions of this world so that I might see today the depths and riches of Your love in Jesus! Amen.

Be Careful, Stay on Course

David Gittings

READY   "So be careful how you live. Don't live like fools, but like those who are wise."—Ephesians 5:15 (NLT)

SET   For the trail runners whose races take them on all types of terrain, staying on course is essential. Normally, plastic streamers hanging from branches and arrows painted on the ground mark the route. Regardless, one thing is sure: finding your way to the finish requires attention, discernment, and focus.

An ultrarunner myself, I was once at mile 94 of a 100-mile race when I passed a struggling runner who asked whether I would mind some company for the last few miles. The long descent traversed back and forth across the mountain. Continuing on, we increased our chatter. Eventually, I realized the roar of the river was not getting closer as it should. Distracted, we'd turned left rather than right at a bend in the trail. We had to turn and run several miles back up the mountain. Sure enough, there were streamers marking the correct direction. Our focus had failed.

This kind of situation is not uncommon in races and in life. Though veering off course can be like a sudden change in direction, most often we are gradually pulled off course without even realizing we are headed the wrong way. Focus and discernment are skills that we must develop. It takes intentionality to stay on God's path for us. Be careful, then, how you walk!

GO   Describe a time when you were "pulled off course." What could you have done to prevent that?

WORKOUT   1 Thessalonians 4:1–9; 1 Peter 1:13–25

OVERTIME   God, You desire us to follow Your paths. Give me the discernment I need to follow Your markings and not lose focus. Grant me the power to live carefully and attentively. Amen.

The Path of Freedom

Clay Meyer

READY   "Now the Lord is the Spirit, and where the Spirit of the Lord is, there is freedom."—2 Corinthians 3:17 (NIV)

SET   Los Angeles Angels All-Star Josh Hamilton's career was initially derailed by the abuse of and addiction to drugs and alcohol. After several stints in rehab, he was still unable to escape those vices under his own power. Once he hit bottom in 2005, his heart was opened to God's love and how much he needed Christ's help to overcome his addictions and heal the brokenness in his life.

Substance abuse can take on different forms, including drugs (illegal and performance-enhancing), alcohol, tobacco, and numerous other things. But the answer to addictions of any kind can only be found by embracing the life and sacrifice of Jesus Christ.

Like Hamilton, we may not be able to overcome substance abuse and addiction under our own strength, but with Christ as our focal point and the support of Christ-followers we can begin walking down the path to freedom and recovery. The road to recovery is long, but once we understand we can never overcome our sin-filled nature on our own and accept God's grace and forgiveness in our lives, we can experience total freedom.

GO   Are you allowing anything in your life to become all-consuming to the point of addiction?

WORKOUT   Psalm 73:23–26; Hebrews 12:1–2

OVERTIME   Father, even though I realize my life and everything in it is Yours, I often place other things at the center. I pray that through Jesus I can be loosened from the chains that are holding me back. May I focus on You being the center of my life. Amen.

Note: If you are currently in the middle of an addiction of any kind, reach out to a trusted friend for help and accountability.

DAY 100

The Audience

Jess Hansen

READY   "Whatever you do, work at it with all your heart, as working for the Lord, not for human masters."—Colossians 3:23 (NIV)

SET   When I got the chance to play my first college basketball game in my home state, I was so excited to play in front of the forty-plus people who had come to watch me. I wanted to play well and prayed that God would help me to do so. Much to my disappointment, I played the worst game of my life. I made only one shot in my team's humiliating thirty-point loss. I was so embarrassed that I didn't want to talk to anyone who had come to cheer me on. I was afraid of what they thought of me and my performance.

But as I left the locker room after that game, I was welcomed by smiling faces and warm hugs. The people that came to see me play didn't care if I had scored three points or thirty points. They just wanted to see the one they loved.

God looks at us in the same way. God loves us enough to call us His children. He loves us unconditionally and does not base His love on our actions or performance. All God wants is for us to do the best we can with the gifts that He's given us.

As athletes, we can either find our worth in our performance or find our worth in something eternal. Sports are what we do, but they do not define who we are or how much we're worth.

GO   What defines you?

WORKOUT   Ephesians 1:3–6; 1 John 3:1

OVERTIME   Lord, thank You for calling me Your child. Help me to live in such a way as to reflect Your perfect love. Amen.

From Fear to Free

Sarah Rennicke

READY "Such love has no fear, because perfect love expels all fear. If we are afraid, it is for fear of punishment, and this shows that we have not fully experienced his perfect love."—1 John 4:18 (NLT)

SET What are you afraid of? Afraid to run the wrong route or turn the ball over? Afraid to look your coach in the eye after striking out? Afraid that at the end of your career no one will remember you? Perhaps you've been hit with heavy disappointment in the past and can't bear to heave your heart up in hope again. Or are you fearful to hand the unknown future to an unseen God?

Fear creates a disconnection in us and covers the truth with lies. The enemy wants to keep us chained to anxiety, weighed down by burdens we were never meant to carry. Jesus calls us into a freedom and peace we can breathe in fresh every day by the power of the Holy Spirit. His great and sacrificial love for us trumps all our doubts and concerns and replaces them with confidence that, in Him and through Him, fear has no hold on us.

We can take this unyielding trust back to our sport and play with abandon, knowing we cannot do anything to make God love us less. We can tuck this truth into our hearts and replace "My fear is . . ." with "What frees me is . . . *Jesus.*"

GO What are your fears? What motivates these fears?

WORKOUT Isaiah 41:10; 2 Timothy 1:7

OVERTIME Father, thank You for seeing me, even in the midst of my fears. Please help me hand over what makes me afraid to You and trust that You have my life under control. Amen.

Do the Deal, No Matter How You Feel

Jenny Burgins

READY   "Now faith is the reality of what is hoped for, the proof of what is not seen."—Hebrews 11:1

SET   After losing every soccer game and almost every basketball game in a season, I was learning a lot about perseverance. It's not easy for coaches whose teams are on a losing streak to encourage players to win when they realistically don't have a chance.

Because I live in a "softball town," most of our best athletes play for the leagues rather than the schools. We have no developmental soccer programs, so it's difficult to be competitive with other schools. Recreational soccer leagues could help develop players, but many never expected that it would work in our town.

Then God began to change things. Our city recreational director said that they would start "rec soccer." Then one of the athletes was offered a scholarship from a nearby college despite the losing season. Just when it looked like nothing good would come out of the year, God reminded me that He is always at work for the sake of His people, even when we're not sure what's happening.

By having faith in God and persevering in what we believe He is asking of us, we can watch Him make good of any situation. As one of my friends says, "Don't give up five minutes before the miracle!"

GO   Are you walking by faith or by sight?

WORKOUT   Philippians 3:13–14; 1 Timothy 6:11–12

OVERTIME   Thank You, Lord, for teaching me to press on toward the goal of knowing You no matter how I feel. Help me to look for Your miracles! Amen.

Priceless

Dan Britton

READY "So if anyone purifies himself from anything dishonorable, he will be a special instrument, set apart, useful to the Master, prepared for every good work."—2 Timothy 2:21

SET Since 1997, MasterCard has received hundreds of awards for their catchy ad campaign featuring the slogan "Priceless." As Christians, I think the slogan for our relationships with Christ should be "Serving Is Priceless." Most people think that *serving* is the same thing as *service*. I believe there is a huge difference between the two. Christ did not come to give good service; He came to serve. As an athlete, I am not supposed to give good service to my teammates—I am to serve them. As a coach, I serve my team; I do not provide them a service. Service is something you pay for or something you expect. But serving involves sacrifice and meeting real needs.

Christ desires that we become servants to our teammates, friends, family, and communities. He has set us apart for a great work. We are His instruments! Today, it seems like everyone in the sports world wants to be a leader, not a servant. Jesus never told us to be leaders, but He did tell us to be servants. To be a leader you must serve, and this is my challenge to you today. Fulfill Christ's calling on your life and become a servant!

GO On a scale of 1 to 5, how well are you serving others (teammates, coaches, friends, family)?

WORKOUT Ephesians 2:10; 2 Timothy 2:14–21

OVERTIME Lord, teach me how to serve. My teammates and friends need to see what Jesus looks like. I pray that when I serve they will be able to see You. Amen.

It Happens

Jere Johnson

READY "Whether I come and see you or am absent, I will hear about you that you are standing firm in one spirit, with one mind, working side by side for the faith that comes from the gospel, not being frightened in any way by your opponents."—Philippians 1:27–28

SET It happens all the time: As an athlete or coach, you are confronted with a situation in which your attitude will dictate your altitude. Someone does you wrong; a promise is broken; a ref makes a horrible call in a game; you are treated poorly.

In his letter to the Philippians, Paul urged the believers to stand firm in their faith in Christ. Paul wanted everyone to stay focused on the glory of the cross, no matter what happened. Though we may be wronged, mistreated, or severely tortured, we must stand firm, knowing that God will provide the victory.

Things happen in sports and in life. Teammates will fail you, coaches will misunderstand you, and officials will make unjust calls against you. But remember, how you respond will show others what is in your heart. Can others tell that Christ is in you? Respect all, fear none. That is God's calling for us. So face it—*it* happens to the best of us. Do your best through Christ to show that He truly rules in your life.

GO Is your attitude flying high in Him, or is it way below His radar?

WORKOUT Philippians 1:20–30; James 1:2–6

OVERTIME Lord, as I compete for You today, help me maintain an attitude that displays Your glory to all. Give me the strength to respect and honor those who do me wrong. Help me to serve You better today than I did yesterday. Amen.

The New Four-Letter Word

Dan Britton

READY   "Dear brothers and sisters, when troubles of any kind come your way, consider it an opportunity for great joy. For you know that when your faith is tested, your endurance has a chance to grow. So let it grow, for when your endurance is fully developed, you will be perfect and complete, needing nothing."—James 1:2–4 (NLT)

SET   Several years ago, the football team at the Oscoda Area High School in Michigan cancelled the last five games of the season as a result of the team's 0–4 record and inability to score even one point. My heart hurts thinking about the possible victories those athletes will never experience because someone gave up on them. And I don't mean on-the-field victories.

Quitting has permeated our society and become a core value by which many people live. Twenty years from now, I can hear those athletes saying that they wish the coaches hadn't given up on them. Even if they had continued the season and went winless and scoreless, it could have been a defining character-building moment for them. Because it's often in the struggle and strain where God shapes and molds us.

Christ didn't quit on the cross. Paul didn't give up preaching the gospel when he was thrown into jail. It is easy to give up when it gets tough. However, when it gets tough and we press on, God is glorified. Keep your eyes fixed on Jesus and finish strong.

GO   When was the last time you stuck it out even though you wanted to quit? What did you learn from that experience?

WORKOUT   1 Peter 1:6–7; Galatians 6:9

OVERTIME   Father, help me when things get tough and I want to quit. Show me the blessing that is waiting for me. Amen.

Giving Your All

Blake Elder

READY "Summoning His disciples, He said to them, 'I assure you: This poor widow has put in more than all those giving to the temple treasury. For they all gave out of their surplus, but she out of her poverty has put in everything she possessed—all she had to live on.'"—Mark 12:43–44

SET There are many things that I count as a privilege in my athletic career. But the greatest privilege I've had was the opportunity to play for Coach Jerry Moore. He is a man of faith, integrity, and passion. He had a slogan that we lived by: "What are you willing to give up?" His giving character fueled me and my teammates to be men who gave our all for what we believed in.

Jesus is attracted to those who give their all, like the poor widow mentioned in Mark 12. She laid her entire livelihood down, believing that it would make a difference. It wasn't the amount as it compared to others or her circumstance that determined what she gave. Out of a selfless commitment to something larger than herself she gave everything that she had, knowing she was being faithful to her calling.

When circumstances get tough and the odds are against you, what you are willing to give will make a difference in your life. It shows the level of your commitment to a cause greater than yourself, inspiring others to do the same.

GO Do you tend to let negative circumstances and momentum determine whether you give your all?

WORKOUT Proverbs 11:24–25; 2 Corinthians 9:6–11

OVERTIME Lord, thank You for giving Your best to me in Your Son, Jesus. I pray that You would give me the strength to give all that I have to constantly represent You. Amen.

Believe

Chris Rich

READY "Do you believe that I can do this?"—Matthew 9:28

SET In the 2014 NCAA Championship, the University of Connecticut men's basketball team was the underdog no one believed could win. But after UConn won, their second-year head coach, Kevin Ollie, said, "They believed in a vision before anyone could see it. They stuck with it through down times, when we were losing. When we were winning, they stayed together, and they believed it was possible."[2]

Just one month prior, UConn lost to Louisville by 33 points. After the game, UConn's point guard, Shabazz Napier, walked into the locker room and told the team that they would be holding the National Championship trophy one month later. Everyone in that locker room believed him.

Often in sports and in life, we face seemingly insurmountable odds. An opponent that seems unbeatable. Injuries, losses, and a whole host of other things try to derail our hope. In life other issues and adversities cause us to doubt God's love.

In Matthew 9:28, Jesus asks two blind men, "Do you believe that I can [make you see]?" When they answered, "Yes, Lord," they did so in faith. Jesus said, "Let it be done for you according to your faith!" (Matt. 9:29). Jesus blessed these two men with this miracle because of their faith. Similarly, in our lives, we must believe that God is powerful enough to overcome any trials we face.

GO In the face of adversity are you instilling belief in those around you?

WORKOUT Matthew 9:27–31; John 16:25–33

OVERTIME Lord, I believe in You and Your plan for my life. Help me to believe in You and Your plan no matter what. Amen.

God's Nutritional Plan

Jimmy Page

READY "Let us be given vegetables to eat and water to drink. Then examine our appearance and the appearance of the young men who are eating the king's food, and deal with your servants based on what you see."—Daniel 1:12–13

SET God created food for our bodies to give us energy, sustain life, prevent disease, and facilitate healing. Our food choices will affect our mood, mental focus, physical performance, weight, immune system function, and more. In order to compete at our best, we must know exactly what to eat and when to eat it!

Daniel also wanted to know what to eat and when to eat it. He knew that the first portion of food served from King Nebuchadnezzar's table was offered to idols and that it would be unacceptable to partake of it. Unwilling to put anything into his body that would dishonor God, he, along with Shadrach, Meshach, and Abednego, stood by his convictions and ate nothing but vegetables and drank nothing but water! God blessed his decision.

In America today, the overweight adult population has arguably been eating the "royal" food—which is now in many cases an idol of self-satisfaction and gluttony. The FCA Competitor's Creed states, "My body is the temple of Jesus Christ. I protect it from within and without. Nothing enters my body that does not honor the Living God."

Isn't it time to truly commit to honoring God through healthy eating? God will bless our decision and our performance on the field will certainly improve!

GO What can you do to get your health back on track?

WORKOUT 1 Corinthians 10:31

OVERTIME Lord, I commit to honoring You through what I eat. Give me the wisdom to eat foods that lead to good health and peak performances. Amen.

The Voice of Truth

Jere Johnson

READY   "Teach me Your way, Yahweh, and I will live by Your truth."
—Psalm 86:11

SET   In a scene from the basketball movie *Hoosiers*, Hickory High needed a sub, and the coach didn't have anyone to put in the game except Ollie, the manager. Ollie went in, immediately got fouled, and had to go to the line for two free throws.

Ollie nailed the first basket. Then, the opposing team called a time-out. Ollie's coach gathered his team together and told them that "*after* Ollie hits the free throw" they would run a certain defense. Because the coach was a voice of truth at that moment in Ollie's life, the unsuspecting player stepped up and hit the next free throw. And his team won!

Throughout the Bible, we see stories of men and women who heard voices of opposition but chose to listen to the voice of truth. What if David had believed those who said that he was too young to defeat Goliath? What if Esther had not gone to the king to intervene on behalf of her people? Hundreds of years later, that same voice fulfilled the promises of their lives when Jesus appeared on the scene and the voice said, "This is My beloved Son . . . Listen to Him!" (Matt. 17:5).

Satan wants us to listen to the voices of opposition in our lives and fail. However, one voice rings louder and truer than any other: God's voice found in His Son and in His Word!

GO   How can you spend more time in the Word or in prayer to better hear the voice of truth?

WORKOUT   Psalm 29:3–4; Psalm 66:18–20

OVERTIME   Living Word, thank You for consistently speaking to me through prayer and the Bible. Please give me ears to hear Your voice all day long! Amen.

Take Off Your Shoe

Matt Yeager

READY   "After all, you have not yet given your lives in your struggle against sin."—Hebrews 12:4 (NLT)

SET   As I would teach younger athletes the game of soccer, I would often have players who constantly kicked the ball with their toe. If I could not get them to change the way they kicked the ball after repeated efforts, I would resort to a fail-proof method: I would ask them to take their shoes off and kick without their shoes. It worked every time because kicking the ball with their bare toe was too painful without the protection of their shoes.

It is much the same in our lives with the sin we struggle to conquer. If we continue to live in certain sin, the method of overcoming that sin can be painful. If we want to become all God created us to be, we have to figure out how to better fight the temptations.

So how do we overcome consistent sins? First and foremost, we need to pray fervently and ask for God's power to resist sin. Second, we need to discover what situations "trigger" those sins and come up with a plan to avoid those situations. Third, we need to determine how we can create a deterrent—something that will make us want to avoid that sin at all costs. So go ahead. Take off your shoe to conquer that sin.

GO   What sin do you constantly struggle with?

WORKOUT   Romans 6

OVERTIME   Lord, please give me the strength to overcome my sin and the wisdom to create a plan that will give me victory over this area of struggle. Amen.

Resist the Devil

Chris Kelsay

READY   "Therefore, submit to God. But resist the Devil, and he will flee from you."—James 4:7

SET   There are many things in this life that can poison your heart. In college, it might be alcohol, drugs, or toxic relationships. As a professional athlete, those temptations are often in the form of material possessions and money. But when I committed my life to Christ during my playing days at the University of Nebraska, I allowed Him to fill the void in my heart that worldly things could never satisfy.

No matter how long you have been serving the Lord, the enemy of your soul is going to tempt you to walk away from the straight and narrow path. Thankfully, when I began playing for the Buffalo Bills, I had a group of like-minded individuals to help me stay the course.

Jesus set the perfect example of how to resist worldly things. He surrounded Himself with a group of men that wanted to please God, and He studied God's Word daily. When He faced a difficult test in the wilderness (Matt. 4:1–11), Jesus was able to stand firm against Satan's temptations.

When you face temptations within sport and life, you don't have to carry those burdens by yourself. Find other believers that will hold you accountable, stay consistent in your Bible devotion, and then you will be able to fully "submit to God" and "resist the Devil."

GO   What are some temptations that you face as a competitor? What can you do to resist those temptations?

WORKOUT   Matthew 4:1–11; Matthew 26:41

OVERTIME   Lord, give me the strength to say no to temptation. Put people in my life that will help me make right choices. Increase my desire to study Your Word so that I might not sin against You. Amen.

An Attitude of Gratitude

Al Schierbaum

READY   "Rejoice always! Pray constantly. Give thanks in everything, for this is God's will for you in Christ Jesus."—1 Thessalonians 5:16–18

SET   If you were to list the qualities of the people you most admire, a thankful attitude would probably be at the top of the list. In his book *Developing the Leader Within You,* John Maxwell says this concerning attitude:

> The disposition of a leader is important because it will influence the way the followers think and feel. Great leaders understand that the right attitude will set the right atmosphere, which enables the right responses from others.

Attitude is always a choice. You may not be able to control circumstances, but you can control how you react to those circumstances. First Thessalonians 5:16–18 implies that our trust in God is directly linked to our attitude. One of the most difficult disciplines in life is that of thankfulness—taking time to adjust your attitude and thank God for the things He has given you.

Paying bills used to be a pain in my side. When I finished, I would be like an angry bear. Then, one day the Lord spoke to my heart about being thankful that He had provided the income to pay those bills. Since that day, as I write each check, I thank God for His provision, and I am no longer like an angry bear when I finish.

GO   How does your attitude create the right atmosphere for your team?

WORKOUT   Psalm 46:10; 1 Thessalonians 5:12–22

OVERTIME   Father, thank You for the way You love me and want Your best for me. Thank You for the peace that surpasses all understanding. Amen.

First Things First

Kerry O' Neill

READY   "Now the end of all things is near; therefore, be serious and disciplined for prayer. Above all, maintain an intense love for each other, since love covers a multitude of sins."—1 Peter 4:7–8

SET   Every day is a challenge. As a competitor, it is a battle to not treat today's practice as just one more in what feels like an endless amount. It seems the only competitors who really value each workout are those who realize there isn't an infinite amount: those returning from injury, at the end of their final season, or especially those who have been told they do not have long to live. These individuals truly make each day count.

A valuable exercise is to write your own obituary. Or picture the final game of your final season, when you are asked to thank your teammates and coaches. This helps you begin with the end in mind. The Bible tells us that the end is near, and we must do two things: be prayerful and loving toward each other. In fact, Jesus knew His death was imminent, and what did He do? He prayed, and His request of the Father was that His followers would be united in love (John 17).

If today was your last, you would not hold back in praying and showing love to those around you. Be a leader. Your teammates and coaches will gain the courage to follow your example. What are you waiting for?

GO   If you knew today's workout was your last, how would you treat it differently?

WORKOUT   John 17:11, 20; Psalm 133:1

OVERTIME   Lord, forgive me for taking things for granted. I want to make today count. Help me demonstrate Your love for others. Amen.

Doing the Right Thing

Michael Wiggins

READY   "For am I now trying to win the favor of people, or of God? Or am I striving to please people? If I were still trying to please people, I would not be a slave of Christ."—Galatians 1:10

SET   Marquette's football team was 10–0 heading into the final game of the season, and it appeared that the program would soon have its first championship. But a few days before the game, the coach received a call: sixteen of his starters had been arrested for underage drinking. Team rules dictated alcohol use as punishable by suspension. The next week, the coach watched his team's hopes evaporate in a 63–0 loss as sixteen of his regular starters stood on the sidelines.

The coach would likely have found support had he imposed a gentle slap on the wrist for his guilty players. Certainly, many coaches overlook such offenses or wait until after the season to enforce discipline. This coach, however, made a difficult decision and placed more importance on citizenship, integrity, and character than on winning a football game.

Doing the right thing may not always be applauded, but that doesn't mean we should avoid it. Why? Because Jesus set the standard for us. When brought before Pilate, who had the power to decide His fate, Christ could have denied who He was or escaped with His life. Instead, He faced the consequences of death for our sin! His grace strengthens us to do what is right and please God, not people!

GO   How do you demonstrate integrity in your relationships?

WORKOUT   Daniel 3:8–30; Hosea 14:9

OVERTIME   Lord, please reveal to me the areas in my life in which I am not doing the right things so that I may have an impact for Your kingdom. Amen.

Leader of the Race

Sarah Roberts

READY   "For that is what God is like. He is our God forever and ever, and he will guide us until we die."—Psalm 48:14 (NLT)

SET   There is a man who runs marathons. Although that doesn't seem like a big deal because many people run marathons, this specific man is blind. Now that's a big deal! His brother runs in front of him, and they have a rope that ties them together. The man is completely dependent on his brother. He goes where his brother goes. He follows the path his brother is on. He cannot see where he is going or how far he has gone, and he doesn't know how long he has left. He can only rely on the words of his brother: "You can do it, we are getting closer."

As Christian athletes, we are tied to God through our relationships with Jesus and by the Holy Spirit. It is this rope that directs us, corrects us, protects us, and inspects us. Too often we try to go down our own path, but the gentle, and sometimes hard, nudge of our Head Coach brings us back.

We don't have to worry about our upcoming season, our teammates, or our futures as coaches or athletes. Jesus is already preparing us for the path ahead. We have peace in the knowledge that we don't have to know where we are going, nor run this race alone. We just have to follow the One in the lead.

GO   What worries do you need God to help you with today?

WORKOUT   Psalm 25:9; Hebrews 12:1

OVERTIME   Lord, lead me in all Your ways as an athlete and follower of You. Amen.

Taking On Defeat

Kyle Shultz

READY "Let us run with perseverance the race marked out for us, fixing our eyes on Jesus, the pioneer and perfecter of faith. For the joy set before him he endured the cross, scorning its shame, and sat down at the right hand of the throne of God."—Hebrews 12:1b–2 (NIV)

SET Carolina Panthers quarterback Jake Delhomme didn't rush into the locker room after losing Super Bowl XXXVIII to the New England Patriots. He stood on the sidelines and forced himself to watch the Patriots in jubilee. "I guess I just wanted it to hurt as much as possible," Delhomme commented afterward. "I wanted to watch the celebration so that it could hurt, so I could remember it, for motivation."

We've all experienced defeat in sports. Sooner or later, all of us will experience defeat in life through hurtful relationships, loss, bad choices, and more. How do we keep the faith during such times in life?

The writer of Hebrews gives us at least one answer: focus our eyes on Jesus. He suffered a painful, suffocating death on the cross—the symbol of utter shame in His day. Remembering Christ's agony on the cross can sometimes push us forward. When we identify ourselves with Him in His death, we'll also identify with His resurrection—which became the hope of the world.

During life's beatings, stand on the sidelines and look to our Savior and His perseverance. The sight of Him will allow us to endure and carry us into tomorrow.

GO What can you learn from Jesus when it comes to dealing with pain in your life?

WORKOUT Romans 8:18–21; Hebrews 12:3

OVERTIME God, when I reflect on the sacrifice You made, the trials in my life pale in comparison. Just as You overcame death, I want to overcome the trials in my life with that same power. Amen.

The Champion's Learning Curve

Steve Fitzhugh

READY "Now these things happened to them as examples, and they were written as a warning to us, on whom the ends of the ages have come."—1 Corinthians 10:11

SET The learning curve: it's a certainty within competitive sports. Champions have to be ready to learn quickly. There's not a lot of extra time during practice for excessive repetition. And sometimes, second- and third-string players get very little practice time and often no reps at all! Their learning comes through observation, and yet they must be ready to jump in the game at a moment's notice.

True champions in life and sport learn how to succeed based on the accomplishments and failures of others. They use everyday examples to strengthen their resolve when facing the temptation to make bad decisions. In Judges 15, we read that Samson took the jawbone of a donkey and killed 1,000 Philistines. One man versus 1,000 and 1,000 men die. When he stood atop the 990 dead men, what do you think the last 10 men thought? Perhaps they whispered among themselves, "He won't kill us, we are smarter than the others!" Regardless, they died too.

We all know people who haven't learned from the bad decisions those around them have made. Why make the same mistakes as others thinking you can escape their regrettable fate? Let's be quick to learn from those around us and not hesitate to make wiser decisions.

GO How can you increase your learning curve?

WORKOUT I Corinthians 11:1, Hebrews 4:11

OVERTIME Lord, forgive me for the times I've chosen to go my own way. Give me the courage to honor Your principles and gain wisdom from the examples You've laid before me. Amen.

Making Courageous Choices

Larry Kerr

READY   "Haven't I commanded you: be strong and courageous? Do not be afraid or discouraged, for the LORD your God is with you wherever you go."—Joshua 1:9

SET   Sometimes I wonder why it is so difficult to be still and listen. We have no problem knowing how to lead, direct others, or give commands. But to whom do we look when we need direction when making tough decisions?

In the Bible, Joshua was a brilliant military leader and had a strong spiritual influence, but his success came because he had learned whom to go to when he faced difficult choices. Joshua knew that unless he first submitted to God, he would never accomplish what he'd been given to do.

Like Joshua, Jesus Christ knew that the greatest gift humankind could receive was the gift of God's presence. Yet He gave that up as well and endured separation from the Father through His death on the cross so that the Lord our God would be with us wherever we go.

How often have we been challenged to make choices that greatly influence the lives of those we love and lead? We all know it can be stressful making the right choices. Thankfully, we have a God who understands our anxieties and promises to be with us wherever we go! As we submit to His counsel, we'll gain the wisdom we need to make courageous choices.

GO   How do you seek God's help in making your decisions?

WORKOUT   Deuteronomy 31:6–8; Matthew 7:13–14

OVERTIME   Father, thank You for Your promise to always be with me wherever I go. Help me to spend time in Your presence so that I will be strong and courageous for Your sake. Amen.

I Was Wrong

Jere Johnson

READY   "Though a righteous man falls seven times, he will get up, but the wicked will stumble into ruin."—Proverbs 24:16

SET   Arguments, fights, and tantrums are a huge part of sports today. At every level, you can see these displays: Little League parents fight in the parking lot; players go into the stands; players and coaches ignore each other for days and weeks at a time. What causes all of this?

Most of the trouble lies within the selfish nature of humans. We have been trained to think that we are always right and that someone else is to blame. "It's not my fault!" is the cry of the selfish warrior in battle. Excuses abound, but the truth is that you are not perfect. In Proverbs 24:16, we read that even a righteous man falls seven times—and just lies there and wallows in his self-pity, right? No! "Though a righteous man falls seven times, *he will get up* . . ."

Tough words like "I was wrong" are hard to say, but we must say them. Admitting our mistakes in life will help us to develop into better people for God's service. So the next time you mess up, own up to your responsibility. And if necessary, also say "I'm sorry."

Your actions and attitudes will make you either better or bitter. No one likes to be wrong, but when you are, don't sit there in your sin and make excuses. Get up, own up, and live up!

GO   What can you do today to be accountable for your actions and attitudes?

WORKOUT   Job 42:1–6; 1 John 1:8–10

OVERTIME   Lord, I don't want to be a bitter person, limited by my pride. Help me to admit when I have made a mistake or wronged another person. Thank You for Your abundant grace. Amen.

What Are My Chances?

Rex Stump

READY   "But Jesus looked at them and said, 'With men this is impossible, but with God all things are possible.'"—Matthew 19:26

SET   The University of Pittsburgh had a commanding lead 31–6 with 10:49 left in the fourth quarter of the Lockheed Martin Armed Forces Bowl. Down 25 points, what were the odds of Houston coming back in ten minutes? Las Vegas gave the odds around 1%!

Houston scored a touchdown on their next offensive drive. Pittsburgh got the ball, moved it down the field, and kicked a field goal, increasing their lead 34–13. But Houston got the ball and scored another touchdown making it 34–20. Down two touchdowns with just a few minutes left, they had no choice but to onside kick. They did, and recovered!

Houston scored again! Excitement was brewing. But they had to onside kick it AGAIN! With just a small chance to repeat the play, they recovered the second onside kick and scored again! Houston trailed 33–34 and had to decide to either kick the extra point to tie the score or go for two points to win. With a 1% chance of coming back, they went for two and won, making it the biggest comeback in college football bowl history!

Choose to be positive when negative surrounds you. Seek opportunities when obstacles slow you down. If God wants it done, it will be! Stay faithful and never give up!

GO   Is it easier to give up or keep going when times are tough?

WORKOUT   Luke 18:27; Matthew 19:25–26

OVERTIME   Father, I admit that the problems I face look like huge obstacles. Thank You for reminding me to trust You with everything. Give me strength to never give up. Amen.

Wear the Colors

Jimmy Page

READY   "For I am not ashamed of the gospel, because it is God's power for salvation to everyone who believes, first to the Jew, and also to the Greek."—Romans 1:16

SET   I can still remember when my coaches handed out uniforms to those of us who had made the cut. We were all so proud to be wearing our school's colors. The best part was being able to wear our jerseys to school on game days. Being identified as part of the team somehow made each one of us walk a little taller.

The reality is that everyone likes to be identified with his or her favorite team. No matter what your favorite teams are, chances are good that you like to wear gear with their logo on it. We all like to "put on the uniform." As competitors for Christ, we are called to put on His uniform. The FCA Competitor's Creed states: "I am a Christian first and last. I am created in the likeness of God Almighty to bring Him glory. I am a member of Team Jesus Christ. I wear the colors of the cross."

If God passed out a jersey to everyone who was a part of His team, would you be proud to wear yours? Would you grow in confidence knowing that you were representing God? Would it make you give everything you've got? Would you be proud to "wear the colors of the cross," or would you be ashamed?

GO   Are you as excited to be identified with Jesus as you are to be identified with your favorite sports team?

WORKOUT   Mark 8:38; 2 Timothy 2:15

OVERTIME   Lord, help me to be eager to be identified with You. Help me to represent You in competition and in life. Amen.

Not Made to Draw Back

Blake Elder

READY "For you need endurance, so that after you have done God's will, you may receive what was promised . . . But My righteous one will live by faith; and if he draws back, I have no pleasure in him. But we are not those who draw back and are destroyed, but those who have faith and obtain life."—Hebrews 10:36, 38–39

SET It was the first game of my senior season at Appalachian State, and we were playing the University of Tennessee Chattanooga. Chattanooga jumped out to a 28–7 halftime lead. With 14:54 left in the game they still led 35–14. Miraculously, we came back to win 42–41. We did not quit or become discouraged by an early deficit. Instead, we fought until we achieved the victory for which we prepared.

Moments like this test us and reveal what we are made of. Times of adversity and uncertainty are opportunities for us to endure in identity, discipline, and purpose. In the middle of our battles, we must stand firm in who we are, what our strategy is, and what we are after.

Endurance is the quality that separates the champions from the rest. As an athlete or coach who follows Christ, stand firm as someone who does not draw back, who endures, and who obtains the promise. God is pleased by your endurance in identity, discipline, and purpose.

GO What are the stressors in your life and during competition that tend to cause you to draw back from your commitments?

WORKOUT James 1:2–4; Hebrews 12:1–3

OVERTIME Lord, help me to keep my eyes fixed on victory like Jesus did when He endured the cross. I pray I bring You pleasure in the way I compete and live by enduring to the finish. Amen.

Troubled?

Clay Elliott

READY "Your heart must not be troubled. Believe in God; believe also in Me."—John 14:1

SET Trouble and being troubled are two completely different things. Trouble is being down by a run, nobody on base, with two outs in the bottom of the ninth and our worst hitter coming to the plate. Being troubled is having no strategy for this scenario and not being prepared to accept the possible consequences that are about to come.

As competitors, there will be many times when we will have to declare to our team, "Don't worry, everything will be okay." As competitors, we need to aim high in becoming trustworthy to help our teammates reach their potential. If our teammates can't trust us, then why should they follow us?

In John 14:1, Jesus told His disciples, "Your heart must not be troubled. Believe in God; believe also in Me." Through His words, Christ offered His followers comfort for the difficult days ahead. He knew that they were about to face some major trouble—serious persecution and, for some, even death. Jesus knew that trouble was coming for Him and for His followers, but He didn't want them to be troubled while facing it. And He doesn't want us to be troubled either.

God invites us in the midst of any trouble that we are experiencing to bring our troubled hearts to our trustworthy God. Even when our hearts are troubled, the ultimate remedy is still the same—totally trusting the Lord!

GO What in the past has helped you face trouble?

WORKOUT Luke 24:36–49; John 14:27–31

OVERTIME Lord, if trouble comes today, help me to come to You, believing that You will work it out according to Your good purposes! Amen.

Help!

Kathy Malone

READY   "Whatever you ask in My name, I will do it so that the Father may be glorified in the Son. If you ask Me anything in My name, I will do it."—John 14:13–14

SET   Why is asking so hard for some of us? Whether it's for a ride to the airport or a few dollars for lunch, many of us avoid asking like the plague. Of course, there are times when even the most self-sufficient among us is willing to swallow all pride and plead before the "throne of grace." I have personally witnessed the amazing transformation of coaches, players, and fans whose circumstances turned them into fervent prayer warriors. This phenomenon typically occurs during a game when their team is down by a point with a few ticks left on the clock.

Maybe it isn't a close game that brings us to our knees. Perhaps it is a life-altering event instead. The truth is that we pray best when we are most helpless. We pray best when, like children, we set aside our pride and self-sufficiency and simply come before our Father with the desires of our hearts.

Jesus said, "Keep asking, and it will be given to you." The Son of God—who intimately knew about asking and giving—intentionally used the word "given." Not "lent." Not "sold." Not "leased." "Given," free of charge. Jesus didn't promise that we would be given exactly what we asked for, but He did say that we would receive. It costs us nothing to ask, but it cost Him everything to give!

GO   What is one desire of your heart that you can take to the Father right now?

WORKOUT   Ephesians 6:18; James 4:2

OVERTIME   Father, thank You that You invite me to ask! Help me to put aside my pride and come to You like a child full of wonder and in need of grace. Amen.

The Win-Win

David Gittings

READY "To me, living means living for Christ, and dying is even better. But if I live, I can do more fruitful work for Christ. So I really don't know which is better. I'm torn between two desires: I long to go and be with Christ, which would be far better for me. But for your sakes, it is better that I continue to live. Knowing this, I am convinced that I will remain alive so I can continue to help all of you grow and experience the joy of your faith."—Philippians 1:21–25 (NLT)

SET In competition, we realize that sometimes we win, and sometimes we lose! No one who truly competes wants to lose. In fact, in the mind of most athletes, losing is not even an option.

In an online issue of *Competitive Advantage*, Sports Performance Consultant Dr. G sums up the emotions felt by both winning and losing: "The winner may experience a broad range of emotions in varying degrees of intensity. He or she may feel ecstatic, satisfied, confident, vindicated, superior, haughty, happy, relaxed . . . or any number of other feelings, even including sad and let-down. Similarly, the loser experiences his own wide array of emotions from distraught, depressed . . . frustrated, inadequate, and cheated."[3]

Paul gives us a view of a win-win situation—a situation most any coach or player would love to be in as many times as possible. Paul said that for him, living is Christ and dying is gain. In Christ, both living and dying is a victory! Because of this truth, followers of Jesus can live this life with great confidence.

GO In what ways are you living and playing your sport with a win-win mentality?

WORKOUT 2 Corinthians 5:1–8

OVERTIME Jesus, thank You for giving me victory in life and in death. Help me, Lord, to live my life with confidence. Amen.

The Gap

Dan Britton

READY "I know, my God, that You test the heart and that You are pleased with what is right. I have willingly given all these things with an upright heart, and now I have seen Your people who are present here giving joyfully and willingly to You."—1 Chronicles 29:17

SET The Competitor's Creed states: "My attitude on and off the field is above reproach—my conduct beyond criticism." This is a tough standard. Legendary Hall of Fame basketball coach John Wooden once said:

> A leader's most powerful ally is his or her own example. There is hypocrisy to the phrase "Do as I say, not as I do." I refused to make demands on my boys that I wasn't willing to live out in my own life.

As athletes and coaches, we too often desire to live a life that we know we have not committed in our hearts to living. We desire for our external life (the life that everyone sees—our wins and accomplishments) to be greater than our internal life (the life that no one sees—our thoughts and desires).

The best definition of hypocrisy that I have ever heard is that it is the gap that exists between the public life and the private life. God doesn't want there to be a gap at all. He wants every aspect of our lives to be filled with integrity.

Oswald Chambers wrote, "My worth to God in public is what I am in private." As a competitor for Christ, be committed to being real—gap free!

GO Where are the gaps in your life?

WORKOUT Psalms 25:21; 78:72

OVERTIME Lord, I pray that You will reveal to me any gaps in my life that must be closed. I desire to live and play for You as an authentic competitor. Amen.

The Squeeze

Amy Richards

READY "Now we have this treasure in clay jars, so that this extraordinary power may be from God and not from us. We are pressured in every way but not crushed; we are perplexed but not in despair; we are persecuted but not abandoned; we are struck down but not destroyed."—2 Corinthians 4:7–9

SET I didn't know if it was a compliment or not, but during my weekly meeting with my college coach she explained that I had a resilient spirit. A few months prior, I had walked on to the team. I had been put through "the squeeze," a series of fitness tests, athletic drills, and competitions to see if I had what it takes to play at the highest level.

Often as competitors, we feel "the squeeze" when it comes to performance. Whether you're competing in a big game, coaching a losing season, or fighting through an injury, we all experience the pressure of performing against outside influences or circumstances. What grows us as competitors is pushing through and learning from those "squeeze" situations.

Yet, as *Christian* competitors, we don't have to rely on our own power to get us through "the squeeze." Rather, we have God's strength and the life of Jesus that empowers and sustains us. Therefore, when we grapple with a season-ending injury, we don't sit in despair. And when we face harsh criticism, we don't feel abandoned. We find encouragement knowing we can tap into the extraordinary power of God that enables us to be "resilient."

GO How can you show a godly, resilient spirit during tough times of competition?

WORKOUT Exodus 15:13; Psalm 46:1

OVERTIME Father, thank You for being with me during my "squeeze" situations and sustaining my spirit. Give me the strength to always focus on and reflect You. Amen.

Power Play

Jere Johnson

READY "When Haman saw that Mordecai would not kneel down or pay him honor, he was enraged."—Esther 3:5 (NIV)

SET Hannah made the varsity tennis team as a sophomore and eventually beat out Mindy, a senior, for the number two singles spot. Hannah soon became arrogant and bossy in her new position of power on the team. But Mindy didn't budge. Angered, Hannah soon began to do anything to make Mindy look bad in front of the coaches. Mindy did not retaliate, but Hannah would not let up. Her dislike for Mindy turned into hatred, and she tried to get Mindy kicked off the team. Sound familiar?

Back in Esther's day, a man named Haman became second in command behind Xerxes. Ruthless and arrogant, he demanded respect and enforced his power over the people. But Mordecai, Esther's cousin, was not about to give in to him. Haman was severely hateful to Mordecai and the entire Jewish race and wanted to kill them all. But Haman was too egotistical, and he soon became his own worst enemy. He died on the very gallows that he had built to hang Mordecai.

Hannah's plan to get rid of Mindy also backfired, and her attitude and hatred got her kicked off the team. Mindy regained her position and began to win for her team. Power and self-importance are the downfall of many. Mindy, like Mordecai, held her ground, had self-respect, and followed a better way.

GO Do you desire to control others or let them control you?

WORKOUT 2 Chronicles 26

OVERTIME Lord, I confess that I often want to be in total control. Forgive me for trying to control people and situations, because I know that You are the only one in total control. Amen.

Play the B.U.G.

Dan Britton

READY   "An honest witness tells the truth, but a false witness tells lies. The words of the reckless pierce like swords, but the tongue of the wise brings healing. Truthful lips endure forever, but a lying tongue lasts only a moment."—Proverbs 12:17–19 (NIV)

SET   Even as the words float off the end of my tongue, I realize that I have blown it. It's so easy for me to become the "cut-down king." It doesn't take much, and it could involve something as simple as calling someone a rude name.

You know the routine: you cut one of your teammates down, and your other teammates laugh. You may try to justify your unkind remarks with the fact that everyone does it, but the truth is that those reckless words pierce like a sword and cause damage. Instead of playing the Cut-Down Game and cutting others down because everyone else is doing it, God desires us to play the B.U.G., or the Build-Up Game. Playing the game doesn't come naturally, but when it's played, it is awesome.

A friend of mine once said that everyone in the world is under-encouraged, and I agree! I ask the Lord to show me ways that I can encourage teammates, friends, family members, and even people I don't know. I want to build others up and show love through my words. I believe that the tongue can heal. Are you ready to play the B.U.G.?

GO   What is one way that you can play the B.U.G. on your team? With your coaches?

WORKOUT   Proverbs 16:21; Colossians 3:16

OVERTIME   Lord, I play the Cut-Down Game way too often. Teach me ways to build others up so that I can be a blessing. I pray for opportunities to bring life with my words. Amen.

The Green Team

Steve Beckerle

READY   "Don't copy the behavior and customs of this world, but let God transform you into a new person by changing the way you think. Then you will learn to know God's will for you, which is good and pleasing and perfect."—Romans 12:2 (NLT)

SET   I recently attended a rec league soccer game for three- to five-year-olds. It soon became clear that both teams were wearing shirts of the same green color! At first, to the observers and the referee, the game appeared chaotic, but as the game went on, it became clear that the color of the shirts did not change the game plan or the goal for the kids, and we could soon easily tell who belonged to what team.

In the same way that each athlete knew what their game plan was and who their teammates were, especially during a time when they were being tested, God calls us to do the same in our lives. The only way to know God's great plan for our lives and be able to fulfill it is to know Him, read His Word, and surround ourselves with people with the same goal.

Peter writes, "Be careful to live properly among your unbelieving neighbors. Then even if they accuse you of doing wrong, they will see your honorable behavior, and they will give honor to God when he judges the world" (1 Pet. 2:12 NLT). We are called to live our lives in such a way that sets us apart—that glorifies God and points others to Him.

GO   How can you develop your relationship with God to have His will become clearer?

WORKOUT   Galatians 5:22–23; Romans 6:4

OVERTIME   Lord, help me see and live the life that You've designed for me. Help me be a light to others through my relationship with You. Amen.

No Excuses

Jimmy Page

READY   "But without exception they all began to make excuses."
—Luke 14:18

SET   When I was twelve, I played second base for an all-star team. I still remember dropping that pop fly that ended up, in part, costing us the win. I made excuses—blaming the rain and even the lights (it was a night game). At the time, I didn't think I was making excuses; I just didn't want the loss to be my fault.

Excuses spread like a virus. We make excuses for why we're late to practice, why we didn't work out, why we missed a shot—you name it. When we justify why we didn't do what we should've, it's easier to make excuses the next time.

In Luke 14, Jesus exposes excuses. Those who had been invited to the Great Banquet feast found many excuses why they couldn't attend, but none of the reasons were genuine.

"But they all alike began to make excuses. The first said, 'I have just bought a field, and I must go see it. Please excuse me.' Another said, 'I have just bought five yoke of oxen, and I'm on my way to try them out. Please excuse me.' Still another said, 'I just got married, so I can't come'" (Luke 14:18–20 NIV).

Excuses never make you better. And they don't change your circumstances; they solidify them. Instead of pointing the finger, we must take responsibility and assume ownership of the problem. We must own both the problem and the solution.

GO   Do you take personal responsibility, or do you make excuses? Why?

WORKOUT   Philippians 2:2–4; Luke 6:41–42

OVERTIME   Father, show me ways that I've become an excuse-maker. Help me to be accountable for my actions and make changes necessary for excellence. Amen.

Some Winning Advice . . . Guaranteed

Clay Elliott

READY "I have told you these things, so that in me you may have peace. In this world you will have trouble.

But take heart! I have overcome the world."—John 16:33 (NIV)

SET Trouble often seems to be waiting around every corner of daily life, especially for coaches. Whether it is a troubled player, an unfair referee, a nagging parent, or an unreasonable principal, coaches can count on difficulties. They come with the territory!

Thankfully, Jesus never pretended that life would be a luxury cruise. "You will have trouble," He told His disciples. In fact, difficulties are guaranteed, an inevitable part of living in a fallen world. Consequently, the best advice that we could heed—and give to others—is not to strive for a trouble-free practice or season. Rather, in the midst of consuming troubles, Jesus invites us to rest in the peace of His presence.

Jesus told His followers that real and lasting peace would come when we walk with Him. And He offered this advice before He went to the cross! Still, He guaranteed this ahead of time because He knew that the "punishment for our peace was on Him" (Isa. 53:5).

True victory comes when we battle through the troubles alongside Jesus. If we know Jesus, we know peace, regardless of what troubles come our way!

GO Are you experiencing peace in the midst of trouble?

WORKOUT Psalm 32; Isaiah 53:5

OVERTIME Father, I am grateful that You gave Your Son so that I could find peace in the midst of my troubles. Envelop me in Your peace as I submit to walking with You. Amen.

Fundamentals for Success

Steve Fitzhugh

READY   "Therefore, everyone who hears these words of Mine and acts on them will be like a sensible man who built his house on the rock."—Matthew 7:24

SET   The foundation for success in any sport relies primarily on the mastery of fundamentals. Champion athletes spend time perfecting their skills by focusing on fundamentals. It doesn't matter at what level you compete; ignore the fundaments and your performance will suffer.

Have you ever seen a wide receiver take his eyes off the ball and drop the pass even though it hit his hands? Or what about a world champion sprinter standing straight up out of her starting blocks, anxious to win but forgetting the fundamental technique of staying low and then losing the race as a result?

In the same manner, if we overlook the foundations to our Christian walk, challenges in life could leave us humiliated. Reading the Word of God and conversing with our Lord through prayer are the one-two punch of Christian fundamentals. Centering our hearts and minds on the truths of God's Word and daily prayer time are practices that will aid in our decision-making, pursuits, passion, and purpose. And when the rushing waters of life come our way, though He may not build a bridge, He will certainly stand with us so the waters will not overcome!

GO   What commitments have you made or will you make to master the two biblical foundations of prayer and reading God's Word?

WORKOUT   Matthew 7:24–27; Acts 17:11

OVERTIME   Lord, give me the strength to commit to reading Your Word and talking with You daily. Allow Your presence to abide in me so I can take on any challenge that comes my way. Amen.

Fire in My Belly

Dan Britton

READY   "The words are fire in my belly, a burning in my bones. I'm worn out trying to hold it in. I can't do it any longer!"—Jeremiah 20:9 (Message)

SET   "Do you have fire in your belly?" is a question I've heard hundreds of times from coaches. It was never really a question that I was supposed to answer; rather, it was a challenge to play harder and tougher. As an athlete, I never had the natural ability of others (speed, strength, size), but I did have the fire in my belly. For me, the fire was hustle, grit, and tenacity to get the job done—I always gave 100 percent, right up until the whistle blew.

Sometimes I wonder if I have the fire in my belly when it comes to my spiritual life. Jeremiah says that he had a fire burning so strong for God that he couldn't contain it. The spiritual hustle, the spiritual grit, and the spiritual tenacity all need to burn within us so fiercely that we can't hold them back, from ourselves or others.

The passion for our Lord should be like a fire that rages within. However, we must also remember that the fire comes from Him. We must lay ourselves on the altar and ask God to consume us with His fire. The great preacher John Wesley said that large crowds came to hear him preach during the Great Awakening because "I set myself on fire and people come to watch me burn." Are you on fire for Jesus?

GO   What does it mean to have spiritual grit and tenacity?

WORKOUT   Psalm 84:1–2

OVERTIME   Lord, I want to be consumed with Your fire. Let the fire that burns within be a light in the darkness that surrounds me. Amen.

Submit. Who, Me?

Rebekah Trittipoe

READY   "Therefore, you must submit, not only because of wrath, but also because of your conscience."—Romans 13:5

SET   The tiny pre-workout room quickly filled with runners, each excited to be through with a long, hard day in the classroom. However, one of the runners disregarded the good-hearted banter and sat off to the side, sullen and solo. Ted didn't want to be there. He was top-notch (at least in his mind), and had little time for this team of "novices." He thought the team coach incapable. That's why he relied on his "real" coach from the running club, ignoring the school's coach. As soon as he could after the waste-of-time meeting, he would go off and do his own workout.

Is Ted right to do as he pleases? Is it okay if he ignores the instructions of the team's coach? Does his talent make it okay to ignore instructions given to the whole team?

Paul speaks of submission to those in any authority: "Everyone must submit to the governing authorities, for there is no authority except from God, and those that exist are instituted by God" (Rom. 13:1). Peter writes, "Submit to every human authority" (1 Pet. 2:13).

Coaches will not always coach perfectly. Athletes may not always like what a coach requires. But when a Christian athlete places himself under the authority of a coach, the obligation is to submit. Why? So that God is glorified.

GO   What is the connection between submission and a clear conscience?

WORKOUT   1 Peter 2:11–25, Hebrews 13:17

OVERTIME   Lord, my ego often gets in the way. Help me to view my coach as an authority placed there by God. Enable me to submit so that You are glorified. Amen.

What Compels Us?

Mike Zatopek

READY "Since we believe that Christ died for all, we also believe that we have all died to our old life. He died for everyone so that those who receive his new life will no longer live for themselves. Instead, they will live for Christ, who died and was raised for them."—2 Corinthians 5:14–15 (NLT)

SET As a sophomore in college, playing baseball was the primary way I found value in life. However, when it turned out that I wasn't cutting it on the baseball field, my coach told me to consider trying football. He'd often said that "we reap what we sow" during his talks about how Jesus could impact our lives and careers. My motivation had always been self-centered. But then I faced the end of something I had depended on since childhood to get the affirmation I craved. Later that day, I accepted Jesus as my Savior. Through Him, I found a greater purpose for life, and as God turned my heart toward pleasing Him, I found something greater to motivate me not only in life but in athletics.

Driving forces in life such as greed, fame, and pride all lead to an empty life. We don't always win in life, and the world seems to only love us when we are on top of our game. But God loves us even "while we [are] sinners" (Rom. 5:8) and "with an everlasting love" (Jer. 31:3)! Are the cheers of the crowd the only compelling reasons you play the game? Or is the pure, everlasting love of God going to be the wind that fills your sails?

GO Is your motivation to play your sport rooted in God's love for you and your love for Him and others?

WORKOUT John 17:20–26; Ephesians 3:14–19

OVERTIME Jesus, help me to find my value in You. May my motivation to play my sport be to bring glory and honor to You. Amen.

The Challenge of Coaching

Jere Johnson

READY "Love is patient, love is kind. Love does not envy, is not boastful, is not conceited, does not act improperly, is not selfish, is not provoked, and does not keep a record of wrongs. Love finds no joy in unrighteousness but rejoices in the truth. It bears all things, believes all things, hopes all things, endures all things."—1 Corinthians 13:4–7

SET During a recent NFL game, I watched as two future Hall of Fame coaches took the field. The announcers shared how they had talked with a player who had played for both coaches and asked him what the difference was between the two coaching styles. The player said that one coached by fear, the other by love. When asked what the player preferred, he shared that both can be effective, but that love lasts forever.

Christ coached a team of men as well. He easily could have used fear as a motivator to get them to do what He wanted them to do—perhaps even successfully. But He chose the path of love. Better yet, He lived and *was* love!

Competing requires wisdom, understanding, and discernment in knowing when to love and listen to your team. A competitor who leads by fear will have success at times, but in the end will lose respect and players will play to spite him or her. A competitor who leads by love will gain respect and admiration, and will build lifelong relationships with players who know they are loved.

GO Do your teammates know that you care about who they are as individuals?

WORKOUT Matthew 22:34–39; John 13:34–35

OVERTIME Lord, help me to care more about the person than the player and show my teammates the love I have for them. Amen.

Desiring and Doing

Rex Stump

READY   "Instead, remain faithful to the LORD your God, as you have done to this day."—Joshua 23:8

SET   Reid Priddy (men's volleyball) and Donny Robinson (BMX) are Olympic athletes whose field of competition receives little attention. These athletes are faithful in their commitment to Jesus Christ and their sport. They fully understand what it's like to work at something with all their hearts, being enthusiastically committed to winning, for the glory of God. But these two men also know that their desire must be accompanied by action.

In Numbers 13, we are introduced to Caleb, somebody just like Priddy and Robinson. Caleb didn't receive much notice and basically stood in the shadow of people who received greater attention. He was one of the twelve spies that brought a correct report to Moses about the Promised Land of Canaan. He wasn't of Jewish background, but his faith was solid in God. He was faithful, knowing he was working for God and not men, and his actions proved it!

Caleb persevered for more than thirty-eight years, and finally attacked and possessed the Promised Land. Even at the age of eighty-five he enthusiastically served God and kicked down the gates of Hebron to move his family into a new home! His desire was accompanied by doing.

What truly matters is a life of disciplined action with a focus on doing things for God, not man. So, make sure your desires are accompanied by action that honors Him!

GO   Do my actions accompany my desire to live and work for God? If not, why not?

WORKOUT   Numbers 13; Deuteronomy 6:5

OVERTIME   Father, help me focus on doing things for You and not praise from man. I pray that my spiritual and athletic desires will be accompanied by actions that honor You. Amen.

Pre-Game Jitters

Michael Hill

READY   "Who of you by worrying can add a single hour to your life? Since you cannot do this very little thing, why do you worry about the rest?"—Luke 12:25–26 (NIV)

SET   We've all been there. It's only a few minutes before "show time." We hear the band playing to get the crowd excited for the game. We look around the locker room and see our players trying to get into the "zone." We've worked hard to get them prepared, but something isn't clicking. They have the pre-game jitters, based on worry and a lack of focus.

All of us who have competed know that feeling in the pit of our stomachs. Sometimes we're not even sure whether it's fear or excitement, or whether we should scream or cry. The men around Jesus had the jitters, too. Like us, they had anxiety about everyday life. But in Luke 12:22–26, Jesus put the "game" in proper perspective for His followers. He told them that if God takes care of the needs of the ravens, He would also take care of those who are worth much more to Him than the birds.

Jesus went on to remind His disciples that worrying would add nothing to their lives. If Jesus reminded His disciples of God's provision in spite of their jitters and proved it with His life, death, and resurrection, why should we worry about our game?

GO   What does Jesus invite us to do when we feel nervous?

WORKOUT   Luke 12:22–34; 1 Peter 5:7

OVERTIME   Lord, please forgive me for worrying and for forgetting how much You love me and care for me. I pray that You would turn my fears into faith as I remember Your provision in Christ. Amen.

Effort

Roger Lipe

READY   "Work willingly at whatever you do, as though you were working for the Lord rather than for people."—Colossians 3:23 (NLT)

SET   Having the motivation to work hard is key for competitors to achieve performance excellence. Everyone who competes in sports finds motivation somewhere—from parents, coaches, teammates, or even from God.

Some of us find ourselves on teams with coaches who really don't suit us that well, and our efforts suffer. For some reason, the coach's attempts to motivate us fall flat, and our performances diminish. Others must deal with divisions among teammates. Regardless of who it is, finding motivation in other people is inconsistent at best.

However, we do find a consistent, steady, and inexhaustible source of motivation in Jesus. His character is consistently excellent, and His reward to those who have a relationship with Him is immeasurable. We can trust Him to come through on every promise and to find great pleasure in our worship as living sacrifices—as we compete and as we live our everyday lives.

Regardless of your relationship with your coach or captain, focus on serving Jesus as you train, practice, and compete. Trust the Lord to reward your efforts with a rich reward of grace, joy, and fulfillment in having served Him well.

GO   How does competing for Jesus motivate you in ways that neither coaches nor teammates can?

WORKOUT   Romans 12:1–2

OVERTIME   Father, I commit every moment, breath, movement, and thought to You. May I focus on finding my motivation in You, above all others. Amen.

Measuring the Heart

Charles Gee

READY   "But the Lord said to Samuel, 'Do not look at his appearance or his stature, because I have rejected him. Man does not see what the Lord sees, for man sees what is visible, but the Lord sees the heart.'"—1 Samuel 16:7

SET   Another signing day has passed. The rankings are out, the top programs have locked down the "best" athletes in the country. The gifts and abilities of these athletes, however, don't guarantee success. If teams are going to be successful, they must also have "heart." Yet, how can we measure "heart"?

God values our heart above our outward appearance or abilities. In 1 Samuel, we read that although Saul had great physical presence, he lost favor with God and was rejected as king. So, the prophet Samuel went to Bethlehem to the home of Jesse where he was to anoint one of Jesse's eight sons as the next king. Jesse lined them up, sure that Eliab, his eldest, would be chosen. While Eliab's appearance was impressive, he was not God's choice. David, the youngest, was out tending sheep, unconsidered. But God knew David's heart was for Him, just as He knew His bigger plan for all humankind: that from the line of King David, another King would come—Jesus.

Over time, many talented athletes—like Saul—will fade, and recruits with less glamour but more heart—like David—will surface. If we stood before our Master Recruiter like Jesse's sons, would He see a heart that crowns Jesus as King?

GO   From a biblical viewpoint, what does it mean to have heart?

WORKOUT   Deuteronomy 8:1–2; 1 Samuel 16:1–13

OVERTIME   Lord, thank You for being more concerned with my heart than with my outward appearance. Help me to crown Jesus as King in all I do. Amen.

Workout Partners

Michael Hill

READY   "For I want very much to see you, so I may impart to you some spiritual gift to strengthen you, that is, to be mutually encouraged by each other's faith, both yours and mine."—Romans 1:11–12

SET   A workout partner is someone who will be there for you. It is a person who has your same desire to succeed and who can't wait to train with you. It is someone who can't wait to be energized by your energy level.

In Paul's letter to the church in Rome, it is apparent that he couldn't wait to see the believers there and spend time with them. He was excited to help them train. He was excited to tell them about Jesus. He was excited to work with them and to be mutually encouraged by them.

We all need a workout partner who will help us in our spiritual training. We need a partner who will commit to growing his or her own relationship with Jesus right alongside of us. We need someone who will give us the support we need when we are going through the rough stretches.

We all need someone who can encourage us and whom we can encourage.

GO   Who is your athletic workout partner? Who is your spiritual workout partner? What similarities do you see in the ways that each of you train?

WORKOUT   Proverbs 27:17; Hebrews 3:13

OVERTIME   Father, let me find encouragement today from my Christian brothers and sisters. Let me be an encouragement to them also. Use me to build Your church. Amen.

Where Is Your Focus?

Rex Stump

READY   "Therefore, since we also have such a large cloud of witnesses surrounding us, let us lay aside every weight and the sin that so easily ensnares us. Let us run with endurance the race that lies before us, keeping our eyes on Jesus."—Hebrews 12:1–2a

SET   The 2004 volleyball season was my toughest as a coach. In just the first month I dealt with gym floor repairs, having items stolen out of the girls' lockers, bus breakdowns, the first losing season of my career, and much more. It was during this time, though, that I found encouragement from Hebrews by remembering to look around, look down, and look up.

Look Around—"*Therefore, since we also have such a large cloud of witnesses surrounding us . . .*" Imagine standing at midcourt in an arena, where every seat is filled with God's people cheering you on. We are not alone.

Look Down—"*let us lay aside every weight and the sin that so easily ensnares us . . .*" The athlete will strip off anything that causes their performance to slack. As God's child, what is causing me to stumble that I should get rid of?

Look Up—"*keeping our eyes on Jesus.*" With every example of how He lived His life, Jesus gives us encouragement to live this life of faith. He is our mentor, the center of our focus.

Endure what is happening in your life by looking around, down, and focusing on our Champion Jesus Christ!

GO   What things do you need to "lay aside"?

WORKOUT   James 1:12; 1 Peter 1:6

OVERTIME   Father, thank You for cheering me on. Help me to stay focused on You as I run this race of faith. Amen.

Six Percent

Dan Britton

READY   "They will turn away from hearing the truth and will turn aside to myths. But as for you, be serious about everything, endure hardship, do the work of an evangelist, fulfill your ministry."—2 Timothy 4:4–5

SET   A recent study reports that only six percent of teens today believe that moral truth is absolute. I knew it wouldn't be high, but that's really low. Not good. Young people today are basically saying that life is a sliding scale. Truth has become relative because it all depends on the situation. In the world of athletics, there are many truths that cannot be relative, such as wins and losses. Fortunately—or unfortunately—winning is defined by the scoreboard. Life without truths, absolutes, and boundaries leads to chaos.

Psalm 31:5 states that the Lord is the God of truth. God is our standard, and His Word isn't just filled with truth, it *is* the truth. Many of us embrace the absolute truth (Jesus), but we find it hard to apply that truth to others. We feel as if we are judging or condemning. It's a hard line to walk, but remember that absolute truth is for everyone.

We must hold fast to the truth and not compromise under any circumstances. As it states in Proverbs 23:23 (NIV), "Buy the truth and do not sell it—wisdom, instruction and insight as well." Stand for the truth—on and off the field of competition.

GO   When do you find it the most difficult to stand for the truth?

WORKOUT   John 18:8; Ephesians 1:13

OVERTIME   Lord, I know You are the Truth. I desire to be Your agent of transformation by living and playing by Your truth with a pure heart. Amen.

After You Suffer

Rebekah Trittipoe

READY   "And after you have suffered a little while, the God of all grace, who has called you to his eternal glory in Christ, will himself restore, confirm, strengthen, and establish you."—1 Peter 5:10 (ESV)

SET   As the runners came through the aid station at 14 miles, most were happy and content despite the deepening darkness and constant downpour for the last several hours. Dry Branch Gap was the second aid station during the grueling 100-mile Grindstone, a footrace that traverses Virginia's Blue Ridge Mountains. Those who would eventually complete the marathon had to first conquer a total of 46,000 feet of elevation changes that tested the runners' muscle fibers, tendons, and ligaments—and their resolves to hold out hope.

By the time they came to the aid station again at 87 miles, the question, "What can I get for you?" was often answered with lengthy pauses. It was as if fatigue caused a fogginess that disconnected their brains from their mouths. Still, most runners persisted in tackling the final distance despite the pain. Why? Because they knew their suffering was temporary. Afterward, they would recover, be strengthened, and be ready to run again.

As Christians, why should we be prepared to suffer? A Christian who suffers for the name of Christ is made stronger. Christians have the hope that temporary pain will bring about sweet restoration. And it will. The God of all grace promises us that.

GO   Can gains in strength and resolve be accomplished without some element of suffering?

WORKOUT   Romans 5:3–5; 2 Corinthians 1:7

OVERTIME   Father, may I be confident that suffering is not without purpose. Help me endure so that I may experience true restoration, strength, and maturity that come only in the aftermath of pain. Amen.

The Power of Joy

Bill Burnett

READY "At the dedication of the wall of Jerusalem, they sent for the Levites wherever they lived and brought them to Jerusalem to celebrate the joyous dedication with thanksgiving and singing accompanied by cymbals, harps, and lyres."—Nehemiah 12:27

SET A large crowd gathered for the memorial service of Coach Whitson, a much-loved junior high coach who had been at the same school for seventeen years. Several former players spoke of his impact on their lives, describing him as happy and joyful. Those close to Coach Whitson knew that he understood what it meant to offer thanksgiving and praise to God regardless of the circumstances. Though he had had his share of pain, his focus on thanksgiving gave him a joy that touched many lives.

Under the leadership of Nehemiah and others, the Jews returned to Jerusalem. They rebuilt the city wall and set up a secure government. They celebrated all that had occurred with joy. Why? Because their eyes were on the Lord and what He had done for them. Nehemiah 12:43 (NASB) says that all the people joined in and that their rejoicing was "heard from afar"—not their *singing*, but their *rejoicing*.

All we have acquired from God through Jesus's life and death is good. Joy is ours when we look to Him in thanksgiving or in expectation of what He has in store for us.

GO Do you bring joy to those you lead?

WORKOUT Nehemiah 12:27–43; Job 8:19–22

OVERTIME God, I have much to be thankful for today. As I reflect on Your many gifts in my life, may others see Your joy! Amen.

Remain in Me

Fleceia Comeaux

READY   "I am the vine; you are the branches. The one who remains in Me and I in him produces much fruit, because you can do nothing without Me . . . If you remain in Me and My words remain in you, ask whatever you want and it will be done for you. My Father is glorified by this: that you produce much fruit and prove to be My disciples."—John 15:5, 7–8

SET   In John 15, Jesus is giving a final charge to his disciples about staying connected to the true vine. He encourages, reiterates, and implores them to stay connected to Him. I often find it significant when Christ repeats himself. There is a fundamental principle that He is trying to relay to the people of God and specifically His disciples.

As the text unfolds, three promises are identified as we remain in Him: we will produce much fruit, we can ask whatever we want and it will be done, and we will glorify the Father.

What athlete or coach doesn't want to produce fruit? Who doesn't want their prayers answered? And which one of us does not have a desire to glorify the Father during our performance? Your effort, work, and striving in sport and life must end in His glory. When we do not remain in Him, we are setting ourselves up for failure. Remain in Him, and let His Word remain in you.

GO   Are you remaining in Him throughout your season?

WORKOUT   1 John 2:5–6; Psalm 119:9–11

OVERTIME   Father, it is Your desire that I remain in You and Your Word remain in me. Let my actions reflect Your principles, and let my decisions reflect Your heart. Amen.

Big Belief Brings Big Reward

Wade Hopkins

READY "But we are not like those who turn away from God to their own destruction. We are the faithful ones, whose souls will be saved."—Hebrews 10:39 (NLT)

SET In 1993, Frank Reich with the Buffalo Bills orchestrated the greatest comeback in NFL history against the Houston Oilers. When Reich entered the huddle, the team down 32 points after the starting quarterback had been injured, there was no doubt in his mind that his team would come back to win the game. Reich had big belief because he had already experienced the greatest comeback in NCAA history. As the quarterback of Maryland, he led the Terrapins back from a 31-point deficit at halftime to beat the Miami Hurricanes.

When you walk with God, you know that "all things are possible" with Him (Matt. 19:26).

Moses experienced the plagues of Egypt and the Exodus. There was no doubt that God could part the Red Sea. David experienced deliverance from the lion and the bear. There was no doubt that God could deliver him and his people from Goliath.

Whatever you are facing, turn your fears and doubts into the belief that nothing is impossible with God. He can turn your life and circumstances around and grant you the greatest reward ever imagined—eternal life in heaven—through faith in Christ.

GO In what areas of your life do you need to trust God and His Word more and stop leaning on and believing in your own understanding?

WORKOUT Hebrews 10:39; John 1:12

OVERTIME Father, give me Your perspective in all my circumstances so that I can simply give my best as I trust in You. Amen.

DAY 149

What Pushes You?

Clay Meyer

READY "Whatever you do, do it enthusiastically, as something done for the Lord and not for men."—Colossians 3:23

SET During the course of a few short years in the MLB, Los Angeles Dodgers pitcher Clayton Kershaw became a household name. Winning the 2011 NL Cy Young Award, Kershaw joined the ranks of all-time Dodger greats. Even though he is known as being an easygoing guy off the field, he flips a switch when stepping on the mound. He becomes a bulldog, pitching with tenacity and intensity. Kershaw feels he is called to do so, playing according to one of his favorite Bible verses, Colossians 3:23.

Kershaw realizes that his faith is reflected on the field through displaying such a competitive nature. He knows that he has to work at directing the part of his God-given talent he can control: his passion and enthusiasm. And with this attitude, Kershaw takes the mound and pitches for God's glory, leaving the results up to the One who put him there. He trusts that no matter the outcome, he has given his all.

As Christian competitors we sweat, bleed, cry, and fight through pain with fierce determination. Not for ourselves, our team, or our coach, but for the Lord. Are you focusing your energy on the field for only God's glory? Don't just give your all, but give your all for your Lord.

GO What does Colossians 3:23 mean to you? How can you apply that to the sport you play or coach?

WORKOUT Ephesians 6:6–8; Colossians 3:17

OVERTIME Father, I pray that as a competitor I would give everything I have for Your glory. Whether in or out of season, I desire to use the abilities and talents You've blessed me with to make Your name known. Amen.

Have Courage

Nate Bliss

READY "But Jesus spoke to them at once. 'Don't be afraid,' he said. 'Take courage. I am here!'"—Matthew 14:27 (NLT)

SET Have you ever encountered something that completely over-whelmed you? Maybe you faced an opponent who seemed way too talented or a circumstance that seemed too overwhelming. Or perhaps you found yourself completely out of your comfort zone, frozen by fear. We've all had those moments when we've felt ourselves sinking into defeat, praying for the courage to rise above the challenge. Like a lifeline in a storm, courage often comes from the inspiration we receive from the words of a teammate, coach, or loved one.

To *inspire* is to breathe into something. *Courage* is what allows a person to continue on despite difficulty, danger, pain, or fear. The word *encourage* combines both *inspire* and *courage* and means "to inspire with hope, courage, and confidence."

As a competitor, when you see a teammate who is struggling or down, do you take some of the courage and confidence you have and give it to them to build them up and fill them with courage and confidence? Teammates must be willing to work together, lean on one another, and be real with one another. A great teammate is able to make the team more confident. A great teammate is an encourager who inspires others to face every obstacle with courage.

GO Find a way to encourage a teammate this week.

WORKOUT 1 Thessalonians 5:11; Hebrews 3:13

OVERTIME Father, thank You for surrounding me with people who are able to fill me with courage when I am afraid. Help me to be the competitor, the teammate, and the friend that You call me to be. Amen.

The Ultimate Goal

Michael Hill

READY "I want to know Christ—yes, to know the power of his resurrection and participation in his sufferings, becoming like him in his death. . . ."—Philippians 3:10 (NIV)

SET As competitors, we challenge each other to set goals. If we were to look in our lockers or playbooks, we might find a list of personal expectations and team goals. Because we need to reinforce our goals once we set them, we often pick up paper and pen to write them down.

The great apostle Paul also had goals, one of which appears in his letter to the church at Philippi. Paul's goal was to know Jesus more. If we wrote this goal down on a list that we had, what would be the result? Would that undefeated team look as daunting if we knew "the power of his resurrection"?

Would the daily challenges, the personal pains of failed relationships, or the real sorrows of daily tragedies seem as unendurable if we knew "the fellowship of sharing in his sufferings"?

An intense love for Jesus such as Paul's could be ours as well. If we set goals to improve our team's performance, why don't we also set goals to improve our relationship with Jesus Christ? And just like we do with our team goals, we can continually assess our progress by bringing them into the light of God's love and remembering His power at work within us!

GO Which of your goals include growing closer to God?

WORKOUT Psalm 51; Philippians 1:27–29

OVERTIME Lord, draw me closer to You today I as walk through the doors that You have opened for me so that I might do Your work. Please help me to know Christ better and reflect His grace. Amen.

Learning: A Lifetime Achievement

Jere Johnson

READY "If you stop listening to correction, my son, you will stray from the words of knowledge."—Proverbs 19:27

SET A wise man once said, "When you are through learning, you are through!" I don't know who actually said that, but my father used to repeat it to me often. As he would patiently try to teach his sons how to play different sports, he would catch us occasionally making simple mistakes due to not paying attention.

Solomon was a wise man. He could've easily thought that he had "arrived" and had gained all the knowledge he needed, but he understood this: If you don't pay attention, listen, and learn, you won't get the knowledge you need to further your understanding in life.

Great men in sports and history, such as John Wooden, Tony Dungy, and my father, Jim Johnson, understand that listening and learning are daily tasks. You should never stop learning. So what are some practical things you can do to continue learning? First, get into God's Word every day. There is no better book to study in order to gain knowledge. Second, surround yourself with people who have "been there" and "done that" in the right ways. They are a wealth of wisdom and knowledge. Third, pray and ask the Lord to point you in the right direction!

GO In what area of your life could you learn more?

WORKOUT Proverbs 1:5; James 1:19–25

OVERTIME Lord, show me where I need to be more teachable in my life, and surround me with men and women who will speak truth to me. As I spend time reading the Bible, open my heart to Your instruction. Amen.

Overcoming Fear

John Crosby

READY   "The LORD is my light and my salvation—whom should I fear? The LORD is the stronghold of my life—of whom should I be afraid?"—Psalm 27:1

SET   Have you ever faced someone who was obviously bigger, faster, stronger, and more experienced than you? When this happens, another even greater obstacle often arises—fear. Fear blinds us to opportunities, disables our reasoning, and can cause momentary paralysis.

"*Fear not*" is the most common command in Scripture. God is concerned about our fear because fear is ultimately a trust issue. God calls us, above all else, to trust Him. Fear and pride are the two greatest obstacles to trusting God—revealing the areas of our life where we trust God the least. They are each about misplaced trust. Fear is about trusting in whatever or whoever you fear. When we are afraid, we put our trust in the ability or power of the source of our fear.

We worship the God who spoke the world into existence, parted the Red Sea, raised a valley of dry bones into a formidable army, raised the dead, and walked out of the grave. He is hardly challenged by our circumstances. In overcoming fear, we must move our trust from the object of our intimidation to God. And to do this, we need to spend time getting to know Him and His Word better. God is completely trustworthy. And if you know Him, you will trust Him.

GO   What areas of your life reveal the most fear? How might spending time with God relieve these fears?

WORKOUT   Psalm 46:1–3; Isaiah 41:10

OVERTIME   Lord, give me a desire to overcome fear by knowing You better. Help me to spend the time in Your Word and prayer needed to fully trust You regardless of my circumstances. Amen.

Test Yourself

Josh Carter

READY "Test yourselves to see if you are in the faith. Examine yourselves. Or do you yourselves not recognize that Jesus Christ is in you?—unless you fail the test."—2 Corinthians 13:5

SET In 2003, LPGA golfer Annika Sorenstam became the first woman in fifty-eight years to compete with men in a PGA tournament. Although she missed the cut by four shots, she had a respectable tournament and finished as well as or better than several of her competitors. "I tested myself from start to finish," she said afterward. "That's why I was here."

If we don't test ourselves, we'll never know how strong we are. Paul's final words to the Corinthians challenged them to test themselves to see whether they are Christians—to take an honest look at their lives to see if they are demonstrating faith in Jesus through their actions. Just because we sin doesn't mean that we are not truly Christians. We all have setbacks with sin, but as Christians, our lifestyle should not be one characterized by willful, habitual sin.

As Sorenstam tested herself on the golf course, we too should examine ourselves to find out where we are in our relationship with Jesus. Some "test" questions that might be helpful include: Have you turned away from sin and committed your life to Jesus Christ, trusting in Him alone for the forgiveness of sins and the gift of eternal life? Does your lifestyle give evidence of your faith in Jesus Christ?

GO What is one of the toughest tests that you have faced in competition?

WORKOUT Psalm 139:23–24; 1 John 1:5–10

OVERTIME God, thank You that today I can walk in the freedom of forgiveness because of Christ. Amen.

That's Gonna Leave a Mark

Christy Cabe

READY   "After the victory, the LORD instructed Moses, 'Write this down on a scroll as a permanent reminder, and read it aloud to Joshua.'" —Exodus 17:14a (NLT)

SET   The Bible records competitions—held on fields of battle. The Book of Exodus tells of when Joshua was called to fight the Amalekites. Moses was instructed by God to stand on top of a mountain that overlooked the battlefield and to hold his staff in the air. When Moses lowered the staff, the battle would turn in favor of the Amalekites, and when he raised the staff, the battle turned to favor the Israelites. The staff was a visual representation of God's power.

As the day wore on, Moses' arms grew weary. So he found a rock to sit on, and Hur and Aaron held his arms up for him. When the battle was over, Israel had won! But the story isn't over. God asked Moses to record what happened that day and to recite it to Joshua so all would understand how God led His people to victory like only He could. God is glorified when we tell of His mighty works. Too bad Moses lacked the great tools we have today to do such telling.

He couldn't tweet: "@EgyptNoMoe helped my army win a big battle, but boy are my 'armies' sore now! #PunIntended #AaronAndHurAre MyWingMen"

He couldn't blog: "Check out my new post, *My Triceps are Killing Me, but the Amalekites Aren't.*"

Even without our modern-day technology, Moses recorded this miraculous story. Because when we tell this story, we tell what God has done for His people. And that's gonna leave a mark.

GO   Do you tell others about what God has done?

WORKOUT   Exodus 17:8–16

OVERTIME   Lord, You are so powerful! May my life bear witness to Your glory. Amen.

What Will You Be Remembered For?

Rex Stump

READY "Therefore, fear the LORD and worship Him in sincerity and truth. Get rid of the gods your fathers worshiped beyond the Euphrates River and in Egypt, and worship Yahweh."—Joshua 24:14

SET Not long ago, I stopped in a nearby town for coffee. When I went to wash my hands, I noticed the shiny new hand dryer on the restroom wall with the words "Feel the Power" printed on it. I pushed the button and got a blast of hot air! It was like one of those huge dryers from the car wash had been compacted into a tiny dryer. Now, whenever someone mentions that town, I think of that silly hand dryer!

Sometimes I wonder how I'll be remembered as a competitor. When someone mentions my athletic career, will they note the wins and losses, the calls I made or failed to make? Or will they remember how I served and acted as a competitor? When people talk about Joshua, the first thing I remember is that he chose to serve the Lord when he could have pursued any other way to live. Joshua's life and leadership clearly reflected what he believed and whom he followed: God. He knew that humans are made to worship and that if we do not worship the one true God, we will worship another.

People might never know just who is behind our actions, but they will remember that something about our lives was different! They might forget records and scores, but they will not forget our Christlike actions.

GO How do you want to be remembered as a competitor?

WORKOUT Psalm 112; Ezekiel 18:21–32

OVERTIME Lord, thank You that Your power works in me to create a life and legacy that reminds others of You! Amen.

Think Before You Speak

Jere Johnson

READY "The one who guards his mouth protects his life; the one who opens his lips invites his own ruin."—Proverbs 13:3

SET As a young coach I had a short fuse, especially when it came to dealing with men in stripes. It was hard to keep my mouth shut. One game in particular, I thought my team was being treated unfairly, and I was quick to point it out. Late in the game, I stood up and yelled, "What?!" It was only one word, but the officials had heard enough. I got a technical foul that cost my team the game.

Controlling the tongue is a problem for many coaches and athletes. Many times, we create more problems with our mouths than with our actions. Why? In my case, it was because I wouldn't think before I spoke. Proverbs 13:3 tells us that if we can control our tongues, it will enhance our lives. But if we speak before we think, we can ruin everything.

Why does God want us to keep our tongues in check? When we speak before thinking, we usually do not honor Him with our speech. He would much rather we say nothing at all than speak too quickly. It's the most difficult thing in the world to tame the tongue, but God's Spirit living in us through the work of Jesus can help us think before we speak—even in the most challenging situations!

GO What actions can you take to start thinking before you speak?

WORKOUT Ephesians 4:29; James 1:19–20

OVERTIME God, please fill me with Your Spirit so that every word that comes out of my mouth today honors You! Amen.

Joy in Victory

Roger Lipe

READY   "LORD, the king finds joy in Your strength. How greatly he rejoices in Your victory! You have given him his heart's desire and have not denied the request of his lips."—Psalm 21:1–2

SET   Is there anything in sport that can match the joy of winning? There is nothing quite like experiencing triumph over one's opponent. And King David, the writer of Psalm 21, was extremely familiar with these emotions as well. In reading verses 1–2, who did David credit as being the source of his victories? It wasn't himself. He said, "Lord, the king finds joy in Your strength."

For everyone, the great joy in victories comes as a gift from God. Like David, we should rejoice in the strength we feel in sport, but not due to our own efforts. It is God that has granted us all the deep desires of our hearts; we're greatly blessed just to be competitors in sport. We must constantly remind ourselves that the joy we feel in victory is an extension of God's blessing and not of our own accomplishments.

As you pray in preparation for competition, seek for God to focus your heart on His strength. Compete in great freedom, knowing God's power is your provision. And be mindful that His joy should be your source of fulfillment, not the final score.

GO   How can you cultivate a sense of joy in your sporting experience?

WORKOUT   Romans 12:1–2; Ephesians 2:10

OVERTIME   Thank You, Father, for Your joy. I pray that I will point to You in victory, knowing You are the source of my strength and the ultimate fulfillment of my life. Amen.

Would You Rather . . . ?

Dan Britton

READY "If anyone wants to be first, he must be last of all and servant of all."—Mark 9:35

SET Our family plays a great game at the dinner table called "Would You Rather?" We ask questions such as, "Would you rather win a World Series or a Super Bowl?" Once, I decided to ask my three kids the following question: "Would you rather be a great leader or a great servant?" My ten-year-old daughter immediately replied, "Dad, they're the same thing. If you serve someone, you are showing and teaching someone what Jesus would do!" Wow! She nailed it. In God's eyes, a great servant is always a great leader, but a great leader is not necessarily a great servant.

In the arena of competition, whether playing or coaching, we must understand what it means to be a great servant. Being a great servant in the athletic world does not mean serving others in order to become a great leader; rather, it means sacrificing and dying to self. This is difficult—it means putting the interests of my teammates first, both on and off the field. It means having an attitude like Christ's as I place their needs before my own. As competitors, we need to realize that this battle to lead or to serve rages every day.

GO What is one way that you can put the needs of your athletes or teammates before your own?

WORKOUT Matthew 23:11–12; Philippians 2:1–11

OVERTIME Lord, teach me today to put the needs of others before my own. Make me a great servant as I seek to follow in Your footsteps. Amen.

Development

Rick Horton

READY "There is so much more I want to tell you, but you can't bear it now."—John 16:12 (NLT)

SET *Development* is a word used extensively in sports when talking about athletes reaching optimal athletic performance. For example, professional baseball teams have minor league systems with trained coaches they call "development people." Prospects need development to acquire the knowledge and master the skills and attitude necessary to move to the next level.

Jesus spent much of His time on earth developing the twelve apostles to not only spread the Good News but also lead the early church. He imparted knowledge, provided skill development opportunities, and constantly taught them about the importance of the attitude of the heart. Like many developing athletes, they too were pushed at times with great care and concern.

As Jesus prepared for Gethsemane and the fulfillment of His mission—to give His life for the sin of man—He passed along wonderful teachings and truths to His disciples. Jesus recognized that the disciples were not fully equipped to handle what lay ahead, despite more than three years of His teachings. What then followed is the great promise to all believers in the gospel of Jesus: He promised to send the Holy Spirit to guide them in all truth.

As we strive to develop as athletes, let us also ask God to develop us as His followers in the power and care of the Holy Spirit.

GO How has God developed you over time in knowledge, skills, and attitude?

WORKOUT Philippians 2:1–5

OVERTIME God, please make me teachable so that I may increase my knowledge of You and learn how to share the Good News with others. Help me to do all of this with the attitude of Jesus. Amen.

Punting into the Wind

Charles Gee

READY "But let him ask in faith without doubting. For the doubter is like the surging sea, driven and tossed by the wind."—James 1:6

SET As a coach, my faith was wavering. As I watched my unpredictable punter jog onto the field, doubt washed over me with every step. With his unpredictable kicks, the ball might go forty yards in a tight spiral or it could be a ten-yard shank off the side of his foot. It was late in the game and field position was critical.

As the punter waited for the snap from center, the gentle night breeze suddenly transformed into a stiff wind. My punter handled the snap cleanly, took two steps, and kicked the ball high into the air. In what seemed to be slow motion, everyone watched as a gust of wind caught the ball in midflight and pushed it backward! When the ball finally came to rest, we realized we had witnessed an unbelievable negative ten-yard punt. My doubts had been confirmed and the untimely wind had managed to make a bad situation worse.

Too often we approach God with the same doubt as I did my punter. Sometimes we're optimistic and sometimes we're pessimistic. We know God can do it, but the results don't always turn out like we want. When doubt creeps into our faith, we often get tossed around and pushed backward like that windblown punt. Our doubt does not honor God. Want better results? Take a firm stand the next time you pray, and talk to God with complete faith in His Word.

GO Why do you think God doesn't give us everything we ask for?

WORKOUT Mark 4:35–41; Philippians 4:4–7

OVERTIME Father, protect me from the winds of doubt. Teach me to be strong in my faith and to trust You in all things. Amen.

Today Is a New Day

Nate Bliss

READY   "This means that anyone who belongs to Christ has become a new person. The old life is gone; a new life has begun!"—2 Corinthians 5:17 (NLT)

SET   I love fresh starts. I can't tell you how many times I've messed up and wished I could hit the reset button. While we can't change what has already happened, God encourages us not to dwell on our past mistakes. We all say things we shouldn't. We all forget assignments, miss shots, and lose games.

God offers every person a reset button. He asks us to believe in Him and rely on Him to take care of the old things and to give us a new start. Ultimately, this occurs eternally when we receive salvation through faith in Jesus. We can also trust God to help us move past our daily mistakes and setbacks. God wants to breathe fresh life into us every day. So how should someone who has new life start a new day?

Psalm 118:24 says we should rejoice in the new day! Each new day is a chance for a fresh start. Are you caught up in what hasn't gone your way? Or, are you ready to approach each new day like a fresh opportunity to be the person God designed you to be?

GO   What is the hardest part about letting go of a bad game or a personal setback?

WORKOUT   Romans 6:4; 1 John 1:9

OVERTIME   Lord, thank You for giving me a fresh start and a new day. Forgive me for dwelling on the past. Please help me to rejoice in today's opportunities and to honor You in all I say, think, and do. Amen.

Constructive Criticism

Jere Johnson

READY   "One who listens to life-giving rebukes will be at home among the wise. Anyone who ignores discipline despises himself, but whoever listens to correction acquires good sense."—Proverbs 15:31–32

SET   One of a coach's toughest jobs is correcting athletes. Most coaches try to do it constructively, but many athletes will still choose to ignore the instruction or make excuses. We all need correction and people who will speak truth into our lives. Although we do not always want to hear what people tell us, we still get to choose how we respond. Many of us choose to take criticism personally, which holds us back from making the necessary changes for the better. Those of us who can listen to this type of correction and react accordingly will be better off in the end.

Christ wants to speak truth into our lives, often in the form of the Holy Spirit's constructive criticism. We have a choice to respond positively or make it personal. When we realize that His criticism is for our own good, our relationship with Him will deepen.

We need to remember that most people who offer constructive criticism truly are trying to help us. Words of encouragement should prod us on to a greater life in Christ, not lead to the bitterness of spirit. So the next time someone gives you constructive criticism, just say, "Thanks for caring enough to tell me what was on your heart."

GO   How can you respond properly to constructive criticism?

WORKOUT   Proverbs 10:17; Proverbs 15

OVERTIME   God, I know that I need to be open to instruction from my coaches if I am going to be a successful athlete. Adjust my attitude and help me as I work to receive instruction with an open heart. Amen.

Fear

Charles Gee

READY   "I am losing all hope; I am paralyzed with fear."—Psalm 143:4 (NLT)

SET   Spiders, flying, storms, and snakes are only a few of the fears that seem to paralyze so many. We all face fears of some kind. Fear is defined as an emotion caused by perceived threats that lead to a change in behavior such as running away, hiding, or freezing.

A trip to the Grand Canyon once brought me face to face with my fear of heights. Standing on the trail and looking out into the vastness of the canyon below made me freeze in my tracks. What do you do when fear shows up? If fear is an emotion, it can be changed; but change comes only as the result of deliberate action. With a little prayer, a personal desire to face my fear, and encouragement from others, I was able to continue on, enjoy the journey, and feel better about myself.

David knew about fear. In Psalm 143:4 (NLT), he said, "I am losing all hope." He was caught up in his fear and depression. He was hiding in caves from King Saul who was trying to kill him. David felt trapped, and his every attempt to escape from the mess was futile. He cried out and told God his true feelings. David turned himself over to God's guidance and put complete trust in God.

What is your fear today? A losing record? What others think? A failing marriage or finances? Tell God your true feelings. Put your fear in His hands and let Him guide your path.

GO   What is your greatest fear? How can God help you overcome this fear?

WORKOUT   Proverbs 1:33; Matthew 8:23–27

OVERTIME   Father, help me to turn my concerns over to You. Teach me to put my complete faith in You. Amen.

Form Follows Function

Christy Cabe

READY "And whatever you do, in word or in deed, do everything in the name of the Lord Jesus, giving thanks to God the Father through Him."—Colossians 3:17

SET The serve in volleyball is a crucial component of the game. The form of the serve, however, is not as important and varies from player to player. Some athletes dribble the ball three times before holding it out in front of themselves for the toss. Some skip the dribble but place their fingertips precisely over a logo or text on the ball's surface. And others step into a jump serve or leap from a standing position. The form is different, but the function is the same: the ball is hit over the net. One's form doesn't really matter if the serve is effective.

In our lives, we serve the Lord in various forms. Some believers work in a professional ministry or a pastoral role. Other believers are college athletes, students, coaches, retail clerks, stay-at-home moms, teachers, etc. The form of our service to the Lord is not what matters. Form follows function. Our function as followers of Jesus is to glorify God and serve Him with all our hearts. As Colossians reminds us, whatever we do, do it in His name. And no matter the form of your service, may you strive to ace the function of bringing glory to God.

GO What does your service to the Lord look like in sport?

WORKOUT Colossians 2:6–7; Philippians 2:14–16

OVERTIME Lord, thank You for the opportunities to serve You. Help me to be faithful in the little details of my life, whatever they may be, so that I may bring glory and honor to Your name. Amen.

Obstacles and Opportunities

Fleceia Comeaux

READY   "'Send some men to explore the land of Canaan, which I am giving to the Israelites. From each ancestral tribe send one of its leaders.' So at the LORD's command Moses sent them out from the Desert of Paran."—Numbers 13:2–3 (NIV)

SET   When you walk onto a court to play a game, do you see obstacles, or opportunities? Do you stare at your opponents while they warm up and begin to wonder why you even laced up your Nikes, or do you focus on giving your all?

In Numbers 13, the spies were sent into Canaan to check out the land. God had already given them great victories in battle and rescued them from tough situations. During the forty days that they were evaluating the land, they could have seen a great opportunity, but they didn't. Only two guys, Joshua and Caleb, thought that they could succeed in acquiring the land.

It's strange that the Israelites didn't remember the situations from which God had delivered them and the victories He had granted. They also forgot that God had commanded them to go into the land and that He had promised to give it to them.

God has already given us much. We only need to receive what He has promised. I pray that we can be like Joshua and Caleb, who received and believed in the opportunity that God had given them.

GO   What practical steps can you take to increase your faith in God's plan for your life?

WORKOUT   Deuteronomy 31:8; 2 Corinthians 12:9

OVERTIME   Lord, help me to remember that through my doubt, I can see only obstacles, but through my faith in You, I can see opportunities. Allow me to increase this faith every day. Amen.

Cheerleaders or Critics

Jim Faulk

READY   "Therefore, since we also have such a large cloud of witnesses surrounding us . . . Consider Him who endured such hostility from sinners against Himself, so that you won't grow weary and lose heart."—Hebrews 12:1, 3

SET   A few years ago, I was privileged to participate in the memorial service of a man who was a faithful servant, dear friend, and former head football coach. Over 2,000 of this man's family, friends, colleagues, and student-athletes attended the service. As I stepped into the pulpit of the church, I thought, *Look at all these people. Everyone here is a cheerleader! What a great send-off for a coach—and a great testimony to a life well lived!*

As we compete in the world of athletics, we'll find people cheering or booing, depending on the circumstances of the moment. When we step into the spiritual realm, we read about that heavenly stadium filled with that "large cloud of witnesses," encouraging and cheering us, God's earthly team, to victory. Imagine them applauding, yelling for us to finish the course, to fight the fight, to keep the faith! They are *shouting* for us to persevere, to fix our eyes on Jesus, and to remember that, as bad as we may think our circumstances are, Jesus's circumstances, for our sake, were far worse.

As we go through our days today, we might encounter both critics and cheerleaders. But we can't let them distract us from our Savior and that heavenly host of fans who've "got our backs"—no matter what!

GO   What could you do today to hear the heavenly cheerleaders' shouts over the jeers of earthly critics?

WORKOUT   Psalm 20:7–8; Hebrews 12:1–3

OVERTIME   Father, thank You that I am never alone in this race. Help me to cheer others on as together we fix our eyes on Jesus! Amen.

True Success

Victor Santa Cruz

READY "The Lord answered her, 'Martha, Martha, you are worried and upset about many things, but one thing is necessary. Mary has made the right choice, and it will not be taken away from her.'"—Luke 10:41–42

SET According to society's standards, a coach or athlete's status is based on his or her win-loss record. Unfortunately, personal worth is often tied into this same evaluation. Feeling down after a losing season, I sought out one of my coaching mentors to discuss my disappointment. He asked if I knew his record from the past season. I apologized that I hadn't followed his season. He informed me of his 11–1 record and a junior college bowl championship. He then asked if I cared about him, since I hadn't followed his team's record. "I certainly do care about you!" I responded. My respect for him was based on who he was as a person, not his football success.

Jesus also provided a unique perspective on success through the story of Mary and Martha. While Martha was busy fulfilling the perceived demands of the moment, Mary sat listening to Jesus. Upset by her sister's lack of help, Martha asked Jesus to tell Mary to lend a hand. Jesus answered by pointing her to what mattered more than worldly accomplishments: a relationship with Him. That's why He came to Earth: to die a death we should have died so that we could have new life in Him!

The rewards of a winning record can be taken away by one "bad" year. But true success—an intimate relationship with God through Jesus—can never be taken away, because of the cross.

GO How do you define success?

WORKOUT Ecclesiastes 2:4–11; Mark 10:17–31

OVERTIME Lord, renew my intimacy with You that I may fulfill my professional responsibilities with excellence and joy. Amen.

One Way 2 Play

Steve Fitzhugh

READY "Be strong and very courageous. Be careful to obey all the law my servant Moses gave you; do not turn from it to the right or to the left, that you may be successful wherever you go."—Joshua 1:7 (NIV)

SET Most students who find themselves in situations or places that they hoped they'd never be do so because of tiny compromises that they made early in their life journey. I have never met a student who has ever identified alcoholism as a career goal. Neither have I met an ambitious student whose "Top 10 Things to Do Before Graduation" included becoming a parent prematurely, or getting kicked off the team.

Although most students would want to avoid these misfortunes like the plague, many engage in behaviors that increase the probability of them experiencing these situations. These compromises are common among all teens, regardless of culture or socioeconomic status. Often, the common denominator is drug use. It doesn't matter if it's a cigarette here or there, an occasional beer or hard liquor drink, weed, blunts, ecstasy, or heroin. Drugs will always diminish the masterpiece that is you!

Most who compromise do so because of the absence of three things: *faith in Christ*, *commitment*, and *accountability*. Make decisions with regard to faith, commitment, and accountability that allow for only "one way 2 play"—drug and alcohol free.

GO Are you compromising in the area of drug and alcohol use? If so, what commitments will you make to be drug and alcohol free?

WORKOUT 1 Corinthians 6:19; Hebrews 12:1–2

OVERTIME God, help me as I make this commitment to remain drug free. Help me identify an accountability partner who will help me to be faithful to my commitment and who will ask me the tough questions each week. Amen.

Sore Loser

Michael Wiggins

READY   "Don't gloat when your enemy falls, and don't let your heart rejoice when he stumbles, or the LORD will see, be displeased, and turn His wrath away from him."—Proverbs 24:17–18

SET   In 2001, golfer Annika Sorenstam dominated the women's professional tour, winning eight tournaments. After that phenomenal year, Annika's chief rival, Karrie Webb, commented that she'd eat her hat if Annika won eight tournaments in the coming year. The following season, Annika won eleven tournaments.

Sometimes the competition is too strong. The fact remains, though, we can't win them all. John Wooden didn't win every basketball game that he coached. Jack Nicklaus didn't win every golf tournament that he entered. Mature coaches and athletes take it a step further; they learn to appreciate the competition's performance.

We all know that even Christians can sometimes struggle to celebrate the victories of others. Perhaps someone else got the job or a crosstown rival won the tournament. Whatever the situation, we have a tendency to focus more on our loss than on the other person's gain. But the mature Christian recognizes God's will in every aspect of life, knowing that His perfect will may involve losses or apparent setbacks.

While the world expects bitterness and resentment in defeat, Christians can stand out by congratulating the victor, knowing that Christ has already won the ultimate victory for us. Not only will this simple act gain the respect of others, it will also make us more gracious on those occasions when we're the victors.

GO   How do you react to your competitor's success?

WORKOUT   Luke 15:11–32; 1 John 2:3–11

OVERTIME   Lord, empower me to live today with the grace and integrity of Your will! Amen.

Taking Care of Business

Kerry O'Neill

READY   "Love the Lord your God with all your heart and with all your soul and with all your mind and with all your strength."—Mark 12:30 (NIV)

SET   For most of my life I have had a problem with these words: *Just do your best. It's not whether you win or lose, it's how you play the game.* It always seemed to me that these words lack a competitive spirit, like something a mom says to her child who has no chance of winning. But it occurred to me recently how few things in sports are within our control. During a basketball game, I cannot control the referees, my opponents, or whether I have a record-breaking game or not. But I *can* control my attitude and my effort.

I cannot control every aspect of my performance or the results. Nor can I control the attitude and effort of others, only my own. That being true, I should only be judged by those things which I have complete control over—my attitude and effort during the game. The same is true in life. What should my attitude be like? "Make your own attitude that of Christ Jesus" (Phil. 2:5). Effort? "Whatever you do, do it enthusiastically, as something done for the Lord and not for men" (Col. 3:23).

Attitude and effort are personal choices that cannot be controlled by other people or circumstances without my permission. I have the sole responsibility to make sure they line up with the words of Christ and no one can change that.

GO   How can you improve your attitude and effort during training or competition?

WORKOUT   Philippians 2:1–8; Colossians 3:23–24

OVERTIME   Lord, I confess that I have focused on things that I cannot control. Help me to focus on giving my best attitude and effort to please You. Amen.

Salty

Amanda Cromwell

READY "You are the salt of the earth. But if the salt loses its saltiness, how can it be made salty again? It is no longer good for anything, except to be thrown out and trampled underfoot."—Matthew 5:13 (NIV)

SET If you run around the soccer field for ninety minutes, you tend to sweat a lot. When you sweat excessively, your body loses much of its natural salt. Without salt in your body, you cannot stay hydrated. Being "salty" is an important part of being able to compete at a high level.

In the same respect, without a relationship with Jesus, you cannot absorb and learn from His Word. Learning God's ways by reading the Bible will impact your approach to competition, but not until you give your life fully to God and accept what His Son did for you on the cross.

Mark 9:50 (NIV) says, "Salt is good, but if it loses its saltiness, how can you make it salty again? Have salt among yourselves, and be at peace with each other." Mark is comparing the importance of having salt in our bodies with the importance of having God in our lives.

When you give your life to Jesus and let the Holy Spirit work in your life, you will begin to understand God's teachings. You will begin to learn what it means to give God glory in all that you do and to be an example of His love to others.

GO How might having more salt in your spiritual diet affect the way you compete?

WORKOUT Luke 14:34; John 6:35

OVERTIME Father, thank You for sending Your Son to die for my sins. I surrender my life to You. Amen.

Self-Esteem

Zach Crowley

READY "And I am certain that God, who began the good work within you, will continue his work until it is finally finished on the day when Christ Jesus returns."—Philippians 1:6 (NLT)

SET In our efforts to achieve high esteem, many of us try to wear the right clothes, drive the right cars, or have the right cell phones. The problem with having the right material items is that, in a month, week, or even a day's time, those will no longer be considered cool. That self-image we thought we could purchase will suddenly be gone.

No matter how hard we try, there will always be someone who doesn't approve of what we are doing. There will always be times when we do or say something that we shouldn't. Because we are imperfect, our constant striving for perfection will eventually wear us out. And when we start to think that we've let God down, we may begin to feel broken, lost, and alone.

Jesus came to earth not only to save us from our sins, but also to save us from the negative thoughts that lead to our low self-esteem. You can get out of the habit of thinking negatively by meditating on the things God says about you in His Word. If you meditate on His Word throughout the day, the Holy Spirit will give you the strength to stay positive in all aspects of your life. Though your problems will likely not simply go away, the Word of God will help you to drive out those negative thoughts and embrace your God-given, Christ-centered, healthy self-esteem.

GO How are negative thoughts separating you from God and His truth?

WORKOUT Romans 8; 2 Timothy 1:7

OVERTIME Father, help me to meditate on Your Word and replace my negative thoughts with positive thoughts. Amen.

Give Me Credit

Michael Hill

READY "The purpose is that none of you will be inflated with pride in favor of one person over another. For who makes you so superior? What do you have that you didn't receive? If, in fact, you did receive it, why do you boast as if you hadn't received it? You are already full! You are already rich! You have begun to reign as kings without us."—1 Corinthians 4:6–8

SET Everybody wants to get the glory. Why shouldn't we? It feels good to have someone say that we played a good game. It feels good to hear our name over the loudspeaker after a good play. The problem is that we haven't done anything to deserve this glory.

Paul told the church at Corinth that everything they possessed came to them because they had received it. This means that they didn't have anything at all that God had not given to them. How many times does a football player score a touchdown and do a celebratory dance that draws attention to himself? How many times does a basketball player make a shot and then draw attention to himself or herself? All of this draws attention to people who don't deserve the glory.

God provided everything we have. If He gives us the talent to score a touchdown, a three-point shot, or a home run, why do we not give Him the credit for allowing us to receive that talent?

GO Who received the glory the last time someone complimented you on a good game?

WORKOUT 1 Corinthians 1:30–31; 2 Corinthians 9:10–11

OVERTIME Father, thank You for using me to build Your kingdom. Today, I pray that my performance will glorify You and You alone. Help me to continually point others to You. Amen.

Don't Make Excuses

Ken Kladnik

READY "If I had not come and spoken to them, they would not be guilty of sin; but now they have no excuse for their sin."—John 15:22 (NIV)

SET I once worked with a head football coach who had a large sign behind his desk that simply read "No Excuses." What this meant to his staff and players was that he would not accept any explanations when something went wrong. He wanted them to be personally responsible and not put the blame on any other people or circumstances.

I see a lack of responsibility today on the part of athletes whenever their coaches call them to be accountable. The players tell their coach that they didn't hear the play, or they blame someone else for making a mistake. Nothing upsets a coach more than a player refusing to be accountable for his or her actions. And nothing is a worse role model to players than when a coach will not accept responsibility for his or her mistakes.

We can't make any excuses for our sin either. If we are believers and followers of Jesus, then we must hate sin as much as He did. To allow ourselves to do what we know is wrong and then justify our actions is to give way to sin. Instead, we can live in the freedom of God's forgiveness by confessing our sins to Him and allowing His righteousness to shine through us so that others may see His love!

GO In what ways can you be more accountable?

WORKOUT Matthew 25:14–30; Luke 14:16–23

OVERTIME Lord, I pray that You will help me to be more obedient to You and to not make excuses for my sinful actions. Amen.

Eternal Focus

Clay Meyer

READY   "So we do not focus on what is seen, but on what is unseen. For what is seen is temporary, but what is unseen is eternal."—2 Corinthians 4:18

SET   Baseball has always been a way of life for Los Angeles Dodgers slugger Adrian Gonzalez. The three-time Gold Glove winner and four-time All-Star has excelled at the game since he was a young boy in San Diego. But make no mistake, when asked to put his life and nine-year MLB career into perspective, he explains how his priorities have always been about so much more than just the game. "No matter what—doing well, doing bad, statistics, box scores—all that stuff matters, but in the big picture it doesn't. I can't try to satisfy anybody here on earth. We're here to satisfy Jesus."

Gonzalez clearly has his priorities in order as a follower of Christ. He's more focused on his relationship with the Lord and sharing Christ's saving message than comparing stat lines and win-loss records.

Where do your priorities lie? Is your athletic career defined by how many wins you can record? Or is the sole focus of your athletic career to bring God glory and lead others to Him through your success and defeat?

GO   Has your faith and foundation in Jesus ever been challenged by the desire to fit in with those around you? How did you respond to that challenge?

WORKOUT   2 Corinthians 4:16–18; Colossians 3

OVERTIME   Father, forgive me for the times that I pursue the praise of man through competition more than deflecting the honor and glory to You. Let it always be my utmost priority to make Your name known as I compete for You, an Audience of One. Amen.

Following the Rules

Michael Hill

READY "Carefully follow them, for this will show your wisdom and understanding in the eyes of the peoples. When they hear about all these statutes, they will say, 'This great nation is indeed a wise and understanding people.' For what great nation is there that has a god near to it as the LORD our God is to us whenever we call to Him?"—Deuteronomy 4:6–7

SET Each new season starts out with a team meeting in which the coach goes over the team rules and states the expectations for the upcoming season. During this time, the coach makes sure that there is no question as to what will be required from the athletes.

The head coach will expect the players to follow the team rules, and he or she will generally set out rewards to the team for doing so. These rewards might include a letterman's patch or pin, or they might include easier conditioning in practice.

God is the Ultimate Head Coach. Just as a good earthly head coach goes over the rules, so does our Ultimate Head Coach. God gave His "team rules" to the Israelites through Moses, and He expected His team to follow those rules. Like our coaches here on Earth, the Ultimate Head Coach also has different rewards for following His rules. But these rewards are not only earthly, they are also eternal. And knowing that you've impacted the kingdom of God is better than a letterman's jacket any day.

GO Are you following team rules?

WORKOUT Matthew 16:27; Colossians 3:23–24

OVERTIME Lord, show me Your ways. Give me an understanding of Your team rules so that I might be a light in the dark world. Amen.

My Father's Eyes

Christy Cabe

READY   "For the word of God is living and effective and sharper than any double-edged sword, penetrating as far as the separation of soul and spirit, joints and marrow. It is able to judge the ideas and thoughts of the heart."—Hebrews 4:12

SET   As a high school freshman, I was chosen to play on the girls' junior varsity team. One week, the JV team did not have a game, so I was "bumped down" to play with the freshman squad. I was arrogant and felt disappointed to be forced to play on what I deemed a "lesser" team.

During a time-out, our coach called us into a huddle. I stood there, a few feet away from the huddle, thinking I didn't need to hear the coach's instructions. Then my eyes met my father's from the stands. That's all it took. Though he didn't say a word, the look in his eyes spoke volumes to my heart. I immediately recognized my attitude as prideful and selfish. I adjusted my perspective and learned a valuable lesson that evening.

Hebrews 4:12 tells us that God's Word has that same penetrating and convicting power as my father's eyes did that evening. Sometimes we fall into sinful attitudes and actions, and we need our heavenly Father to help us get back on the track. By fixing our eyes on God's Word, we can constantly adjust our hearts and lives in a way that is pleasing to Him.

GO   Are there sinful attitudes or actions in your life that you need His help adjusting?

WORKOUT   Psalm 51:10; Psalm 25:4–5

OVERTIME   Lord, forgive me for my pride, selfish attitude, and sinful actions. Teach me from Your Word, Father, that I may learn to please and honor You. Amen.

DAY 179

Who, Me?

Jere Johnson

READY "Whatever happens, conduct yourselves in a manner worthy of the gospel of Christ."—Philippians 1:27 (NIV)

SET Every team needs leaders on and off the field who set examples at practice, in the classroom, and with their friends. However, many players do not want that responsibility. When I encourage athletes to be leaders, I usually get the same response: "Who, me?" They feel unwatched, and that nobody cares what they do on or off the field. I beg to differ. Athletes are under the microscope. People, peers, and fellow athletes are watching.

Paul knew this well. He understood that, as believers in Christ, we are all called to lead. He challenges us in Philippians to live in a way that brings honor to Christ—not just to live our faith, but also to be an example to others. We are all called to be spiritual leaders. Not all are called to lead a church or join international missions, but we all have a mission field that surrounds us daily.

So, the next time you are offered an opportunity to lead as an athlete or believer, remember that others are watching closely. Don't ruin your opportunity to show Christlike leadership by living a life that is displeasing to God. Don't be the person that no one wants to follow because you talk one way and act another.

Who, me? Yes, *you!* People want to follow the leadership of someone who will take them higher than ever before. So let your actions be those that people will want to follow.

GO How can you start to lead effectively for Christ today?

WORKOUT Matthew 5:13–16; James 2:14–26

OVERTIME Lord, please give me the strength to stand up for You each day. Help me to be not of this world, but of You only, Lord. Amen.

A Given Victory

David Gittings

READY "But thank God! He gives us victory over sin and death through our Lord Jesus Christ."—1 Corinthians 15:57 (NLT)

SET Have you ever experienced victory in a fierce competition with an older brother or sister? What happens when they then say, "I gave you that win"? Hearing those words can quickly drain our confidence because even after all the effort, we didn't really earn the victory. It was given to us.

As competitors, we want our opponents to be in their best possible shape and to compete as best they can. We want to know that we've earned our victories!

In life, we are in a battle—or game, if you will—that has winners and losers. Some will be "given" eternal life, and others will have chosen eternal death. I don't know about you, but when it comes to my eternity, this is one instance in which I'd rather be given the victory! Jesus is the only one who can give us this victory. Receive it and walk in the confidence the Holy Spirit gives you. That way, no matter who or what you face in life, victory has been given to those who are in Christ.

GO In what ways do you experience or live out the victory God has given you on a daily basis?

WORKOUT Matthew 25:31–46; Romans 6:23

OVERTIME Lord, I thank You for giving me victory over sin and death! Amen.

Team Player

Carl Miller

READY "Then he called the crowd to him . . . and said: 'Whoever wants to be my disciple must deny themselves and take up their cross and follow me. For whoever wants to save their life will lose it, but whoever loses their life for me and for the gospel will save it.'"—Mark 8:34–35 (NIV)

SET Before an intersquad scrimmage, I stood waiting to hear the team assignments. I was sure I would be placed on the team with the school's best athletes, who were also my best friends. But instead, I was chosen to join the "underdog" team. In anger and disgust, I told the coach that I was going to quit and began walking off the field.

I was sure the coach would stop me, but he let me go. As I continued walking away, I thought, *What am I going to tell my parents? What are my friends going to think?* Suddenly, I came to my senses, went back, and joined the team. Guess what? Our team won the scrimmage, and I apologized to the coach for not trusting his wisdom.

In the big picture, being on God's team means denying what we want and following Him. He strategically places us in situations in life in which we can make the greatest impact, even if this sometimes means being separated from things we want and the people who are most familiar to us. You were created to make a difference, and your team's ability to win may possibly lie within you.

GO What traits do you bring to your team that will make a difference?

WORKOUT John 15:16; 1 Corinthians 1:27–29

OVERTIME God, help me to look past what I want so that I can use the talent You gave me to make a difference for the team assigned to me. I want to honor You in everything I do. Amen.

Become a Cheerleader

Clay Elliott

READY   "For you have made me rejoice, LORD, by what You have done; I will shout for joy because of the works of Your hands."—Psalm 92:4

SET   In 1936 the US Bureau of Reclamation and thousands of American workers completed an incredible man-made piece of work that cost $165 million dollars to construct. It was the Hoover Dam, located on the border of Nevada and Arizona. It is 660 feet from end to end, 726 feet tall, and took 4.5 million yards of concrete to complete.

Think about incredible athletic efforts that also took major work. Though it was thought impossible by many experts, in 1954 Roger Bannister ran the first sub-four minute mile. Now, fifty years later many are running it fifteen seconds faster than that. Now, compare these kinds of work to God's. In the beginning God spoke the entire existence of all life in just six days! Galaxies, light, plants, creatures, and his crowning achievement—man!

Work, by definition, means to take effort. To compare the work of man in the Hoover Dam to God's efforts is a joke. There is no comparison, but somehow we marvel at these major earthly accomplishments while almost forgetting the unbelievable works God has completed. It should come as no surprise that when the author of Psalm 92 spent a few minutes reflecting on God's work, he cheered. I encourage you to do the same. Take time today to marvel at all of God's work and become His cheerleader!

GO   What earthly pieces of work amaze you? How do they point to God?

WORKOUT   Genesis 1–2; Psalm 19

OVERTIME   Father, today I commit to be Your cheerleader. Thank You for the work You have done and continue to do within me! Amen.

Most Powerful Tool

Jere Johnson

READY "All Scripture is inspired by God and is profitable for teaching, for rebuking, for correcting, for training in righteousness, so that the man of God may be complete, equipped for every good work."—2 Timothy 3:16–17

SET What is your most powerful athletic tool? The strength of your bench press? The speed you've acquired from agility training? These are important, but I think that the *most* powerful tool in most sports today is simply the ball.

Think about it. You need the ball to score. Without the ball, Tiger Woods is just Eldrick, and the Rocket Clemens is just Roger. It's what these men do with the powerful tool that makes them champions. So if the ball is the most powerful tool in sport, what is the most powerful tool in life? It's the Bible.

God's Word teaches us many things. It teaches us what is right and what is wrong, then helps us get it right and prepares us to keep it right in our lives. The Bible can save us, free us, change us, protect us, and make us what we are meant to be: children of Christ.

In most sports, without the ball, the game could not be what it is intended to be. In your life with Christ, without His Word, you cannot be what you are intended to be. In the same way that football without the ball is not football, the Christian life without God's Word is not truly a Christian life.

GO How can you begin to use God's Word as a tool to bring greater meaning and purpose to your life?

WORKOUT Ephesians 6:10–17; Hebrews 4:12

OVERTIME God, I want my most powerful tool to be the Bible. Teach me how to use Your Word as the sword of the Spirit that equips me. Amen.

DAY 184

The Play That Changes Everything

David Vailes

READY   "We are pressed on every side by troubles, but we are not crushed. We are perplexed, but not driven to despair. We are hunted down, but never abandoned by God. We get knocked down, but we are not destroyed."—2 Corinthians 4:8–9 (NLT)

SET   The odds seem stacked against you. The score is not in your favor. The other team has an unstoppable momentum. Then, out of nowhere, your team makes a simple game-changing play that turns imminent defeat to potential victory.

Every athlete knows that something small can change a game's outcome. The greatest sports stories are about the underdogs—the ones who have no chance of winning but come from behind and win! Those are the stories movies are made of.

When we follow Christ, there can be times when we sit and wait for something major to happen in our walks with Jesus. We forget that something small can have a major impact on our lives and change our hearts forever. There will be times when we will feel defeated; there will be times we will want to give up; and there will be times we will think there is no hope. But those are the times in which God can mature us. As Christians, we must always seek out the opportunities (big or small) to have big impacts—for our teams, our communities, and our world.

GO   How can you search for the small things God is trying to show you?

WORKOUT   John 16:33; 2 Corinthians 7:4

OVERTIME   God, help me remember to seek You when I feel defeated, and to see You in the little things in life. Mature me to be a better follower of You. Amen.

Don't Mess Up a Good Thing

Rex Stump

READY "Wisdom is better than weapons of war, but one sinner can destroy much good."—Ecclesiastes 9:18

SET Imagine a football stadium full of excited fans. The home team is losing by six points. It's 4th down and they have the ball with less than a minute left on the game clock. The offensive line provides great protection as the quarterback drops back and throws the ball to his receiver in the end zone. It's good—touchdown! Wait, there is a flag on the field. An offensive lineman was called for holding. The touchdown doesn't count. All it took was one mistake and a would-be victory is out of reach.

In Ecclesiastes 9:18 we are reminded that "one" sinner can destroy much that is good. To sin is to miss the mark, to mess up. We are all guilty of making bad decisions and have the potential to destroy much good. And it just takes one. One sinful act can really make a mess of something good. One spouse wanders away and suddenly an entire family is a mess. One driver wanders out of his lane and destroys the life of an innocent passenger.

The writer of Ecclesiastes says that having wisdom (the ability to make great choices) is better than a weapon (something that ultimately makes you feel powerful). It is through wisdom—which comes from God—that we find great power to turn from sin.

GO How can you make more of an effort to gain godly wisdom?

WORKOUT James 1:5–6; Psalm 111:10

OVERTIME Father, I don't want to be mastered by sin. I pray for Your wisdom to avoid bad decisions. Keep me from destroying "much good." Amen.

Right or Left?

Dan Britton

READY   "But a man named Ananias, with his wife Sapphira, sold a piece of property. However, he kept back part of the proceeds with his wife's knowledge, and brought a portion of it and laid it at the apostles' feet. Then Peter said, 'Ananias, why has Satan filled your heart to lie to the Holy Spirit and keep back part of the proceeds from the field?'"—Acts 5:1–3

SET   When I played little league football, my team had an undefeated season. Not a single team even scored against us. Not bad for eight-year-olds! After our games, our coach would hand out the coveted "110%" helmet stickers to players who had played with all their heart and had given that extra effort on the field.

As competitors, we can sometimes be tempted to hold back what is God's for our own pleasure. But God wants us to give Him what is right, not what's left. In Luke 6:38, Jesus says:

Give, and it will be given to you; a good measure—pressed down, shaken together, and running over—will be poured into your lap. For with the measure you use, it will be measured back to you.

Ananias gave what was left, not what was right. Abel gave what was right; Cain gave what was left. God is not honored by our leftovers. The challenge when competing is to surrender all of your talents, gifts, and abilities to become more like Christ on and off the field.

GO   How can you make sure that you always give God what is right?

WORKOUT   Leviticus 23:10; 1 Timothy 6:7–9

OVERTIME   Lord, it is hard to surrender all my abilities for You. Please renew my mind and help me to give You 100 percent of the glory when I compete. Amen.

God and the Apple

Laura Crawford

READY   "After Jesus was baptized . . . the heavens suddenly opened for Him, and He saw the Spirit of God descending like a dove and coming down on Him. And there came a voice from heaven: This is My beloved Son. I take delight in Him!"—Matthew 3:16–17

SET   One day in the teachers' lounge, I overheard an office aide talking with her friend. The aide could not understand how God could be God and Jesus at the same time—how He could be in heaven and on Earth simultaneously! Her friend didn't know how to respond.

I asked God to give me the words to help them understand this difficult concept, and the Lord brought an idea to my mind. Feeling confident, I got up and went to tell them about God and an apple.

I started by explaining how an apple has a core, an inside white part, and an outer peel. I then explained that God the Father is like the apple core; all things are created from Him. God the Holy Spirit is like the white part of the apple; He comes to live inside us at the point of salvation and guides us. God the Son, Jesus, is like the apple's exterior; He took on a human "peeling" to show us that He experienced the same sufferings and temptations that we do. Yet He remained blameless. So Jesus, in human peeling, took our blame and sin so that we could be blameless in the Father's sight.

As competitors, we often have teachable moments like these that allow us to help our teammates understand Christian truths. After hearing the example of the apple, how do you respond? Is God the Father the core of your life?

GO   In what ways can God the Son's example direct you today?

WORKOUT   Matthew 7:17–20; 1 Corinthians 1:9

OVERTIME   Lord, help me take in all that You are in order for me to be all that You want me to be! Amen.

Speak Up

Dan Britton

READY "But one of them, seeing that he was healed, returned and, with a loud voice, gave glory to God. He fell facedown at His feet, thanking Him. And he was a Samaritan."—Luke 17:15–16

SET After every practice and every game, Jessie would approach me before leaving the field and say: "Thank you, Coach!" During the entire two years she played on our high school girls' lacrosse team, she never missed a single day of saying those three powerful words. Jessie understood the value of gratitude, and she wanted to make sure I knew that she did not take a single practice or game for granted.

Jessie was like the one leper in Luke 17 who returned and thanked Jesus. Out of the ten lepers healed by Jesus, only one man scrambled back to say thanks. And it's noted that he said it loudly. The other nine may have had an attitude of thanks, but never applied their gratitude. A friend of mine says that unexpressed gratitude can often be interpreted as being unthankful.

Thankfulness overflows if we have deep roots in Jesus and if our lives are built on Him. As Christian competitors, if we are *over-full* with God, then we *overflow* with thankfulness. Make sure you tell others how grateful you are for them. The power of thankfulness is in the action. Say it loudly!

GO List three teammates or coaches you are thankful for and why.

WORKOUT 1 Thessalonians 5:16–18; 1 Corinthians 1:4

OVERTIME Lord, I desire to be someone who not only prays for those I am thankful for, but who also takes action and tells them. Fill me up so that I can overflow with thanksgiving. Amen.

Tunnel Vision

Michael Hill

READY "Brothers, I do not consider myself to have taken hold of it. But one thing I do: Forgetting what is behind and reaching forward to what is ahead, I pursue as my goal the prize promised by God's heavenly call in Christ Jesus."—Philippians 3:13–14

SET "That's never been done here before."

"We've never been to the state playoffs."

"We've never beaten them before."

How many times have we as athletes looked at past seasons as the standard for potential success in the current season?

At times we get caught up in it. We often think that what we did last year has a bearing on what we can do this year. Yes, that is true to an extent. But you also have to learn how to block past seasons out of your mind in order to reach your full potential.

Paul, the ultimate bad guy, knew this all too well. He not only persecuted Christians, but he also sought permission to kill them. How could someone with such a past be of any use in building up the kingdom of God? By "forgetting what is behind." Paul accepted God's grace and forgiveness and pressed on to the goal of what the Lord had for him. He refused to allow past mistakes to keep him from doing the will of the Father.

If Paul, a former persecutor of Christians, could accept God's forgiveness and put his past behind him, don't you think you can?

GO What from your past is keeping you from doing God's will for your life?

WORKOUT Romans 6:1–14; Hebrews 6:1

OVERTIME Father, forgive me for my past mistakes and free me from the guilt that comes with them. Help me to focus on what is ahead instead of what is behind. Amen.

Advantage of Adversity

Harry Flaherty

READY "You intended to harm me, but God intended it for good to accomplish what is now being done, the saving of many lives. So then, don't be afraid."—Genesis 50:20–21 (NIV)

SET Athletes typically respect one another. We all share a single-minded, committed lifestyle that tends to be laced with adversity, but the adversity is the price we pay to excel. An athlete's identity and purpose all too often hinge on performance, so what happens when adversity strikes, making our performance less than ideal?

It's important to remember that what we see as adversity, God sees as opportunity. Joseph was sold into slavery by his brothers (Genesis 38), and was imprisoned for thirteen years for a crime he did not commit. Nevertheless, in the end, Joseph was able to say, "You intended to harm me, but God intended it for good . . ." He was right. Joseph became second in command over all of Egypt.

When I was a young man, playing ball meant the world to me. God blessed me with natural ability, and I excelled at my sport. Then adversity struck. The first NFL team that signed me, cut me. Feeling like a failure, I grudgingly headed to Tampa Bay to play for the Bandits, part of the USFL. It was there, through the Bandits' chapel program, that I met Jesus, and then God called me to do youth ministry. Whether we are deceived, beaten, jailed, surrounded by lions, or cut from a team, we are being prepped through adversities for divine opportunity.

GO How will you choose to respond to the current adversities you are facing?

WORKOUT Psalm 23; Jeremiah 29:11

OVERTIME Lord, I pray for grace and humility to see my troubles as opportunity for blessing, and as a means for You to be glorified through my life. Amen.

A Bulldog's Nose

Rex Stump

READY "Therefore, since we have this ministry because we were shown mercy, we do not give up."—2 Corinthians 4:1

SET Winston Churchill once said, "The nose of the bulldog has been slanted backwards so that he can continue to breathe without letting go!" I'm not sure if this is true, but I love it. Think about that mean-looking, stubborn dog that has clamped onto an object and just won't let go! Talk about persistence!

In Luke 18, Jesus tells us about a woman who was being treated unfairly. She persistently and repeatedly came to the judge asking for justice. Like a tough bulldog, she wouldn't let go! It got to the point where she drove the judge crazy with her requests. The judge said, "I will give her justice, so she doesn't wear me out by her persistent coming" (Luke 18:5).

This is not just a story, but it is also a life principle that Jesus wants us to learn. When you know that what you are holding on to is true and right, don't let go! Be persistent in your prayers. Be persistent in living for God. As a competitor, be persistent with your work ethic, with your dedication to your game and team, and with how you respect your coach staff, teammates, and opponents. Honor God by completing the tasks that He gives you with a determined, persistent resolve.

GO How can you be more persistent in your spiritual life? How about within sports?

WORKOUT Luke 18:1–7; 2 Corinthians 4:16–17

OVERTIME Father, give me strength to be persistent in living for You. Help me to take a bold stand for You each day. Amen.

Grieving with Hope

Josh Carter

READY   "Brothers and sisters, we do not want you to be uninformed about those who sleep in death, so that you do not grieve like the rest of mankind, who have no hope."—1 Thessalonians 4:13 (NIV)

SET   How do you go on after experiencing the unexpected death of a friend and loved one? The Illinois Wesleyan University football team was faced with this difficult task after the death of 21-year-old offensive lineman and co-captain, Doug Schmied. Schmied passed away in 2005, after suffering complications from heatstroke. "This is a devastating loss for everyone who knew Doug," said Illinois Wesleyan head football coach Norm Eash.

The Christians in Thessalonica were eagerly anticipating the return of the Lord Jesus. However, when fellow believers died and Christ had not returned yet, they began to fear that those believers would miss His return. In 1 Thessalonians, Paul assures them and us that we will one day be united with our brothers and sisters in Christ when He returns. He doesn't tell us not to grieve when a brother or sister in Christ passes on; he just encourages us to grieve with hope, knowing we will see them again.

The greatest decision that you or I will ever make (or not make) is to receive Christ into our lives. This choice will either make or break your eternity.

GO   How can Paul's words encourage you when it comes to dealing with death?

WORKOUT   1 Thessalonians 4:16–18; 2 Timothy 4:7–8

OVERTIME   God, dealing with death is unavoidable. I thank You for the hope You have given me through Your Son. Create in me an urgency to share about Jesus's sacrifice and the eternal life so that I can see my loved ones in heaven one day. Amen.

Looking Forward

Jo Kadlecek

READY   "Dear friends, we are God's children now, and what we will be has not yet been revealed. We know that when He appears, we will be like Him because we will see Him as He is. And everyone who has this hope in Him purifies himself just as He is pure."—1 John 3:2–3

SET   Teresa was an athlete who was all spirit, gifted with more determination than natural talent. But her Christian faith and love for soccer had a powerful effect on the other high school players. If we needed a surge of enthusiasm, we looked to Teresa. During a difficult practice one day, Teresa struggled to finish a long-distance run. As I jogged to the end of the line to encourage her, she glanced upward and shouted,

"Take me now, Lord Jesus! Take me now so I don't have to finish!"

Though we laughed hard at the time, I've often thought back to her plea. Teresa instinctively knew that there was something far better in life than earthly struggles or physical pain. She knew that as God's child, the hope of heaven awaited her.

As an eyewitness to Jesus's crucifixion, the apostle John must have been crushed by the pain of such an event. But then he witnessed the Lord's powerful resurrection. John's hope sustained him during days of great persecution; it purified him and empowered him to live in expectation of Christ's return.

For competitors who want their teammates to experience God's love, there's no greater gift we can give than the hope of eternal life!

GO   What does it mean to be "God's child now"?

WORKOUT   1 Corinthians 15:17–18; Revelation 1:4–7

OVERTIME   Lord, may our contemplation of the gift of eternal life renew our love for You today! Amen.

Following Your Dreams

Dan Frost

READY "For I know the plans I have for you," declares the LORD, "plans to prosper you and not to harm you, plans to give you hope and a future."—Jeremiah 29:11 (NIV)

SET I stood in the phone booth with tears in my eyes. I had just called my parents to let them know I would be flying home that night to Los Angeles. The Cleveland Cavaliers had become the third straight NBA team that I had failed to make. I had such high hopes of realizing my dream to play in the NBA when I was drafted out of the University of Iowa, but it was becoming clear to me that dreams don't always come true.

I thought my days as a basketball player were over. I had lost my identity. Basketball was my life. What would the future hold now? I should have known that my future was in the hands of Someone bigger than myself. Shortly thereafter, I received an invitation to play full-time with a sports ministry team. For the next nine years I traveled the world and played basketball, sharing my faith with thousands of people. God began using me in ways that I had never imagined.

Today, as I minister to leaders in our nation's capital, I am reminded daily that God still holds my future. I now know to hold plans loosely, resting securely in the knowledge that my Father may have a far different plan from my own.

GO Are you willing to give up your plans and dreams if God's plans and dreams for you are different?

WORKOUT Proverbs 16:9; Matthew 6:33–34

OVERTIME Lord, thank You for setting the path before me, even if I don't realize that it is the best road for me to take. Amen.

Buy In. Sell Out.

Chris Rich

READY "If you try to hang on to your life, you will lose it. But if you give up your life for my sake, you will save it."—Matthew 16:25 (NLT)

SET The Clemson football program, led by head coach Dabo Swinney, has created a culture of being "All In." In 2014, while celebrating their Orange Bowl win, the team wore T-shirts that read "All In Win." Coach Swinney has made it a part of the culture that in order to win you must be "all in," surrendering it all to be great.

Being "all in" begins with "buying in" to the vision your coach lays in front of you. It's more than simply doing what your coach says. It means believing in the plan and its ability to get you to your goal. The second part takes action; you have to "sell out." You have to be willing to give it all.

Scripture tells us of God's big plan for a young boy named David. At the beginning of God's plan, David was to save the Israelites from a giant named Goliath—a man who terrified the army of Israel. But David trusted and bought in to God's plan. He also sold out by taking only a slingshot and five stones to battle the giant.

Because of David's faith and trust in God's plan, he went all in. David was successful and defeated Goliath! In our faith, we must be willing to buy in and sell out to achieve all that God has for us.

GO Are you fully "bought in" to the plan God has for you?

WORKOUT 1 Samuel 17

OVERTIME Lord, I want to go "all in" for You. Give me faith to "buy in" and strength to "sell out." Amen.

Commitment 101

Jere Johnson

READY "All a man's ways seem right to him, but the LORD evaluates the motives. Commit your activities to the LORD, and your plans will be achieved."—Proverbs 16:2–3

SET "Commitment" is a big buzz word in sports. Coaches are asking for commitment, players want to be committed, and schools are looking for a four-year commitment. But commitment is a word that is used very loosely today.

When it comes to commitment, Jesus wants us to be committed as well. He desires our commitment. When is the last time you said, "Lord, I am committing this to You"? In the verse above from Proverbs, we read that if we commit our work to the Lord, our plans will succeed. Now, that does not mean we will win, but that we will be successful. When we walk with the Lord, we are guaranteed ultimate victory with Him in the end.

Committing everything to the Lord is a moment-by-moment adventure, not just a "one and done." Everything we do, everything we are, and everything about us needs to be completely committed to Christ. You might say that sounds like a lot to ask, but it is the *only* way that we can be totally committed to Christ.

GO How can you start being committed to Christ with all that you are?

WORKOUT Psalm 37:4–6; Revelation 3:15–16

OVERTIME Lord, today I commit to You. Help me to integrate this commitment into every part of my life so that I will be successful. Amen.

Nibbled to Death

Michael Wiggins

READY ". . . don't give the Devil an opportunity."—Ephesians 4:27

SET In the 1980s, the San Francisco 49ers made popular what became known as the West Coast Offense, an offense characterized by short, controlled-pass plays that gained only five to six yards. By running such low-risk plays, San Francisco nibbled away at their opponents. Their strategy earned them five Super Bowl titles between 1982 and 1995.

Sports highlight shows are filled with replays of big plays. Although these are exciting, rarely is a sporting event won in a single play. Certainly, the big play may put the nail in the coffin of an opponent, but often there are several small plays that lead to the loser's demise. The key to winning often involves staying close to the opposing team, nibbling away at them until success is reached. This allows the team to capitalize on the mistakes of their opponents and benefit from the opportunities that they are given.

As Christians, our opponent uses a similar strategy. If we allow Satan to "stay close," he'll find a way to break down our defense. He doesn't need the big play to be successful, only enough small plays to capitalize on our mistakes. To overcome this strategy, we have to put him away early in the game, remembering that Jesus has already won the victory.

Every questionable move, small lie, and fit of anger keeps our opponent in the game. But by confessing our sins and focusing our lives on the power of the cross, we leave the enemy in the dust!

GO Are there people or things in your life that are nibbling away at you?

WORKOUT Proverbs 1:10–19; 1 Peter 5:8–9

OVERTIME Lord, help me to stay close to You today and live in the freedom of Your grace! Amen.

Quiet Gives Birth to Momentum

Scott Ashton

READY "So Jotham strengthened himself because he did not waver in obeying the LORD his God."—2 Chronicles 27:6

SET It's the last at-bat of the 2003 American League Division Series. Red Sox outfielder Trot Nixon steps up to the plate with millions watching around the world. If he fails to get on base, the season's over for him, his teammates, coaches, and the entire Red Sox Nation. Nixon takes a deep breath and prays that God would calm his nerves. He calmly looks for a pitch to hammer and hits one of the biggest walk-off home runs in Red Sox history, setting off a mob scene at Fenway Park. In the midst of chaos and pressure, Nixon was quiet.

Jesus sets the ultimate example of the need to experience quiet moments with God in times of pressure. In Luke 6, He went away before making the important decision of choosing the disciples. Maybe the best example is in Luke 22, when Jesus prayed in the garden before the crucifixion. It was here He experienced the Father's presence and gained momentum to fulfill His purpose on the cross.

In the quietness of your heart, remember that God the Father is available to you today. Whether you are facing a game- or life-changing situation, God is able to provide you with the peace and momentum needed to fulfill His callings in your life.

GO In what areas of life do you need quietness with God to help fulfill His callings?

WORKOUT Luke 6:12–16; Mark 1:35–37

OVERTIME Lord, I ask for You to calm my spirit today. Help me to seek Your Spirit for direction and the momentum needed to complete all You've called me to. Amen.

Protect the House

Jimmy Page

READY "Don't you know that your body is a sanctuary of the Holy Spirit who is in you, whom you have from God? You are not your own, for you were bought at a price. Therefore glorify God in your body."—1 Corinthians 6:19–20

SET When the NFL's Baltimore Ravens prepare to play on their home field, the sound system blasts music and the giant screens exhort the team to "Protect this House." This same scene is replayed in stadiums all around the league.

God refers to our bodies as His house. Because we are believers, the Holy Spirit actually lives inside of us. And because God lives within us, He expects us to protect His house! Because the pressure to win is so great, many athletes resort to trying just about anything that will take their game to the next level. Each year, hundreds of athletes test positive for illegal or banned substances.

God calls us to a different standard, wanting nothing to harm our bodies or dishonor his name. The reputation of athletes who test positive for drug use is forever tarnished. For believers, the name and reputation of Jesus also will be harmed. Instead of putting our confidence in banned or illegal substances to boost our performance, we must put our confidence in the power of God to give us the discipline, determination, drive, or talent to compete at our best.

GO What would Jesus think about what you are willing to do in order to succeed in your sport?

WORKOUT Philippians 1:20–21; 2 Timothy 1:7

OVERTIME Lord, I know Your Holy Spirit lives in me. Help me to protect Your house from anything that is harmful to my body or that dishonors Your name. Amen.

Rise Up

Hal Hiatt

READY "Don't copy the behavior and customs of this world, but let God transform you into a new person by changing the way you think. Then you will learn to know God's will for you, which is good and pleasing and perfect."—Romans 12:2 (NLT)

SET God gives us positions of influence so that we can change the world for Him. In order for that to happen, we must always remember that His principles for living are often very different from the way we see others living. Knowing this fact offers us great opportunities to be "game changers" in the lives of those who do not know Jesus. But doing so requires a great deal of strength (which comes from the Holy Spirit) to stand firm for what is right when others are not willing to do the same.

When we are willing to be different from the world for God, He begins a process of transformation in our lives that shows us more about His plan and purpose for us. It is this process that begins with personal obedience, which unfolds a new and exciting relationship with Jesus. We no longer go from day to day questioning His plan. Instead, we live in His truth, which gives amazing purpose and clarity for every step of life.

It's not important whether you're the best player on your team. It *is* important to recognize the opportunities you have to make a difference for Jesus and take advantage of them.

GO When do you have the most difficulty being obedient to God's principles for life?

WORKOUT James 4:17; Galatians 6:9

OVERTIME Father, give me strength to stand for You when others are not. Help me to love all people and through that love to be Your instrument of change in the world. Amen.

Finish Line

Jere Johnson

READY   "I am sure of this, that He who started a good work in you will carry it on to completion until the day of Christ Jesus."—Philippians 1:6

SET   In college, my friends and I referred to long-distance runners, in good fun, as "jar heads." We figured that each day they would unscrew their heads, take out their brains, and then run an unbelievable amount of miles before returning and putting their brains back in. I've always admired distance runners and their amazing abilities. When these runners race, they strain through sore muscles and tough conditions lap after lap with determination to finish what they started.

In a way, we're all distance runners. At birth, our race of life begins. And there can be an amazing prize at the finish line. Christ will one day return. At the finish line, He will be waiting to congratulate those whom He recognizes.

If you believe in Him and He has found residence in your heart and life, you will receive the prize of heaven. But if you have lived for yourself and have denied Him through sinful choices, when you cross over the finish line, you will be finished. Give your all for God all the time. Never give up or give in to what the world holds on to today. You are a warrior. If you belong to Him, He will complete the work in you at the finish line!

GO   Are you running as a member of His team, or running for yourself?

WORKOUT   Matthew 5:12; 1 Corinthians 1:8

OVERTIME   Lord, as I live my life for You today, help me run with endurance to the finish line. Help me run for You and only You until my final breath. Amen.

Single-Handed

Charles Gee

READY "For as the body is one and has many parts, and all the parts of that body, though many, are one body—so also is Christ." —1 Corinthians 12:12

SET Have you ever tried to coach single-handedly? If you have, you know from experience that it's not the most efficient or effective way to get things done. As a young head coach, I had the attitude that if it were going to get done the way I wanted, I had to do it myself. I wanted to prove my capabilities. Little did I realize that not only was I wearing myself out, I was also denying my coaching staff the opportunity to grow and develop their own coaching skills. As I matured, I began to understand that trying to do things by myself would always limit the scope of what could be done.

The apostle Paul reminds us that we need each other. We can do so much more if we connect our gifts with the gifts of others. There is something about a common goal that naturally connects people. This is true in athletics, business, and ministry. We stop thinking about ourselves and start thinking about how we can get the job done. We stop trying to do it all on our own and simply begin to do our part. God intended us to be unified. Regardless of where God has placed us, He has others ready to join the team as we pursue our common goal.

GO Have you tried to accomplish an athletic goal single-handedly? What was the outcome?

WORKOUT John 17:20–23; Philippians 2:1–3

OVERTIME Lord, forgive me for trying to do it all by myself. Teach me to trust the teammates You put beside me each day. Amen.

Self-Sacrifice

Donna Miller

READY "Peter began to tell Him, 'Look, we have left everything and followed You.'"—Mark 10:28

SET When most sport seasons end, numbers are crunched. As competitors, it's easy for us to get caught up in this number-crunching, especially as the media highlights our career wins, the titles we've won, and the number of awards we've received. But any true competitor knows that records are not what is important. Having the opportunity to work with fellow competitors and make a difference in their lives is what is important.

In the Christian life, we make sacrifices as well. Instead of sitting in front of the television after a long day, we volunteer for church committees, sing in the choir, or work in the soup kitchen. What motivates us to do these things? If it is to build up a store of good deeds, then we're more concerned with building a record as Christians than with honoring Christ. In other words, our "sacrificial" serving isn't really serving anyone but ourselves.

As a Christian, I am called to serve Christ because I love Him, not because I need to earn His love. In fact, there is nothing that I could do to earn His love—Christ already paid the price for that love on the cross! We are not called to serve Christ for personal gain, for like Peter, we have left everything to follow Jesus! For Christian competitors, genuine love for fellow competitors motivates a selfless commitment to them. Winning takes care of itself.

GO What steps can you take to keep your motives on track—both as a competitor and as a child of God?

WORKOUT Acts 20:24; Philippians 3:7–11

OVERTIME God, please remind me that nothing compares to knowing Christ Jesus my Lord! Amen.

Hooked Up

Ken Bakewell

READY   "Suddenly a sound like the blowing of a violent wind came from heaven and filled the whole house where they were sitting. They saw what seemed to be tongues of fire that separated and came to rest on each of them."—Acts 2:2–3 (NIV)

SET   As athletes, we train to become faster and stronger. We try to bring as much power to our sport as we can. But even more important than our physical training is our spiritual training. Consider a plain, ordinary lightbulb. On its own, it puts out no power. It has to be hooked up to a power source in order to produce light.

This reminds me of the apostle Peter. He was a common man (a fisherman) but also a powerful man who was dedicated to his calling. In Matthew 26, Peter said he would never be drawn away from the Lord. Yet after Jesus was arrested, Peter denied Him—not once but three times. However, later on, at Pentecost, Peter boldly proclaimed the gospel and was instrumental in bringing thousands to the Lord (Acts 2:14–41).

What made the difference? The time spent waiting on the Lord and the indwelling of the Holy Spirit. Isaiah 40:31 (NIV) states: "Those who hope in the LORD will renew their strength. They will soar on wings like eagles; they will run and not grow weary, they will walk and not be faint." Today, make sure you're connected to the Power Source.

GO   What happens when you wait on the Lord? How can you be hooked up to the Power Source?

WORKOUT   Matthew 26:31–75; Philippians 4:13,19

OVERTIME   Lord, You are my power source. Please forgive me for the times that I have tried to replace You with some other source. Anoint me with boldness to proclaim Your message. Amen.

Playing for the Lord

Jennifer Ruddell

READY "Work willingly at whatever you do, as though you were working for the Lord rather than for people."—Colossians 3:23 (NLT)

SET As athletes, we play with the abilities God has given us. But what really drives us to play the game? For some it's the praise of parents, coaches, and friends, or awards and medals. Often our self-worth and dedication to the game is driven purely on the thoughts, praises, and criticisms of others.

One of the toughest parts of an athlete's performance is to be mentally focused on the game. Letting outside praise and distractions guide us will often lead to inconsistently good or poor performances. To stay mentally tough, we need to remember the race set before us—the eternal race for God's glory, not our own. This means playing with good sportsmanship, integrity, a competitive spirit, and using our talents to the best of our abilities. Focusing on Christ in sport takes a positive attitude and willingness to work harder even when we feel unnoticed.

In the end, God gives out the rewards. Christ calls us to be competitors for Him. He loves us when we use what He has given us to be the best we possibly can—working and playing for Him, not for others.

GO What are some tangible goals you could set to focus on playing for the Lord?

WORKOUT Matthew 25:14–30; Mark 9:35

OVERTIME Father, help me to focus on You and the abilities You have blessed me with—to train, compete, and strive to be the best while competing for You. Amen.

Not What It Seems

Loren Thornburg

READY "A man who endures trials is blessed, because when he passes the test he will receive the crown of life that God has promised to those who love Him."—James 1:12

SET God doesn't always work the way we think He should. Sometimes the things that we think are tragedies turn out to be blessings. In the Bible, when Joseph received a dream foreshadowing his role to reign over his brothers, his brothers grew angry and sold him into slavery. When Joseph was later falsely accused of a crime and thrown into prison, it seemed that his dream would never come true.

But the Lord proved faithful and present. While in prison, Joseph's God-given ability to interpret dreams attracted Pharaoh, and Joseph interpreted Pharaoh's dream. Through that interpretation, he gave Pharaoh the advice he needed to save his people from years of famine. As a result, Pharaoh put Joseph in charge of all of Egypt. Joseph went from being a slave to being the ruler of Egypt. Not only was Joseph blessed—all of Egypt was spared from a famine as well.

Often, God takes everything away to show that He has so much more in store for us if we will only have patience and faith. When we are in the middle of the trial, it seems interminable and hopeless. But that is where patience and faith come in. We must believe in God's promises to bring us through and into something better—His ultimate blessing.

GO Can you remember an event that seemed like a tragedy but turned out to be a blessing?

WORKOUT Romans 5:1–5; James 1:2–6

OVERTIME God, I choose to stand on Your promises in faith by delighting myself in You. I'll wait expectantly for what You are going to do in my life. Amen.

No Knick Knocking!

Kathy Malone

READY   "Keep asking, and it will be given to you. Keep searching, and you will find. Keep knocking, and the door will be opened to you."—Matthew 7:7

SET   Of all silly childhood games, the one I remember best was a game some of the older, mischievous kids in my neighborhood played. "Knick Knocking" was the practice of approaching a neighbor's front door, knocking loudly several times, and then running away. Serious Knick Knockers would retreat to a nearby hideaway so that they could watch the unsuspecting neighbor open the door in confusion.

As I've grown in faith, I've come to realize how many of us play Knick Knocking when it comes to prayer. We bring a request before God and "knock" loudly, only to drop the prayer and run away before the door opens or an answer comes. But Jesus tells us to "keep knocking." He invites us to come right up to His doorstep and make noise. The key to knocking is repetition. We're supposed to keep at it until the door opens.

P. T. Forsyth wrote, "The chief failure of prayer is its cessation." Sometimes we simply stop praying too soon. But the truth of the gospel says that because Jesus made a way for us on the cross, we can come to our Father's house at any hour of the day or night and call on Him! He never slumbers or sleeps (Ps. 121:4), so don't give up knocking or run away and wonder if He'll answer. He will!

GO   How do you deal with prayers that seem to go unanswered?

WORKOUT   Luke 11:5–8; James 5:13–18

OVERTIME   God, stir in me a desire to come to You repeatedly. Teach me to pray and not give up even when the answer seems far off. Amen.

No Pain, No Gain

Jay Beard

READY   "I do not run like one who runs aimlessly or box like one beating the air. Instead, I discipline my body and bring it under strict control, so that after preaching to others, I myself will not be disqualified."—1 Corinthians 9:26–27

SET   All athletes need to go through this, but most would probably rather skip it if it were possible. It's probably the least fun part of sports. Yet it's also the part that separates average athletes from top athletes. Have you figured it out yet? It's training. Athletic training involves many different things. Proper eating, weight training, and practicing are all necessary in order to get into top playing condition.

As Christians, we need to train ourselves spiritually. This involves omitting sin from our lives and removing things that may not be sin but are a hindrance in our respective walks with Christ. An example of this is when sports in your life begin to take away from time that you need to be devoting to God.

Paul tells us in 1 Corinthians 9:27 that he trained spiritually so that he wouldn't become disqualified for the prize. If a person comes into a game when he hasn't been practicing or is out of shape, he is not qualified to play. The same is true in our spiritual lives: we need to continually bring ourselves under God's command so that we remain qualified for what He has for us.

GO   Are there any sins in your life that you realize you need to remove?

WORKOUT   Hebrews 12:1–3

OVERTIME   God, I want to win the prize. Please open my heart to Your Holy Spirit and show me the areas in my life where I need to train harder. Amen.

Grace and Glory

David Lyons

READY   "But I count my life of no value to myself, so that I may finish my course and the ministry I received from the Lord Jesus, to testify to the gospel of God's grace."—Acts 20:24

SET   As I recently watched a bodybuilding competition and saw the victories and defeats of the athletes, my thoughts went to the effect our relationship with Christ has on us as competitors. I think about my life as an athlete, the training I have endured, the elation at my victories and the devastation of my defeats, and I am reminded of the role God has played in this journey. Our lives are an absolute result of our relationship with Him and how we conduct ourselves as Christians as well as athletes.

I know now, after the years of competition, that it was God's grace that allowed me to stay healthy through it all. I also know that it is God's grace that covers me while I now train and compete as an over fifty-year-old bodybuilder with multiple sclerosis. I am often asked how I can consider my life under the grace of God when I am afflicted by an incurable disease. My answer is that the grace of our Lord is not about our physical existence; it's about the blood He has covered us with that allows us the gift of eternity in heaven. No matter how tough life on Earth is, we as believers are blessed with God's grace.

GO   Do you see and feel God's grace in your life, win or lose?

WORKOUT   Romans 5:17; Ephesians 1:7

OVERTIME   Thank You, Father, for Your constant grace and guidance in my life. Help my attitude, actions, and words reflect Your glory during competition. Amen.

Sometimes You Win, Sometimes You Learn

Rex Stump

READY   "Hold firmly to the message of life. Then I can boast in the day of Christ that I didn't run or labor for nothing."—Philippians 2:16

SET   In the spring of 2015 many witnessed an incredible finish at the Pepsi Team Invitational in Eugene, Oregon, as the margin of victory in the men's steeplechase was only .10 seconds! In a close sprint finish, Oregon University's Tanguy Pepiot came down the final straight of the track with a large lead over Washington University's Meron Simon. In the last few yards, Tanguy slowed down and motioned to the crowd to start cheering, believing he was going to finish first without a problem. What Tanguy didn't know is that Meron was charging hard to the finish line. As Tanguy prematurely celebrated, Meron sprinted past him for the first place finish.

Sometimes you win, sometimes you . . . learn! Tanguy lost, but he learned a great deal that day! Anyone can start something—a job, a relationship, a season . . . but it takes a great deal to finish! Athletes who may not have much to strive for since their league aspirations are gone and tournament opportunities are bleak will struggle with finishing strong. Even FCA Huddles, ministries, and church youth groups can be tempted to fade out in the month of May, giving way to various excuses.

It's so easy to slow down, forget about our opposition, or even become apathetic in living. Learn now how to finish strong by running the race of life with determination and desire to finish strong!

GO   Ask yourself: "Am I firmly grounded in God's Word to help me finish strong?"

WORKOUT   Philippians 3:14; Hebrews 12:1

OVERTIME   Father, help me to stay focused, committed, and not distracted away from the finish line. Amen.

Higher Standard

Jere Johnson

READY "But just as he who called you is holy, so be holy in all you do."—1 Peter 1:15 (NIV)

SET In the height of his playing days, Charles Barkley *claimed* that he was not a role model. The University of Colorado *claimed* that the troubles with its football program were not as bad as they seemed. The people involved in these situations didn't want to be held to a higher standard. Why? Because they felt that athletics and off-the-field issues should be kept separate.

In many ways, that may be true. However, as athletes, we need to remember that we are who we are. People don't view Alex Rodriguez as just another guy who lives in New York; they see him as a future Hall of Famer who plays third base for the Yankees. As an athlete at any level, we are held to a higher standard. How we react to the spotlight demonstrates to others who we truly are.

Likewise, as believers in Christ, we are held to a higher standard by which we all will be measured one day, and we should strive to live up to that standard every day. Too many Christians compare themselves to others and just get by in their faith. But that is not God's standard for us. Our plan may be to slide by, but His plan for us is perfection. So set your sights upward, plant your feet on the straight and narrow path, and make your actions worthy of Christ.

GO Are you living your life below God's standard?

WORKOUT Romans 12:2; 1 Corinthians 3:18–19

OVERTIME God, I want to live by a higher standard, and I know that I will only be able to do this by allowing You to have complete control in my life. Guide me in Your ways. Amen.

Fighting for God

Fleceia Comeaux

READY "And this whole assembly will know that it is not by sword or by spear that the Lord saves, for the battle is the Lord's. He will hand you over to us."—1 Samuel 17:47

SET For forty days, Goliath stood on a hill across from the army of God, mocking, challenging, and taunting the Israelites to fight. And every time he came to the battle line God's army would cower and flee with terror back to their camp. But one day, a shepherd boy named David came to visit his brothers at the camp. After listening to the soldiers talk about the giant and hearing Goliath mock God, David volunteered to fight the giant and get rid of Israel's disgrace. He knew that God would be with him.

David did not prepare for battle to simply beat his opponent, but for the honor and glory of the one true God. He did not focus on what his opponent was saying, but rather on what his God could do. And out of a *pure motive came a pure victory*. With the power of God in him and the army of the Lord behind him, he defeated the giant with ease. He believed that God could do anything in him and through him.

We must believe the same as David. With God on our side, we can compete with confidence, knowing His glory will be revealed, regardless of the outcome.

GO What can you learn from David's example that can help you and your team?

WORKOUT 1 Samuel 17

OVERTIME God, help me to remember that it is not about my strength but about Your power in me. Encourage me to give my all when facing seemingly impossible situations, but to recognize that You determine the outcome. Amen.

First Response

Lisa Fisher

READY "Listen to my words, LORD; consider my sighing. Pay attention to the sound of my cry, my King and my God, for I pray to You. At daybreak, LORD, You hear my voice; at daybreak I plead my case to You and watch expectantly."—Psalm 5:1–3

SET We all respond to problems in various ways. A "thinker" looks at the problem from every possible angle. A "talker" seeks the wisdom and advice of others. A "doer" goes at the problem head-on. A "reactor" has a negative emotional outburst in the midst of difficulty.

God wants our first response to be prayer. No matter how big or small our problems are, He wants us to present our requests to Him first. As Psalm 55:22 says, "Cast your burden on the LORD, and He will sustain you; He will never allow the righteous to be shaken."

The daily situations that cross my path as a coach are many: recruiting battles, disciplinary action, staff member conflicts, and so on. As a role model to my players and fellow coaches, I am convicted daily as to how I respond when problems arise. The Lord wants nothing more than for our first response to be to lay our requests at His feet and to open our hearts to hear His voice.

GO By changing your first response, how can you see this affecting your life in a positive way?

WORKOUT Matthew 11:28–29; Philippians 4:6

OVERTIME Lord, I pray that my first response today would be to come to You in challenging times. By doing so, may I be an example to my team of the peace, love, and grace that come through Your Son. Amen.

Leave Your Mark

Brad Holloway

READY "You yourselves are our letter, written on our hearts, recognized and read by everyone. It is clear that you are Christ's letter, produced by us, not written with ink but with the Spirit of the living God."—2 Corinthians 3:2–3

SET On my eleventh birthday I received a gift that set me head and shoulders above everyone else in the neighborhood. It was the coolest bicycle in the world. It was shiny and bright, with a white frame and a blue glitter banana seat, blue glitter handles, and tassels. It did indeed make me the envy of all my friends. I might as well have been flying an F-16 fighter jet.

But the coolest thing about that bike was its blue tires. I was the only kid in town who could lay blue streaks on the sidewalk. We'd all line up together, race down the sidewalk, and then slam on our brakes to see who could leave the longest mark. If there was a blue streak on the sidewalk, you'd know I'd been there. I'd left my mark for all to see.

As Christians, God calls us to leave marks on the places that we've been, influencing others for Christ. Whether at work, home, or around the neighborhood, God calls us to live a life that reaches out to others every day and glorifies Him. What kind of mark are you leaving?

GO What opportunities do you have today to leave your mark?

WORKOUT 1 Corinthians 2:1–5; Philippians 1:13

OVERTIME Lord, help me to realize that the greatest goal I can reach is to make an eternal impact on the lives of those whom You have put in my path. Amen.

Tossing Up a Prayer

Christy Cabe

READY "And the Holy Spirit helps us in our weakness. For example, we don't know what God wants us to pray for. But the Holy Spirit prays for us with groanings that cannot be expressed in words."—Romans 8:26 (NLT)

SET I'd give my kindergarteners the same halftime speech: "You guys are doing well, but what have I told you about passing the basketball?" They'd squirm and giggle, and a few little shoulders would shrug. Coaching five-year-olds is not for the faint of heart.

"When you pass the ball, you need to pass it to someone instead of just tossing it in the air and hoping that one of your teammates will catch it," I'd continue. "Okay!" they'd shout. But then the second half would begin, and they'd toss up almost every pass with the hope that someone wearing the same color jersey would be paying attention. At least we had fun!

When we pray, we are in a sense tossing up prayers to God. Sometimes we pray with clarity and conviction, and at other times we feel a yearning and desire to connect with God, yet we don't know what words to say. In those moments, we toss up a prayer, and the Holy Spirit intercedes with the perfect "alley-oop." Romans 8 tells us that the Holy Spirit Himself intercedes for us. When all we can offer is an imperfect and incomplete mess of words, we can trust that God will receive it perfectly. Even through our weaknesses and humanity, God has provided a way.

GO Is prayer a habit in your life?

WORKOUT Romans 12:12; Ephesians 3:16

OVERTIME Lord, sometimes I don't know the right words to pray, yet I trust that through Your Holy Spirit, You understand perfectly. Amen.

Lasting Leadership

Jere Johnson

READY   "Teach a youth about the way he should go; even when he is old he will not depart from it."—Proverbs 22:6

SET   Coaches are always looking for the winning edge. They go to clinics, conferences, and seminars to improve their programs and learn how it should be done. No coach is successful 100 percent of the time. But I know one coach who always did it right.

The Master Coach personally selected His own team. He poured His life into a team of twelve, worked with them for three years, and then sent them out to teach and prepare others for future good work. He instilled lasting leadership skills among His team in five ways: (1) He empowered them—He gave them confidence to be bold in Him; (2) He equipped them—He prepared them for future ministry for Him; (3) He educated them—He gave them wisdom to direct others to Him; (4) He edified them—He built them up in the Word to share about Him; (5) He encouraged them—He blessed their lives by a relationship with Him.

Jesus is the Master Coach. His teachings are the only foolproof way to find meaning, peace, and victory in life. Because the young people in our programs deserve the best, we can help them learn from the best coach there ever was or will be—Jesus. Would your teammates say that you empower, equip, educate, edify, and encourage them daily? Remember, the only legacy that will last forever with them is Him!

GO   How can you help your teammates learn from the Master Coach?

WORKOUT   John 14:6; Ephesians 6:4

OVERTIME   Thank You, Jesus, that You have empowered me with Your Spirit so that I may equip and encourage others for Your work. Amen.

Looking Ahead

Kyle Shultz

READY   "Not that I have already reached the goal or am already fully mature, but I make every effort to take hold of it because I also have been taken hold of by Christ Jesus."—Philippians 3:12

SET   After routing Oklahoma University for its second straight national title, USC coach Pete Carroll was asked when preparation for the next season would begin. Carroll replied, "It's already going. We live this thing. If you're competing, then you're always competing." Carroll had just led his team to an undefeated championship season, yet he already had his sights set on the highest goals for the following year.

Athletes set goals all the time with the belief that good goals will help them live up to their potential. At the beginning of the year, many are doing the same thing with life in general. Some look ahead without passion or vision at all. And some have a dream and, like Pete Carroll, want to be active in accomplishing it.

What would you like to see happen over the next year? I encourage you to do two things: First, give it serious thought. What do you truly want to see happen? Second, write these things down and stay focused. If you have something else in mind, something less than total commitment, God will clear your blurred vision.

GO   What is God telling you to set as a goal for your life?

WORKOUT   2 Corinthians 5:17; Philippians 3:12–21

OVERTIME   Lord, reveal to me what Your goals are for me on the road ahead, not what my goals are for You. Stretch my vision and show me not what is, but what can be. Amen.

Followership

Dan Britton

READY   "For even the Son of Man did not come to be served, but to serve, and to give his life as a ransom for many."—Mark 10:45 (NIV)

SET   NBA point guard Chauncey Billups said, "To be a good leader, at some point you have to be a good follower." So, what about you?

"Are you a leader or a follower?" I heard that question constantly from my youth pastor, parents, coaches, and friends. A subtle principle was communicated through that question: be a leader, not a follower! But if everyone is leading, then who is following? In our recognition-driven society, we all want to lead. Volumes have been written on leadership, but very little on followership.

What society is missing is that followership is the beginning of leadership. The best competitors have mastered the art of following. Following does not mean doing what everyone else is doing. Following means intentionally watching and learning from others. You observe those who are walking in a manner worthy of the Lord, who live with humility and courage, who exhibit integrity and compassion, who make wise decisions, and then you choose to follow in their footsteps. Followership starts at the foot of the cross. We must be willing to pick up our cross and follow Him daily. Remember, when you follow well, you lead well.

GO   How can followership change your team, family, school, church, and community?

WORKOUT   Luke 9:23–24

OVERTIME   God, I desire to lead before following. Teach me how to let go of my pride and be a good follower. Amen.

In Him

Jere Johnson

READY   "Some take pride in chariots, and others in horses, but we take pride in the name of Yahweh our God."—Psalm 20:7

SET   On the second Sunday of every March, you'll hear teams all over the country proclaiming how they should be invited to the NCAA Basketball Tournament. More than thirty teams get automatic bids through conference tournament championships, but thirty-four other teams have to be invited. These teams boast of the great things they have done—and how they deserve to be in the tournament.

During the Old Testament times nations would boast of their great armies or warriors and how powerful they had become—as if they had risen to power on their own. Countless passages in Scripture describe how vain these people were and how God brought them to their knees each time. God wants us to understand that all we are and all we can become are only because of His work in our lives. It is only in Him that we can boast.

The FCA Competitor's Creed states: "I do not trust in myself. I do not boast in my own abilities or believe in my own strength. I rely solely on the power of God."

It is through God alone that we receive the power to perform. When we stop looking for praise and start giving it to Him, we will fully understand His power and goodness in our lives.

GO   How can you start to live and compete for God today?

WORKOUT   Acts 8:4–25; Romans 3:27–31

OVERTIME   Lord, as I compete today, may I give You all of the credit for what You have created me to do in You. I desire to honor only You with my performance. Amen.

Fresh New Start

Rachel Pace

READY   "This means that anyone who belongs to Christ has become a new person. The old life is gone; a new life has begun!"—2 Corinthians 5:17 (NLT)

SET   Nothing beats the start to a new season. Fans desperately watch to see who will be the star players and which teams will make it to the end, or, best of all, which teams will have a perfect record. Despite how poorly a team played the previous season, there is a moment when the playing field evens, and last year's losers are no better or worse than last year's state champs.

When you become a Christian, you get the same fresh start. Even though you may feel like a complete failure with your sins and scars from the past, Christ died so that He could wipe those completely clean. In John 3, Jesus used the term *born again* to describe a Christian's new start. Like a baby, we get a fresh start in life.

Unlike a sports team, Christians do not have to worry about a blemished record in the future. Once you ask Jesus to lead your life, your sins, your past, and your future are completely wiped clean. So, the only one holding on to that list of wrongs is you. Are you willing to give up that list and live freely in the forgiveness that is given to all who believe in Jesus?

GO   How can you give up sins of the past?

WORKOUT   Romans 11:6; Isaiah 1:18

OVERTIME   Lord, thank You for making me a new creation. May I live a forgiven life and forgive others in the same way You forgive me. Amen.

The Word

Judy Siegle

READY   The tempter came to him and said, "If You are the Son of God, tell these stones to become bread." Jesus answered, "It is written: 'Man does not live on bread alone, but on every word that comes from the mouth of God.'"—Matthew 4:3–4 (NIV)

SET   Throughout my years of training as a wheelchair athlete, I've found that memorizing and reciting Bible verses helps me in many ways. It helps me to stay focused, get to sleep, and stay calm in anxious moments.

Prior to a race, I often recite a verse in my mind to calm my heart. I know that God is going with me as I race and that He will give me what I need on that particular day. One of my strengths as a wheelchair racer is my endurance, but I'm usually slow off the start. Once, one of my coaches shouted at me after a race about my slow start. "What were you thinking? Where was your mind, anyway?" she asked.

I didn't tell her that my thoughts were fixed on God and His Word, which gave me power that day. His Word continues to give me that same power every day as I compete and strive to live up to my highest potential.

GO   What are the distractions in your life that make it difficult for you to focus on His Word?

WORKOUT   Proverbs 30:5; Ephesians 6:10–18

OVERTIME   Father, help me to realize the importance of Your Word. Let my mind retain what I read so that I may carry Your wisdom in my heart and apply it to each new situation. Amen.

Setting an Example

Josh Carter

READY   "Don't let anyone look down on you because you are young, but set an example for the believers in speech, in conduct, in love, in faith and in purity."—1 Timothy 4:12 (NIV)

SET   On January 16, 2004, two fourteen-year-old athletes made a big splash in their respective sports. Michelle Wie played in the Sony Open on the PGA tour and missed the cut by one stroke, tying two men who had won major championships the previous year. Freddy Adu, in a move that shocked no one, was chosen as the top pick in the Major League Soccer draft by DC United.

While Michelle Wie and Freddy Adu were competing with and against athletes twice their age, they still made an impact by the example they set. When Adu was given the number 9 on his jersey, he responded by saying, "I would rather have number 11, but you can't always get what you want. You have to earn it."

It would have been easy for the fourteen-year-old phenom to whine and complain about not getting his number. Doing so may have stripped credibility and influence that Adu had with his coaches, teammates, and fans. Instead, he set an example that revealed a desire to work hard and be a team player. Whether you are young in age or young at heart, people are watching you to see how you live, not how you say you live.

GO   What kind of example are you setting for others on your team?

WORKOUT   Psalm 119:9; 2 Timothy 2:22

OVERTIME   God, I want to be an example for the believers in speech, in life, in love, in faith, and in purity. As I spend time with You in the Word daily, I pray to get closer to this goal. Amen.

Soul Food

Alex Hagler McCraney

READY "Like newborn infants, desire the pure spiritual milk, so that you may grow by it for your salvation."—1 Peter 2:2

SET One of the most crucial moments in a newborn's life is the first act of taking in milk, their sole source of nutrition. Babies enter the world hungry and begin seeking the sustenance they were created to receive. The nutrients milk provides are vital to the health of the baby.

When Nicodemus came to Jesus by night to secretly inquire how to go to heaven, Jesus plainly replied, "I assure you: Unless someone is born again, he cannot see the kingdom of God" (John 3:3). After we experience the supernatural rebirth of salvation, there is also a crucial moment that affects our spiritual well-being: desiring the pure milk of the Word of God.

Before being born again, our souls fed on the things of this world with hopes of satisfaction. After hearing the gospel one night at a college FCA Huddle, my eyes were opened to the truth and I came alive. I wanted to know and do what pleased Jesus and I found myself feasting on the Bread of Life. As I consistently read God's Word I grew in my relationship with Him, which also transformed how I lived. The Bible nourishes our spirit as God speaks into our hearts and minds. As born again children of God, let us not neglect the real "soul food." Let us seek God daily by meditating on the everlasting truth.

GO Why is consistency important in studying God's Word?

WORKOUT Hebrews 4:12

OVERTIME Father, help me to hunger for more knowledge of You and Your Word. Help me to consistently read Scripture and apply it to my life as a competitor. Amen.

Trust

Judy Siegle

READY "Take delight in the LORD, and He will give you your heart's desires. Commit your way to the LORD; trust in Him, and He will act, making your righteousness shine like the dawn, your justice like the noonday."—Psalm 37:4–6

SET Upon arriving in Atlanta for the National Wheelchair Championships, I was informed by the stewardess that they had forgotten my manual wheelchair in Minneapolis when I had changed planes. Fortunately, they had remembered to load my racing chair, but it arrived with a huge crack in the back wheel frame. There was no way I'd be racing with that!

As I sat in the claims office filing reports on these two wheelchairs, I thought back to some verses from Psalm 56:3–4 : "When I am afraid, I will trust in You. In God, whose word I praise, in God I trust; I will not fear. What can man do to me?" These verses calmed my heart. I didn't know if I'd be racing, but I knew that God was in control of everything. The next day, my daily wheelchair arrived at camp. As it happened, my racing wheelchair manufacturer was also at the meet and had, on hand, an exact replacement for my broken wheel.

I was able to compete at that event and ended up setting national records in four events. But the most exciting part of this experience was confirming that I could trust God, even when circumstances seemed out of control.

GO Can you list some of the occasions when God has provided for you during challenging times?

WORKOUT Joshua 1:9; Philippians 4:6–7

OVERTIME God, many times I allow my frustration to control my attitude and actions. Help me to trust You more and remain flexible when things aren't going my way. Amen.

Lost

Charles Gee

READY "My people have been lost sheep. Their shepherds have led them astray and turned them loose in the mountains."—Jeremiah 50:6a (NLT)

SET Yogi Berra was a Hall of Fame baseball player with a wit worthy of the Hall of Fame too. He had a gift for saying the smartest things in the funniest ways.

Though he played on ten world championship teams and won the American MVP Award three times, Yogi is best known and beloved for his Yogi-isms. He had a knack for saying something that made no sense; yet, with a little perspective, it made perfect sense. Once, while traveling to Cooperstown, New York, for his 1972 induction into the MLB Hall of Fame, Yogi got lost, and his wife, Carmen, was giving him a hard time. As only Yogi could, he gave it right back, saying, "We're lost, but we're making good time!"[4]

Honestly, Yogi's wisdom could also apply to our spiritual lives. As competitors, how often have we let our to-do lists take priority over family time? The truth is this: we will never finish everything that needs to be done! I have seen many competitors who were "making great time" in their careers but were totally lost to their families.

Like sheep, we can lose our way. Jeremiah reminds us how easy it is to follow poor shepherds, chase foolish idols, and lose the things that matter the most. Be careful. Stay focused. Keep your eyes on Jesus.

GO Are your priorities what they should be? If not, what can you do to revise them?

WORKOUT Proverbs 5:23; Luke 15:11–32

OVERTIME Father, keep me from losing myself in the things that don't matter. Give me the wisdom to seek Your guidance in all that I do. Amen.

Together

Clay Meyer

READY   "For as the body is one and has many parts, and all the parts of that body, though many, are one body—so also is Christ."—1 Corinthians 12:12

SET   Former University of Southern California quarterback Matt Barkley will forever be remembered by the cardinal and gold faithful for rewriting the USC and Pac-12 record books during his four years at Southern Cal. But in a spirit of humility, Barkley realizes those accomplishments would have never been possible without his Trojan teammates.

"Football is such a unique sport because of the team aspect of the game," Barkley said. "Every play there has to be eleven guys doing the exact right thing or else it won't work. But, when all those things do come together, all the hard work you put together as teammates collides in a perfect play; it's [exhilarating]."

Each of us plays a certain position or role on our team because of the abilities we possess. The same applies to our responsibilities as a Christ-follower. We each play an important role in doing God's kingdom work with our spiritual gifts. And when we team up with other believers, He is able to do even mightier works through us.

How can you use your spiritual gifts on your team? As an encourager or maybe a servant-leader? When your gifts are combined with the gifts of those around you, the Spirit of the Lord will be alive and active and your impact unstoppable.

GO   What role do you fill on your team?

WORKOUT   1 Corinthians 1:10; 1 Corinthians 12

OVERTIME   God, thank You for giving me unique gifts to fill a specific role on my team in Your kingdom. I pray for wisdom to know how to best do my part to reflect You in my life. Amen.

Game Face

Sean McNamara

READY "The Lord God will help Me; therefore I have not been humiliated; therefore I have set My face like flint, and I know I will not be put to shame."—Isaiah 50:7

SET The lacrosse game was heading in the wrong direction fast. As a goalie, I was frustrated that our defense had allowed three quick goals in a short period of time. Our coach pulled me aside and said, "Wipe that look off your face! If your teammates see or think that you, as our leader, doubt for one second that we can't win this game, they will be discouraged and give up." I obviously had lost my "game face."

Although circumstances continually change, we need to have resolve like Isaiah and make our faces like flint or stone. Today, we wouldn't say "get your flint face on," but rather "put your game face on." As competitors, we know what it means to have a game face. However, do we know what it means to put on our game face when it comes to our spiritual lives?

As followers of Christ, our spiritual game face doesn't come from our own resolve, perseverance, or tenacity. Instead, our game face comes from putting our trust in God. We don't know what tomorrow may bring, but as Christians, our countenance and demeanor should be unwavering, because we trust the promises of God's Word.

GO What can you do today to move your confidence as a competitor from yourself to Christ?

WORKOUT Romans 5:35; Revelation 12:11

OVERTIME Lord, I desire to put on a spiritual game face all the time. I place my trust and confidence in Your character and in the promises of Your Word. Amen.

One Thing

Dan Britton

READY "Brothers, I do not consider myself to have taken hold of it. But one thing I do: Forgetting what is behind and reaching forward to what is ahead, I pursue as my goal the prize promised by God's heavenly call in Christ Jesus."—Philippians 3:13–14

SET Paul uses the phrase "one thing" to bring focus and clarity to his calling. This phrase appears five times in the NIV Bible translation—once in the verse above in Philippians and four times in the Gospels:

- Jesus says to Martha, "Only one thing is needed" (Luke 10:42).
- Jesus tells the rich man that he still lacks "one thing" (Luke 18:22 and Mark 10:21).
- The blind man who was healed by Christ tells the Pharisees, "One thing I do know. I was blind but now I see!" (John 9:25).

As competitors for Christ, the *one thing* that God desires is for us to focus on Him. The FCA Competitor's Creed states: "I am a Competitor now and forever. I am made to strive, to strain, to stretch, and to succeed in the arena of competition. I am a Christian Competitor and as such, I face my challenger with the face of Christ."

The one thing that we need to focus on as competitors for Christ is the fact that we have been created in the likeness of God in order to bring glory to Him on and off the field. Anything else takes our focus off the Master.

GO What would you describe as the one thing on which the Lord wants you to focus?

WORKOUT Luke 10:38–42; John 9:13–34

OVERTIME Lord, please forgive me for the times when I have not fixed my eyes on You. Help me to focus on You and glorify You alone in all that I do. Amen.

Trust in God

Jonathan Byrd

READY   "Trust in the LORD with all your heart, and do not rely on your own understanding; think about Him in all your ways, and He will guide you on the right paths."—Proverbs 3:5–6

SET   As a professional athlete, I've been entrusted with a measure of talent by God. That talent has allowed me to achieve a certain amount of success on the golf course. If I'm not vigilant against prideful thoughts, it can be tempting to trust in my own ability. That's why one of the greatest lessons I've learned in my life is dependence upon God.

There have been times in my life when I haven't trusted God completely and I've done things on my own. When I lean on my own understanding, it doesn't make sense to give when finances are tight. When I trust in my own abilities, it might be easier to succumb to temptations on the golf course and hedge in areas of competitive integrity.

But when I put everything in God's hands, I'm telling Him that I trust Him no matter what happens and no matter how bad things might seem. It's that surrendered attitude of trust that allows me to have the freedom and peace to compete at a high level, play golf to God's glory, and let Him take care of the rest.

GO   As a Christian competitor, what does having a "surrendered attitude of trust" look like? What can you do today to put complete trust in God in every area of your life?

WORKOUT   Deuteronomy 28:1–14; Romans 8:28

OVERTIME   Lord, help me trust You no matter the success or failure I might experience. I trust You with every area of my life. Amen.

Remember

Rex Stump

READY   "He causes us to remember his wonderful works. How gracious and merciful is our LORD!"—Psalm 111:4 (NLT)

SET   In the early 1980s, Eric Davis joined the Cincinnati Reds. He had finally made it to the top, so this was an exciting night. Unfortunately, Eric began his debut on the road in St. Louis and grounded out in the fifth inning. His team lost 9–1. Worse yet, Eric was forced to wear a numberless jersey because Cincinnati forgot to pack extra road uniforms. They *forgot*?

"I forgot" are two infamous words that plague my life.

- "I forgot" to call today like I promised.
- "I forgot" to send the email I promised.
- "I forgot" his name again.

Forgetfulness is frustrating for everyone. Forgetting God is more than frustrating—it's dangerous! We often forget God and what He has done for us because we have too many other things occupying our thoughts and our time. So today, *stop* and *remember*.

- **Remember** that we are saved by the grace of God, not by our good deeds (Eph. 2:8–9).
- **Remember** to give thanks! When you give thanks to God, the focus is off you (1 Thess. 5:18).
- **Remember** that God loves you and has a plan for you (John 3:16).

God has not forgotten you. He loves you and longs to meet with you today.

GO   What practical steps can you take to remember that God loves you?

WORKOUT   Deuteronomy 32:17–19; Psalm 106:20–22

OVERTIME   Father, let me never forget Your love for me and Your plans for me. Clear my mind of things that clutter my view of Your truths. Amen.

The Real Teachers

Jenny Johnson

READY "Therefore, God's chosen ones, holy and loved, put on heart-felt compassion, kindness, humility, gentleness, and patience."—Colossians 3:12

SET As practice was about to end on my very first day of coaching high school girls' tennis, the only thing left was our distance run. It would be a tough first day; nobody was in great shape at the end of the summer—too many afternoons spent relaxing on the couch.

When the first runner crossed the finish line, I called out her time with my stopwatch in hand. Immediately, she turned around to see how far back the other players were and saw one young player far behind everyone else. Without hesitating, she sprinted back to that last runner and began to run alongside her for the last leg. Our fastest runner didn't want anyone to have to finish last or alone!

I was amazed. I remembered my own days playing high school basketball. If I had finished my laps first, I wouldn't have thought about anyone else. Instead, I would have rested on a nice cool spot on the gym floor. But on this first day of coaching high school tennis, I suddenly realized that I'd be learning a lot more than I'd be teaching.

Through that young player, God taught me a lesson about kindness and sensitivity. Just as Jesus amazed the local leaders with His deeds and words, God used the unexpected to change me in a way that I could never have imagined.

GO How has God used the unexpected to teach you something He wanted you to learn?

WORKOUT Ephesians 4:31–32; 1 John 3:8–20

OVERTIME Thank You, God, for coming to Earth in the person of Jesus to "run" beside me in some amazing ways! Amen.

Eyes on the Target

Charlotte Smith

READY   "And climbing out of the boat, Peter started walking on the water and came toward Jesus. But when he saw the strength of the wind, he was afraid. And beginning to sink he cried out, 'Lord, save me!'"—Matthew 14:29–30

SET   One of the oldest acrostics in basketball is B.E.E.F. The "B" is for "balance." The first "E" is for "eyes on target." The second "E" is for "elbow straight." And the "F" is for "follow through." Each one is important, though plenty of shots go into the basket even when the shooter is off balance, has bent elbows, or doesn't follow through. But seldom will a ball find the hoop if the shooter's eyes aren't fixed on the target.

As important as goals are within sports, at the heart of every great Christian competitor should be the discipline of focusing on a greater purpose. In Matthew 14, the disciple Peter wanted to walk on water with Jesus and did so until he shifted his eyes from Christ to the fierce wind. He became fearful and began to sink.

Likewise, we will start sinking in our lives if we focus on the tumult that surrounds us. We must allow the Holy Spirit to be our guide, reminding us that with Christ, all is well with our souls. No matter the final score, injury, or pressure, if we fix our eyes on Christ, our target, and trust His faithful provision, we will be able to accomplish His purposes, both in our game and our life.

GO   How can you keep yourself from shifting your eyes off God?

WORKOUT   John 10:27; 1 Corinthians 16:13

OVERTIME   Lord, help me to always fix my eyes on You so that my faith will never waver. Amen.

Far More Important

Dan Britton

READY "You shall love the Lord your God with all your heart, with all your soul, with all your mind, and with all your strength . . . 'You shall love your neighbor as yourself.' There is no other commandment greater than these."—Mark 12:30–31 (NKJV)

SET As a young athlete, I thought winning was everything. Whether it was a big high school game against our rivals or just a pick-up basketball game against my brothers, I wanted to win. One of the greatest NFL coaches of all time, Vincent Lombardi, once said, "Winning isn't everything—but wanting to win is."

In Mark 12:33, a religious teacher summarized Jesus's words by saying, "To love Him with all the heart, with all the understanding, and with all the strength, and to love one's neighbor as oneself, is more than all the burnt offerings and sacrifices" (NKJV). At that time, burnt offerings and sacrifices were important. But this man realized that there was nothing more important than loving God.

What could possibly be more important than loving God? Maybe for you it's not burnt offerings, but it could be your sport, your friends, your family, schoolwork, winning, or anything in your life that tries to crowd out Jesus. Examine your heart today and ask God to show you what is keeping you from loving Him above all else.

GO Is there anything or anyone in your life more important than Jesus?

WORKOUT Deuteronomy 6:4–9

OVERTIME Lord, I want nothing in my life to be more important than You. Pour out Your wisdom and help me to see what those things are. You are far more important than anything. Amen.

Unconditional Respect

Bill Buckley

READY   "Love each other with genuine affection, and take delight in honoring each other."—Romans 12:10 (NLT)

SET   During a losing season or bad game, it's easy to give up on each other. In the Bible, Peter made a lot of mistakes. He made empty claims; did things recklessly; talked when he should have listened; and lied, cried, and almost died because of his immaturity. But Jesus never gave up on him, and he became a world-changer.

When teammates quit believing in one another, the fight is over. But when our respect for one another is unconditional, all things become possible. There is a respect that must be earned. But there is also a respect that must be unconditional. Unconditional respect is honoring one another no matter what. The following words are the Team Covenant my teams adopted:

"To my teammates and coaches: I will believe in you and your potential regardless of your ability, performance, or past failures. I will trust you to grow, to rise to the occasion, to do the right thing. If you fail my trust, I will not give up on you and will do whatever I can to help you succeed. If I see a weakness in you, I will honor you enough to pray for you, and, if necessary, challenge you face to face to rise up to our higher calling. I commit to always treat you better than I treat myself. I will fight for your honor if you are attacked in any way. I will stick by you and stick up for you, always."

God promises He will never give up on us. We must offer our coaches and teammates the same unconditional respect.

GO   Do you show unconditional respect?

WORKOUT   Romans 12

OVERTIME   Lord, teach me to see Your potential in each of my coaches and teammates. Amen.

Learning from the Best

John Crosby

READY "Now if any of you lacks wisdom, he should ask God, who gives to all generously and without criticizing, and it will be given to him."—James 1:5

SET John Wooden, the legendary basketball coach who led UCLA to ten NCAA National Championships, spent every off-season focused on learning a specific aspect of the game from those he considered to be the best in that area. He became the most successful collegiate coach by recognizing there was a lot he didn't know and that improvement could be gained by gleaning wisdom from experts in each facet of the game.

When the Bible speaks of wisdom, it is referring to God's perspective. James says that gaining God's perspective starts with recognizing that we need it. See the sarcasm in *"if any of you lacks wisdom"*? We all lack wisdom. To gain wisdom, we must acknowledge that we don't have all the answers, that we don't even have all the questions.

The great news is that when we realize our need for God's perspective on our game, our relationships, our circumstances, and our lives, we simply need to ask. Not for God to fill our prescriptions for solving our problems, but for Him to show us how to receive more of His wisdom. We are not asked to jump through hoops or meet minimal requirements. God knows that when we see the gap between our lives and His will, the Holy Spirit will provide us with the wisdom needed for change.

GO How do we ask God for His perspective?

WORKOUT 1 Kings 3:5–14; Proverbs 1:7

OVERTIME Lord, help me to recognize the gap between my limited perspective and Your perfect wisdom, and give me the courage to align my life with Your will. Amen.

Praising God through Pain

John Register

READY   "You show that you are a letter from Christ, the result of our ministry, written not with ink but with the Spirit of the living God, not on tablets of stone but on tablets of human hearts."—2 Corinthians 3:3 (NIV)

SET   As I approached the third hurdle, I knew I was a little too far away to take it with my right leg. So in a split second, I decided to alternate and go over with my left foot leading. I had done this a thousand times in my career, but this time when I landed I felt my knee shift out of the socket. I had hyperextended my knee, and I knew my running days were over.

Surrounded by my teammates, I had a choice. My team knew me as a Christian who had led them in Bible studies, and now they waited expectantly to see what would proceed out of my mouth. From sheer pain, I screamed, "Hallelujah!"

The apostle Paul writes that as believers, we must be a living testimony—an open book for the world to see the glorious gospel of Christ. Sometimes this is painful. It could be physically or even psychologically painful.

Although I would later need to have my left leg amputated, there was a greater outcome than I could have anticipated: Two people gave their lives to Christ as a result of seeing the way that I reacted to the situation. As Paul said, it was not I but Christ who lives inside who won the victory that day (Gal. 2:20).

GO   Are you a living testimony for the gospel of Christ? Why or why not?

WORKOUT   John 15:2; Philippians 3:8

OVERTIME   Father, help me to grow in You so that all aspects of my life will bring You glory and honor. Amen.

My House

Alex Hagler McCraney

READY "And the things that you have heard from me among many witnesses, commit these to faithful men who will be able to teach others also."—2 Timothy 2:2 (NKJV)

SET I think we would all agree that Moses was a man of God. Though he had his mishaps along the way, God had this testimony about him, "He *is* faithful in all My house" (Numbers 12:7 NKJV). So what caused God to say this about Moses? Well, not only did he lead God's chosen people out of their slavery in Egypt, build the tabernacle (the place where God's glory would dwell), and receive from God's hand the Ten Commandments, he also did not neglect to make disciples.

Moses was faithful to pass on the Word of God to the next generation and reminded the people of God's mighty acts on their behalf. He invested in the leaders among the people, specifically a young man named Joshua. Moses noticed his heart for God and took this young man under his wing. Joshua learned much from his mentor, including how to lead and serve people, and about God's character: His faithfulness, loving kindness, and mercy. Things he would soon learn firsthand.

After Moses's death, God appointed Joshua to be Israel's new leader. Like Moses, Joshua was faithful. He was victorious in bringing the people into the land of promise. His famous last words still echo in our homes today: "As for me and my house, we will serve the LORD" (Josh. 24:15 NKJV).

GO Have you ever been a disciple? If not, seek out someone whose walk with the Lord you respect and admire and ask them to disciple you.

WORKOUT Psalm 145:4; Matthew 28:18–20

OVERTIME Father, please help me see the opportunities to be a disciple and to disciple others on my team and in my community. Amen.

In the Zone

Dan Britton

READY   "Walk as children of light—for the fruit of the light results in all goodness, righteousness, and truth—discerning what is pleasing to the Lord."—Ephesians 5:8–10

SET   If someone walked up to you and asked, "What does it mean to play 'in the zone'?" how would you respond? As an athlete, you have certainly been in the zone at least once. To play in the zone means that you are unstoppable. You can't miss.

What does "in the zone" mean when you relate it to your spiritual life? What does it take to get "in the zone"? Here are a few questions based on Ephesians 5:1–10.

- Who in the Bible lived "in the zone"? Why?
- Paul says to be an imitator of God (v. 1). What does it mean to imitate someone?
- What things does Paul say someone should do to imitate God (vv. 3–7)?
- When you are living in the zone for Christ, what does your life look like (vv. 8–10)?

The 1924 Olympic runner Eric Liddell said, "God made me fast. And when I run, I feel God's pleasure. To win is to honor Him." Ask God to show you what it means to play in the zone for Christ. Pray that you will discover more ways to please Him and not yourself. The FCA Competitor's Creed states: "I give my all—all of the time." When you're giving your all for Christ, you can bet that you're spiritually in the zone.

GO   What can you do to please God during competition?

WORKOUT   3 John 11

OVERTIME   Lord, I am consumed with my own performance. Break me of the hold that competition has on me and help me to compete for Your glory alone. Amen.

DAY 239

Know the Source

Michael Wiggins

READY "No wisdom, no understanding, and no counsel will prevail against the LORD. A horse is prepared for the day of battle, but victory comes from the LORD."—Proverbs 21:30–31

SET In 1982, the Miami Dolphins faced the New England Patriots in Foxboro, Massachusetts. Snow began to fall during the game, and by the fourth quarter the wintry conditions had contributed to a scoreless tie. But late in the game, the Patriots drove down the field and came within field-goal range, where a successful kick would likely win the game. The New England coach ordered a snowplow to clear a spot for the kicking team, enabling the kicker to set his foot firmly on the turf. As a result, he kicked the game-winning field goal.

Tremendous preparation goes into competing at high levels. Still, many of the variables associated with winning, such as weather conditions or travel situations, are outside the coach's control. Experienced coaches prepare for the factors that are within their control and accept those that are not.

As Christians, we are faced with the reality of uncontrollable factors when we share our faith with others. We can say all the right words at all the right times, and yet we may never see someone make a decision for Christ. Even so, we must take every opportunity to testify to Christ by living out our faith with integrity, trusting that God's Spirit will work according to His purposes!

GO Who are some people in your life for whom you can pray to receive Jesus?

WORKOUT Matthew 13:1–23; 28:16–20

OVERTIME God, Your ways are perfect and Your love is unconditional. Help me to reflect that love to others today that they may know You! Amen.

250

Jesus's Jobs

Nate Bliss

READY "I am the good shepherd. The good shepherd sacrifices his life for the sheep."—John 10:11 (NLT)

SET Jesus has a lot of jobs. The Bible says Jesus's many roles include Advocate, High Priest, and King. Jesus is also our Shepherd, and it's this job that reveals some amazing truths about how God wants to help us live our lives. Recognizing these truths can also help you reach your full potential as a competitor.

A shepherd's job is to take care of the sheep by providing:

1. Protection and Safety
   - **Read Psalm 27:1.** What would you be afraid of if you believed that God always has your back?
2. Guidance and Blessing
   - **Read Psalm 23:1–4.** A good shepherd will lead his sheep to the greenest pastures and the cleanest water so that the sheep will be strong and well fed. In the same way, Jesus offers us the tools and resources to live overcoming and abundantly blessed lives, ones He designed us to live.
3. Training and Wisdom
   - **Read John 10:3–5.** The best coaches and trainers help you reach your full potential. You want to be in the best position to achieve competitive success. As we read the Bible and talk with God (pray), we develop a lifestyle of following Jesus. By getting closer to Him, we position ourselves to succeed in the things God wants us to accomplish.

As you compete today, let Jesus protect, lead, guide, and train you.

GO What are some things keeping you from letting God be your Shepherd?

WORKOUT John 10:1–11; Psalm 23

OVERTIME Lord, as I follow You, teach me who I am and how You want me to live my life in a way that brings You glory. Amen.

DAY 241

God's Love

Al Schierbaum

READY "For Christ's love compels us . . ."—2 Corinthians 5:14

SET As an athlete and a coach I have spent most of my life thinking God either loved me or was mad at me based upon wins or losses, good or bad performances, injury or health. Intellectually, I believed that God loved me unconditionally, but practically, my sense of self-worth and idea of God's love was dictated by performance. When I lost or failed I thought I was worthless, and that God was punishing me for my sins. Repentance was motivated more out of the hope of receiving God's favor and a future win rather than true remorse.

There are numbers of athletes and coaches who are very successful because their entire identity is based upon their performance. This performance-based identity has driven them to levels way above the average because they have had to perform to feel validated or loved by God. Does this describe you?

Instead of our self-worth being based upon performance, performance should be based on God's unconditional love for us. We should compete because God made us to do so. With a heart of gratitude we should express the gifts He gave us. It is Christ's unconditional love and our relationship with Him as a child of God that give us our true identity. With an identity founded in Christ, our self-worth does not fluctuate based upon performance. God's love for us never changes!

GO Why do you think self-worth is connected to performance?

WORKOUT 2 Corinthians 5:14–21; 1 John 4:7–21

OVERTIME Jesus, may You cleanse me of a performance-based mentality and help me to be secure in Your love alone. Amen.

What Do You Sow?

Josh Carter

READY   "A man reaps what he sows. Whoever sows to please their flesh, from the flesh will reap destruction; whoever sows to please the Spirit, from the Spirit will reap eternal life."—Galatians 6:7–8 (NIV)

SET   After injuries to ligaments in both knees cut his 2001 and 2002 seasons short, Oklahoma quarterback Jason White wanted desperately to get back on the field. White not only got back on the field in 2003, but he also led the Sooners to a 12–1 record and won the Heisman Trophy. When reflecting on the grueling rehab that he had gone through to get to this point, White said, "I'd go through it all again."

God's principle of reaping what we sow is often evident in athletics. Those who sow the seeds of hard work and mental preparation will generally reap a harvest of success in competition. Those who sow seeds of physical and mental laziness will reap a harvest of disappointment.

You are going to sow many seeds today, and at some point in the future you will reap a harvest according to what was sown. The key is to first know what kind of harvest you want to reap and then sow the seeds that will produce it. I challenge you today to sow seeds in competition and in life that bring glory and honor to God, and know that you will be rewarded with a great harvest.

GO   What kind of harvest do you want to reap in life? Are you sowing seeds that will produce it?

WORKOUT   Proverbs 11:18; Romans 6:21–22

OVERTIME   Father, I want to reap a bountiful harvest, and I know that this will be accomplished only when I give You complete control. May each seed I plant be pleasing to You. Amen.

Every Day Principle

Sean McNamara

READY "Very early in the morning, while it was still dark, He got up, went out, and made His way to a deserted place. And He was praying there."—Mark 1:35

SET As an athlete, I always looked forward to the off-season. During the off-season, I could customize my training to improve my skills and make the most of the opportunities God presented to me as an athlete, elevating my game to the next level.

Every competitor would like to experience similar growth in the off-season, but for some, the discipline, focus, and desire is lacking. As a result, they get out of shape when their season is over. To excel in sports, athletes and coaches understand the "Every Day Principle." Every day, I need to discipline myself in every area (spiritually, mentally, and physically) to compete at my best.

The Christian life can be viewed similarly. To experience all that is promised in God's Word, we must realize the importance of being in prayer and strengthening our understanding of God's Word and character every day. As an athlete, you cannot see change or growth in your skills overnight and the same goes for your spiritual life. To see growth in your faith, you have to intentionally carve out time every day to allow God's Spirit to transform your life. Jesus modeled this daily, as He would continually withdraw to be in God's presence. Make it a priority every day to discipline yourself and engage with God!

GO Do you have a time and a place set aside for daily fellowship with God?

WORKOUT Philippians 1:5–7; Revelation 3:20

OVERTIME Lord, thank You for the power of prayer. Give me the desire and discipline to fellowship with You daily. Amen.

Fuel to the Fire

Amy Cullum

READY "Fire goes out without wood . . ."—Proverbs 26:20a (NLT)

SET Fall has always been a wonderful season for me. Campfires are one of my favorite things. I love the sound, the smell, and the fellowship that usually comes with a good campfire.

Recently, this short yet powerful verse from Proverbs caught my attention. Proverbs 26:20a says, "Without wood, fire goes out." When I read this verse, the Lord seemed to ask me, "What are you fueling your fire with?"

To keep our fire for the Lord, we must continually fuel it with good things—solid pieces of wood that will sustain our fire for Him. At times, my fuel is like a dead twig. Am I lying? Gossiping? Am I trying to fuel the fire with activities and duties for God instead of just getting to know Him better? As an athlete or coach, am I fueling my fire with stats and scores instead of simply deepening my spiritual intimacy with the Lord through competition?

Each of us has to face these and many other issues in our own lives. But the Lord wants us to give Him all of our firewood, no matter how rotten, wet, or small it might be. With it, He will bless each of us with a fire to warm the cold places in our hearts, a peace to calm our souls, and a comfort to know that when we give Christ our all He will enlighten us through His grace and mercy.

GO What is fueling your spiritual fire?

WORKOUT Jeremiah 29:13; Matthew 25:14–30

OVERTIME Lord, fuel my fire for You even when I feel like I have nothing to give. Amen.

The Right Choice

By Amy Walz

READY "As for me and my family, we will serve the LORD."—Joshua 24:15 (NLT)

SET What does it take to win the game? Under ever-increasing pressure to win, every coach and player has been encouraged to bend or break the rules. In the sports world, why is it so difficult to discern what constitutes cheating?

In the 1999 Women's Soccer World Cup, USA goalkeeper Brianna Scurry stepped off her goal line to make the game-winning save on a penalty kick. While the rules allow a goalkeeper to move sideways along the line, he or she is not allowed to step forward until the ball is kicked. In the championship match that day, the referee did not rule against the save. It is still a point of contention whether the right choices were made.

Making the right choice and acting with integrity become even more challenging when it appears that our competitors are not doing the same. How can our players be expected to compete against a team that practices extra days or uses ineligible players or illegal equipment?

As believers in Christ, God calls us to a higher standard, which He proved by sending Jesus to Earth so that we might come to Him. He desires that we act with integrity in every aspect of our lives, but He did not leave us on our own to fulfill that call to live by His standards. He provided a way through a personal relationship in Christ.

GO What does it mean for you as a competitor to serve the Lord with integrity?

WORKOUT Psalm 37; Proverbs 24:10

OVERTIME Lord, I desire to serve You. Help me to make the right choices and encourage others to do the same. Give me the strength to act with integrity at all times. Amen.

Not Top Ten

Rex Stump

READY "And My people who are called by My name humble themselves, pray and seek My face, and turn from their evil ways, then I will hear from heaven, forgive their sin, and heal their land."—2 Chronicles 7:14

SET Many of us enjoy watching the "Top Ten" athletic highlights shown on television. Those plays are always the talk of the day, but what about those "Not Top Ten" plays? The highlights of an athlete's most embarrassing moments caught on tape.

In 2 Chronicles 32–33, there is a story of a father and his son, both kings who are humbled by their mistakes. The first king, Hezekiah, seemed to be on the right track in leading his nation toward God. The problem occurred when he prayed for healing, and in his pride he never thanked God for the miracle that occurred. God humbled Hezekiah; the king repented and got things right with God.

King Manasseh replaced worshiping God with the sin of sorcery and witchcraft. Manasseh ignored God's warnings, so God allowed an opposing army to defeat Manasseh. They put a ring through his nose, bound him in chains, and took him to a foreign land. Manasseh sincerely humbled himself to God and asked for forgiveness.

Just like some athletes, these kings experienced a "Not Top Ten" moment in life. Haven't we all? If you find yourself humbled by a mistake, pray for forgiveness, pick yourself up, and turn back to God. Don't allow a "Not Top Ten" moment to define your life.

GO What is one of your "Not Top Ten" moments in life? What did you learn?

WORKOUT 2 Chronicles 32–33; Psalm 147:5–7

OVERTIME Father, forgive me for my pride and for the times I tried to rule my life. Help me today to live in a way that pleases You! Amen.

Put On Your Armor!

Jimmy Page

READY "Finally, be strengthened by the Lord and by His vast strength. Put on the full armor of God so that you can stand against the tactics of the Devil."—Ephesians 6:10–11

SET Under Armour sports performance apparel has become one of the hottest brands in sports. The company has "engineered" apparel for athletes to protect them from the cold, the heat, and the turf. Athletes from the NFL to NASCAR—and even members of the military—wear Under Armour gear in order to "arm" and protect themselves from the elements and to enhance performance.

As competitors for Christ, we are given a different kind of armor. The FCA Competitor's Creed states, "My body is the temple of Jesus Christ. I protect it from within and without." Just as we protect our bodies through intense physical training, we must also protect our hearts and minds by putting on our spiritual armor.

If we step onto the playing field without being physically prepared, our opponent is likely to dominate the competition. We are at a greater risk for injury, and we become a liability to our team. If we step onto life's playing field without the full armor of God, then our opponent, the devil, is likely to push us all over the field. We are at a greater risk for moral failure, and we become a liability to our team, Team Jesus Christ.

GO Do you put on your spiritual armor each day?

WORKOUT 1 Thessalonians 5:8; Ephesians 6:10–17

OVERTIME Lord, help me put on Your spiritual armor so that I can stand against the schemes of the devil and be protected from within. Amen.

DAY 248

Seizing Opportunities

Steve Keenum

READY "David said to Saul, 'Don't let anyone be discouraged by him; your servant will go and fight this Philistine!'"—1 Samuel 17:32

SET When I was recruiting, it was critical for me to judge if a potential player was a true competitor or not. True competitors are easy to spot. They are the ones who are willing to do the things most people shy away from.

According to 1 Samuel, David was a competitor. All he wanted was for Saul to give him the chance to fight Goliath. He wasn't fearful of a big challenge because he had prepared himself to seize the moment. He had already faced obstacles as a shepherd, defending his flock from lions and bears, which developed his confidence. And like a true competitor, David knew where his strength came from. When facing Goliath, he boldly told him that he came to fight in the name of the Lord.

Just like David, we have the opportunity to be true competitors both in our sport and spiritual life. We must continually prepare ourselves physically and spiritually to take on any obstacles we may face. It is the willingness to sacrifice and train ourselves to grab hold of opportunities that separates a true competitor from the rest of the crowd.

GO If presented with the chance, would you be ready to take a stand for God?

WORKOUT 1 Samuel 17; Revelation 3:20

OVERTIME Lord, I ask for the opportunity to make a stand for You. I pray for the wisdom and strength to seize each moment You present to tell others about Your love and grace. Amen.

Hand in Glove

Charles Gee

READY "Remain in Me, and I in you. Just as a branch is unable to produce fruit by itself unless it remains on the vine, so neither can you unless you remain in Me."—John 15:4

SET Do you remember your first baseball glove? Mine was a "genuine" Tony Taylor that I purchased when I was eight years old. It rarely left my hand during the day, and each night I would rub it down with a generous application of saddle soap to soften the leather. To help shape the glove's pocket, I would put a baseball in the center and pull it tight with my Sunday belt. I knew this glove was going to make me a better player, and my confidence soared. As time passed, I learned that the glove held no magic—it was only as good as the hand that went inside.

We can easily apply this principle to our Christian lives. Without a masterful hand inside, the greatest of gloves cannot accomplish what it was designed to do. If we think of ourselves as baseball gloves, our ability is limited without God's masterful hand working inside us. Jesus said that we can't accomplish anything unless we are connected to our heavenly Father. The challenge is in our allowing God to constantly keep His hand in our lives. We must fully trust Him in every area. It's only then that our gifts and talents can fully be used according to His will.

GO Why do you think it can be hard to fully rely on God?

WORKOUT John 3:16; Hebrews 11:1–3

OVERTIME Father, thank You for helping me understand that when I allow You to be the hand in my glove, You can use me to accomplish great things. Amen.

The Big Game

Kristy Makris

READY   "For he satisfies the thirsty and fills the hungry with good things."—Psalm 107:9 (NLT)

SET   When I was a young girl, I was given a ticket to The Big Game. I stuck it in my pocket, kept it close, but never used it. Many years passed before a friend reminded me of the ticket tucked away in my pocket. Years later, the ticket was still good, so we went to the game. But I became enamored with the tailgate. I spent a lot of time with people who were outside the stadium, where the roars of the crowd could be heard, but not a play could be seen. Finally, I became restless and ventured inside the stadium. I handed over my tattered ticket.

Once inside, I saw distracted friends hanging out in the upper deck, but my seat was down closer to the field. As I took my seat, I noticed everyone looking at a book. I was told it was the "playbook," and that by reading it I could know all that was happening on the field. I purchased one and studied it, taking copious notes and watching the game unfold.

Suddenly, a hand was extended to me from the field, and I was invited to be a participant in The Big Game rather than simply a spectator. I was told I had to trust the Coach, study the playbook, and take my place on the team. Since then, my life has never been the same, and I will never be satisfied at the tailgate or as a spectator again.

GO   What does this story teach you about how God can satisfy your longing soul?

WORKOUT   Exodus 9:16; Philippians 2:13

OVERTIME   Father, satisfy my longing soul with Your good things. Amen.

$10 Million Tongue

Dan Britton

READY "With the tongue we praise our Lord and Father, and with it we curse human beings, who have been made in God's likeness. Out of the same mouth come praise and cursing. My brothers and sisters, this should not be."—James 3:9–10 (NIV)

SET As competitors, it is often hard to guard our mouths. Carson Palmer, a Heisman Trophy winner, signed a $49 million, six-year contract with the Cincinnati Bengals in 2003.

A total of $10 million of the deal was for his signing bonus. However, that $10 million wasn't contingent upon his great talent or intelligence. It was contingent upon his tongue and whether or not he would say anything negative about his team, coaches, or management—a loyalty pledge.

There are two types of people in the world: builders and tearers. Builders use their words to lift up those around them. They pour goodness into the emotional bank accounts of others. Tearers are people who berate those around them. They are the cut-down kings, usually saying things to make themselves look better in front of others.

The tongue is only a reflection of what is in the heart. When the pressure comes, we speak what is in our heart. God desires not only for us to keep our mouths from cursing but also to abstain from being critical. When you are under pressure, what comes out? Criticism or godliness? You might not get paid $10 million for having a Christlike tongue, but your Savior will be glorified!

GO What came out of your heart the last time you were under pressure? How will you respond differently next time?

WORKOUT Proverbs 15:4; Ephesians 4:29

OVERTIME Lord, help me to be a person whose words build up those around me. I desire to glorify You in all I say. Amen.

Encouragement

Bill Burnett

READY "And let us be concerned about one another in order to promote love and good works."—Hebrews 10:24

SET Coach Peacock's team had just won a state championship. They were celebrating in the locker room, and Coach was hugging his players right and left. As the congratulations continued, the coach noticed one player in particular sitting alone on a bench, watching him. Coach Peacock knew that the young man's parents were divorced and also that his dad was an alcoholic who never attended any of his son's games. So he walked over to the player and asked if he was okay. The young man responded, "Yes, Coach, but I was just wondering . . . could I have another hug?"

The experience was a milestone in Coach Peacock's life, so much so that he began a campaign to be a "team of huggers." He started with the coaching staff. Soon, the coaches began sharing hugs with their players, and Coach Peacock found that hugs were a tremendously effective form of encouragement.

There are many ways we can encourage others. Hebrews 10:24 says that we are to consider how to stimulate and encourage one another to good deeds. Why? Because Jesus, the Son of God, willingly took on all of our discouragement on the cross so that we might experience the embrace of God's love. Because of that truth, let's consider all the ways that we might encourage our fellow coaches, teachers, players, family members, and neighbors.

GO What are some specific ways that you could encourage your team?

WORKOUT Romans 15:4–6; Hebrews 3:12–13

OVERTIME God, thank You for inviting me to experience the embrace of Your love! May Your love always lead me as I consider how to encourage others. Amen.

Grace and Strength

Kerry O'Neill

READY "But He said to me, 'My grace is sufficient for you, for power is perfected in weakness.' Therefore, I will most gladly boast all the more about my weaknesses, so that Christ's power may reside in me."—2 Corinthians 12:9

SET The one thing competitors strive to never be is weak! Being mentally and physically tough for your sport is a good thing. However, strength often leads to self-sufficiency and an unwillingness to admit the need for help. In fact, it often goes a step further and the coach or competitor ends up pretending. Rather than feeling vulnerable, one chooses to hide behind a mask of confidence and capability.

This negatively affects teammates as they deal with feelings of inadequacy from playing the comparison game, worship at the altar of performance, and eventually learn to wear their own masks of self-sufficiency. Sadly, this can also describe some Christian circles.

We all need help, and we will never grow if we are too proud to admit it. We all need God's grace, but we must humble ourselves in order to receive it. Is there an area where you have been too embarrassed to admit you need help? Don't let pride stand in the way of receiving the greatest gift in the universe—God's grace. Your strength is no match for His.

GO Which weakness in your life could be an opportunity for God's grace and power?

WORKOUT 2 Corinthians 12:1–10; James 4:6

OVERTIME Lord, I admit that I have avoided weakness and vulnerability. I've tried to be self-reliant and I've fallen into the trap of pretending and comparing. Forgive me. Soften my heart to seek Your grace and strength in my weakness. Amen.

Failing?

Alex Harb

READY   "Dear friends, let us love one another, for love comes from God. Everyone who loves has been born of God and knows God. Whoever does not love does not know God, because God is love."—1 John 4:7–8 (NIV)

SET   It doesn't matter how good or how bad you are at sports. God is love. But what exactly is love?

Love is patient, love is kind. It does not envy, it does not boast, it is not proud. It does not dishonor others, it is not self-seeking, it is not easily angered, it keeps no record of wrongs. Love does not delight in evil but rejoices with the truth. It always protects, always trusts, always hopes, always perseveres. Love never fails (1 Cor. 13:4–8 NIV).

Since God is referred to in the Bible as the very essence of love, this means that God Himself is patient and kind. God does not envy. He is not prideful. He does not behave rudely, does not seek His own, is not provoked, and does not rejoice in evil.

God rejoices in the truth. He bears all things, believes all things, hopes all things, and endures all things. God never fails! Even when *you* fail, God never fails to love you, His child. So as you go through your day, think about how much God loves you—enough that He gave us His Son so that we may have eternal life (John 3:16).

GO   How have you shown love to others? How can you improve on showing love to others?

WORKOUT   Romans 8:38–39; 1 John 4:7–21

OVERTIME   God, thank You for Your perfect, nonjudgmental love. Help me to be a walking example of this love and show me practical ways that I can love my friends and family. Amen.

We Are Family

Jimmy Page

READY   "Both the one who makes people holy and those who are made holy are of the same family. So Jesus is not ashamed to call them brothers and sisters."—Hebrews 2:11 (NIV)

SET   In the 1979 World Series, the Pittsburgh Pirates adopted the wildly popular disco hit "We Are Family" by Sister Sledge as their theme song. The song was good, but I believe there is something powerful about family, especially when it's a healthy one.

In Genesis 1 and 2, we learn that we were all created as part of God's original family—in His image, for His purpose. We are said to be His masterpiece made for the Master's purpose. But then we were separated from Him because of sin. By disobeying God, we choose to walk away and abandon God's best for our lives. Only through Jesus are we restored to God's family once again and forevermore.

As believers who have been saved by grace, we are all once again part of the same family—God's family. Since this is true, there are some things I believe healthy families do.

Healthy families:

- cultivate a safe environment of love, care, forgiveness, and encouragement,
- serve one another out of humility,
- challenge one another to be our best for God,
- and hold one another accountable.

Each family member's unique personality, gifts, and strengths benefit the others. Every team and family needs players who play their part. So let's bring our best to our "family" on the field and in our homes.

GO   Pick one action this week to improve your "family."

WORKOUT   Ephesians 2:8–9; 1 Corinthians 12:4–14

OVERTIME   Lord, thank You for designing me to be part of Your family. Help me to play my part and bring my unique gifts and strengths to use for Your glory and to benefit others. Amen.

DAY 256

I'm Tired . . . He's Not

Cheryl Baird

READY   "Although my spirit is weak within me, You know my way. Along this path I travel they have hidden a trap for me."—Psalm 142:3

SET   When David wrote this instructive psalm, he was in trouble. He was most likely cowering in a hole dug deeply into a hill, hiding from enemies that were pursuing him. As he hid, he felt out of control and uncertain of the future. So David implored the Lord for guidance, acknowledging in this time of distress that his trust and confidence had to come from God.

Many of us can echo David's cry in this psalm. As coaches, we often experience periods in a season when it feels like people are out to trap us, athletes are disinterested or uninvolved, and administrators are demanding wins. The rough times can be draining, leaving us feeling empty or without sufficient resources to survive another season, let alone another off-season.

But David teaches us from a dark cave that though we can only see this very moment, God can see the entire future. If we relinquish our desire to control our destiny, God promises to walk faithfully ahead of us and light the way. Jesus experienced fatigue, felt the abandonment of those closest to Him, and was burdened by the self-serving demands of people. That's why He understands our cries to Him in the midst of dark, lonely, and tiring times!

GO   Do you resist allowing God to take over when you feel tired?

WORKOUT   Psalm 107:1–9; Isaiah 2:5; 1 Peter 2:9

OVERTIME   God, You alone can fill me with strength and grace today. I receive both from You now in Your faithful name! Amen.

The Right Spot

Michael Wiggins

READY   "There are different kinds of gifts, but the same Spirit distributes them."—1 Corinthians 12:4 (NIV)

SET   The Boston Red Sox saw little potential in their twenty-four-year-old pitcher. He'd had a couple of decent years, but showed little sign of improvement. Eventually, he was traded to the New York Yankees, who moved him to the outfield to utilize his strong arm. The Yankees also believed he could become a good hitter. They were right. Years later, few people remember that Babe Ruth began his career as a mediocre pitcher in Boston!

Different athletes are blessed with different skills and physical traits, and each makes them more effective in some positions than others. A football player who is 5'10" and 200 pounds might be a tremendous running back, but he would struggle as a wide receiver. It is vitally important for a coach to find the position that allows the athlete to use his or her skills to the fullest. Athletes in the wrong position may still perform adequately, but they will never reach their full potential.

Christians must also find the right position. Paul teaches us in 1 Corinthians 12 that different Christians are given different gifts. For example, some are gifted teachers, while others are gifted administrators. When the right talent is matched with the right job, great things happen. As Christians, we should never feel compelled to work in an area in which we are not gifted. Rather, we should wait on the Lord and His counsel. God will give us the opportunity and grace through Jesus to use our God-given gifts.

GO   What gifts or talents has God provided you with and how do you use them?

WORKOUT   Romans 12:3–8; 1 Corinthians 12

OVERTIME   Thank You, Lord, that each of Your children is gifted and equally important. Enable me today to use my gifts to serve You! Amen.

Conformity

Heather Price

READY "Do not conform to the pattern of this world, but be transformed by the renewing of your mind. Then you will be able to test and approve what God's will is—his good, pleasing and perfect will." —Romans 12:2 (NIV)

SET Abby was on cloud nine. As a freshman, she had just made the varsity girls' soccer team. She played hard during that freshman year, but when tryouts came at the beginning of her sophomore year, she assumed that she was guaranteed a spot on the team and put very little effort into what she was doing. As a result, Abby was cut from the team.

Abby's story has a clear parallel with our Christian walk. So many times we become complacent and feel that because we've accepted Christ, we've done our job. It's easy to just sit in FCA or in our youth groups, but what really matters is how we are pushing ourselves to become better Christians.

In Revelation 3:15–16 (NIV) God tells us:

I know your deeds, that you are neither cold nor hot. I wish you were either one or the other! So, because you are lukewarm—neither hot nor cold—I am about to spit you out of my mouth.

Halfway doesn't cut it with God. We have a world to save. We can't afford to be complacent!

GO What do you need to do today to allow God to light a fire in your heart?

WORKOUT Matthew 25:1–13; Hebrews 6:9–12

OVERTIME Lord, place in my heart an unquenchable fire for You. Please renew my mind and heart each day as I spend time with You and read Your Word. Amen.

Sweaty Worship

Kallie Britton

READY   "And whatever you do, in word or in deed, do everything in the name of the Lord Jesus, giving thanks to God the Father through Him."—Colossians 3:17

SET   In the midst of a workout, athletes need to be intensely focused on the task at hand. Sometimes it can be difficult to focus on God when we are in the heat of a game. Often, I find myself losing focus on God and channeling all of my thoughts and effort towards my performance. At the end of games or practices, sometimes I feel guilty for not giving God the glory He deserves and instead focusing on my personal performance.

God has blessed each and every one of us with certain talents and gifts that He desires for us to use to glorify Him. Worshiping God should not only take place at church on Sunday morning. We can use the athletic talents God has given us to bring him glory and praise on the field.

By focusing our attention and efforts on God throughout our workouts, it's easier to remember that we are playing for an audience of one. When we can compete with an understanding that our hard work is viewed as worship in God's eyes, the drudgery of workouts suddenly becomes more enjoyable.

Just as it takes time to train physically to become a great competitor, it will take time to train your mind to view your performance as worship. Don't be discouraged if you find it difficult to focus on God all the time. It takes practice!

GO   Have you ever experienced a moment of worship while competing?

WORKOUT   1 Corinthians 10:31; Romans 12:1–2

OVERTIME   Father, teach me to use the talents and gifts You have blessed me with to bring You glory and praise on and off the athletic field. Amen.

No Fear

Eileen F. Sommi

READY   "There is no fear in love, but perfect love casts out fear."
—1 John 4:18 (ESV)

SET   I was in graduate school when the dean from a Christian college where I worked asked me to coach the women's field hockey team (the team's head coach was ill). Although I loved playing the game and knew it well, I'd never considered coaching. But the players would arrive in two days, the dean looked desperate, and I didn't have the heart to say no. How hard could it be?

Staring at the twenty-five women on that hot August morning—and with a week of training and a season of games ahead—I realized that I didn't have a clue as to what I was doing! Fear gripped me. Finally I prayed for help, telling God that I needed an experienced assistant. Two weeks later, the dean found my assistant. On the day of practice, he walked toward the field with a guitar and a smile. He said he knew nothing about field hockey but that he was ready to help!

My minstrel/assistant coach decided to begin each practice and game with a team song he wrote called "No Fear," which was based on 1 John 4:18 and 2 Timothy 1:7. Ironic choice, I thought. Every day, I sang those verses and remembered to love, not fear—to claim God's spirit of power and not be timid.

God didn't send what I thought I needed that season, but He gave me what got me through: His promises in Jesus. He even had the good humor to set it all to music on a hockey field!

GO   How can you love your team and help them to have a spirit of love instead of timidity?

WORKOUT   Psalm 121:1–2; Isaiah 41:10–14

OVERTIME   Lord, take my fear and fill me with Your spirit of love, power, and discipline. Amen.

What Is at Your Core?

Kristy Makris and Alex Hagler McCraney

READY "She is energetic and strong, a hard worker."—Proverbs 31:17 (NLT)

SET Strength, both physical and spiritual, is not something that occurs overnight or happens by osmosis. It is developed over time through discipline, intentionality, and hard work. The Proverbs 31 woman possessed both physical and spiritual strength, which equipped her to not only be the woman God created her to be but also to fulfill the Kingdom work He had for her to do.

The NKJV translates Proverbs 31:17 this way: "She girds herself with strength, and strengthens her arms." The phrase "gird yourself" usually refers to making your core strong. Most physical trainers agree that the most important part of your body to strengthen is your core, which gives the rest of your body the stability it needs to perform well. The Proverbs 31 woman was diligent to make sure her core was strong (her physical being), but more important, she made sure that the core of her soul (her spiritual being) was strengthened regularly.

In 1 Timothy 4:8 it says, "For bodily exercise profits a little, but godliness is profitable for all things, having promise of the life that now is and of that which is to come" (NKJV). God deeply desires to use each of us to accomplish His Kingdom work. Let us be men and women who train ourselves both physically and spiritually that we may be prepared to be used by God!

GO When you face challenges in your life, where do you look for strength?

WORKOUT 1 Timothy 4:7–8; 1 John 2:14

OVERTIME Look up Proverbs 31:17 in three different translations (NIV, NKJV, The Message, etc.) and write down any additional understanding you receive through the differences in the wording. Incorporate your findings into a prayer.

Winning Decisions

Wade Hopkins

READY   "As for me and my family, we will worship Yahweh."—Joshua 24:15b

SET   It was my rookie year with the Houston Oilers, and we were playing the Dallas Cowboys at Texas Stadium. We were losing late in the game, and I caught three balls in a row, the last one for a game-winning touchdown. Looking back, I see that the catch itself wasn't the win. That was simply the result of all the "winning" decisions I had made to get to that point.

Winning is all about your decisions. There is a big "I" in the middle of "win." For a team to be the best, you must be the best you can be. Winning isn't always about talent, but your commitment. There is a big "I" in the middle of commitment. Commitment is all about your attitude, and there is a big "I" in the middle of attitude. Attitude is all about your choice. By the way, there is a big "I" in the middle of choice too.

Joshua didn't say, "Let's all serve the Lord." He said, "As for me and my family . . ." You can't choose for everyone, but you can and must decide for yourself. It all starts with God's Word, which has the power to transform your thoughts, actions, and circumstances. Never allow others to dictate your life, never allow your current situation to determine your future, and always trust God to accomplish the purposes that He has placed in your heart.

GO   According to God's Word, how should you respond to challenging times?

WORKOUT   1 Kings 18; Colossians 1:16

OVERTIME   Father, I know You have a wonderful plan for my life. Help me make wise decisions when facing struggles and choose to trust Your Word. Amen.

Brothers and Sisters

Roxanne Robbins

READY "Therefore, be imitators of God, as dearly loved children. And walk in love, as the Messiah also loved us and gave Himself for us, a sacrificial and fragrant offering to God."—Ephesians 5:1–2

SET Speed skater Kristen Talbot made headlines in 1992 when she gave up her Olympic dreams to donate bone marrow to her critically ill brother. Talbot demonstrated extreme personal sacrifice to support him during his physical illness, even at the expense of the hard work and practice she had put in on the ice over the years.

Often we take our brothers and sisters for granted. We don't carve out time from our schedule to spend with them, or invite them to join us in activities. We don't ask about their days or show interest in their lives. Consider ways that you can live out Paul's instruction in Ephesians 5:1–2 by serving your family members.

For example, you might want to surprise your brothers or sisters by doing their chores for them. Take the time to listen to them. Invite them to join you and your friends for an activity. Ask forgiveness for times when you treated them unkindly. As you sacrifice something for a family member, think about what Jesus gave up for you: His life. And in doing so, He made it possible for you to experience ultimate forgiveness and a personal, eternal relationship with God.

GO How does this lesson apply to the rest of your brothers and sisters in Christ?

WORKOUT 1 Peter 3:8–9; 1 John 3:11–24

OVERTIME Jesus, thank You for Your sacrifice on the cross. Please help me demonstrate that sacrificial love with my own actions to my friends and family, and show me how I can serve them in love. Amen.

Tough Questions

Dan Britton

READY "Search me, God, and know my heart; test me and know my concerns. See if there is any offensive way in me; lead me in the everlasting way."—Psalm 139:23–24

SET Being on FCA staff, I have the opportunity to spend time with amazing leaders from around the world. One of my goals is to be a sponge and ask them as many questions as possible. However, few people maximize the opportunity to ask questions. Like the Chinese proverb says, "One who asks a question is a fool for five minutes; one who does not ask a question remains a fool forever." Asking the right questions in the right way at the right time can reveal powerful insight.

To better ourselves as Christian competitors, we must be willing to ask ourselves tough questions. This isn't questioning yourself, but rather asking yourself questions. One is a matter of doubting, the other discovery. Here's an example of some tough questions to start with. Let each question sink in before rushing to the next one.

Tough Questions Competitors Must Ask:

1. Do I realize it is impossible to glorify Christ and myself at the same time? *(Compete with humility)*
2. Am I doing the things I expect of others? *(Compete with integrity)*
3. Do others experience God's love through me? *(Compete with love)*

Let God have complete access to your heart. Allow Him to ask you tough questions like these and mold you more into the image of Jesus.

GO Do you ask yourself tough questions? If so, what?

WORKOUT Proverbs 1:5; Proverbs 9:9

OVERTIME God, I want to be a life-learner. Help me to be quick to listen and slow to speak. Give me a teachable spirit. Amen.

Trash Talking

Pat Street

READY   "For whatever is in your heart determines what you say."
—Matthew 12:34b (NLT)

SET   In 1998, the Ohio State Buckeyes beat Northwestern 36–10, but personal fouls and unsportsmanlike conduct tainted the win. OSU's coach at the time, John Cooper, made a point to his number-one ranked team, emphasizing that there is no place in football for trash talking and taunting and that it can be a distraction more than a help.

Discussing the numerous flags that were thrown during the game, Cooper demanded that the trash-talk behavior stop. "You can have a good, tough, hard-nosed football game without all that stuff," Cooper said. "I think college football would want to do more to prevent trash talking. It seems like we're more worried about a guy celebrating in the end zone after a touchdown than with what else is going on during the game."

Jesus said, "For the mouth speaks from the overflow of the heart" (Matt. 12:34b). Play with the character that's reflective of a heart surrendered to the Lord. It is not our accomplishments that influence others, but our character. Trash talking means we must belittle our opponents in order to build ourselves up as greater and better than them. That type of behavior is both unsportsmanlike and unworthy of a follower of Christ.

GO   Is it easy for you to trash talk? If so, how do you think the Lord wants you to change such behavior?

WORKOUT   Matthew 12:34; James 3:1–12

OVERTIME   Lord, I need help with my mouth. Take total control of my heart. Amen.

Teammates

Josh Carter

READY   "Watch your life and doctrine closely. Persevere in them, because if you do, you will save both yourself and your hearers."—1 Timothy 4:16 (NIV)

SET   Chad was the consummate team player. He worked harder than everyone else. He was humble and unselfish, and I never heard him trash talk an opponent. I knew there was something different about Chad, but I couldn't quite figure out what it was.

At age sixteen, I began to search for the purpose of my existence. Sports were gratifying, but I knew they wouldn't last forever. Around this time, I learned that the difference between Chad and me was that he had a personal relationship with Jesus. This influenced his life on and off the field. Through the connection I had with Chad as a teammate, his life had a huge influence on my decision to give my life (sports and all) to Christ.

The celebration of victories, the disappointment of tough losses, the sweat and the sacrifices all helped us to develop a strong relationship and opened my heart to see and hear the message of Christ through Chad. I encourage you, as a Christian competitor, to view your team as your mission field. Jesus is calling you to be His ambassador and to help reconcile your teammates to God.

GO   How have your teammates influenced your life? In what ways are you influencing your teammates?

WORKOUT   2 Corinthians 5:16–6:2; Colossians 4:2–6

OVERTIME   God, please help me live in such a way that my teammates notice that there is something different about me. Open up opportunities for me to share about Your love and unconditional grace. Amen.

A New Way

Michael Wiggins

READY "Although I am a free man and not anyone's slave, I have made myself a slave to everyone, in order to win more people."—1 Corinthians 9:19

SET In the 1964 Tokyo Olympic Games, sprinter Bob Hayes tied the Olympic record on his way to winning the gold medal in the 100-meter dash. Just a few months later, Hayes was dashing past defensive backs as a wide receiver for the Dallas Cowboys. It was a radical idea at the time: taking a world-class sprinter and turning him into a football player. Hayes's success altered defensive strategy and changed how football was played.

Coaches design drills to improve players' technique and help them gain strength and increase their speed. These improvements are typically made in small increments, and hours of work can go into making the smallest advance. But sometimes, an innovation occurs that radically redefines the way a sport is played, causing such a drastic change that teams and players are forced to adapt. Those who refuse to adjust are defeated.

Christians must also acknowledge the power of innovation. While God is unchanging, the people who need Him are forever changing. As Christians, we must recognize this and alter the way we communicate God's message of love and forgiveness to others. We must be creative in how we reach those who don't know about Jesus. If we fail to be innovative in our presentation of God's message, the world will assume that the message is no longer relevant to their lives. So let's explore new ways of spreading God's message of love and forgiveness.

GO What adjustment is God asking you to make in your life plan?

WORKOUT Matthew 5:43–48; 1 Corinthians 9:19–23

OVERTIME God, thank You that You never change. Lead me into new areas of growth for Your sake! Amen.

Mourning into Dancing

Josh Carter

READY   "You turned my lament into dancing; You removed my sack-cloth and clothed me with gladness, so that I can sing to You and not be silent. Lord my God, I will praise You forever."—Psalm 30:11–12

SET   One of the Division I schools in my area entered its conference tournament as the number eight seed and appeared to be a long shot to win it all. The head coach for the team admitted they fell short of expectations, but that the one goal they could hold on to was winning a conference tournament championship. Despite the odds, the team achieved that goal by knocking off the first-, second-, and fourth-seeded teams, earning an automatic berth in the NCAA tournament in the process.

We all know that falling short of our expectations can bring about many disappointments on and off the court. However, if we, like this team, keep looking forward to even a small hope of success, we'll often be glad we made the effort.

Jesus faced far greater trials when He came to Earth. He endured the cross, submitting Himself to God for the joy that was set before Him (Heb. 12:2). He also knew that the mourning would soon be turned to dancing! Likewise, God sometimes gives us a new outlook in difficult situations so that we might endure them (2 Cor. 12:7–9), or He relieves us entirely by removing us from the situation (Exod. 6:6). Whatever the circumstance, we can submit ourselves to Him and be thankful that His joy is our strength!

GO   How have you seen God turn sorrow into joy in your life?

WORKOUT   Ecclesiastes 3:1–4; Jeremiah 31:4

OVERTIME   Lord, be the reason that I dance and sing today so that I might praise You forever! Amen.

Positive Goals

Kerry O'Neill

READY   "I pursue as my goal the prize promised by God's heavenly call in Christ Jesus."—Philippians 3:14

SET   Goals give competitors and teams purpose and direction, and serve as a reminder of the potential rewards ahead. One essential element to achieving a goal is that it must be stated in a positive manner. There is a part of our brain called the reticular activating system (RAS). One function of this system is to filter incoming stimuli and determine where one focuses attention. And when it comes to setting goals, the RAS plays a part in how they're interpreted.

For example, a football placekicker can word his goal in one of two ways. Either "my goal is to make this kick" or "my goal is to not miss this kick." There is a huge difference in those statements. Your RAS will choose to focus on one thing. In the first case, the focus is on making the kick. In the second, it is on missing the kick, even though the goal is to *not* miss it. The last thing a competitor should be thinking about is the potential of failure.

The apostle Paul stated his goal regarding God was "to know Him" (Phil. 3:10). The thought of knowing God and His calling was stuck in his head rather than the idea of "not missing out" on his relationship with God. And Paul pursued that goal (v. 14) with a reckless abandon. So, begin stating your spiritual and physical goals in the positive, allowing your intricate brain process to focus on reaching them.

GO   What is one goal you have for sports? For your relationship with God? For your life?

WORKOUT   Philippians 3:10–14; Matthew 6:33

OVERTIME   Father, give me the wisdom to set goals that will bring You honor and bring me closer to You. Amen.

Conquering the Idol

David Vailes

READY "Those who worship false gods turn their backs on all God's mercies. But I will offer sacrifices to you with songs of praise, and I will fulfill all my vows. For my salvation comes from the LORD alone."—Jonah 2:8–9 (NLT)

SET Being an athlete is tough. It requires waking up early, staying late, and working hard—and sometimes the results don't truly show how much work you've done and time you have invested. However, being an athlete can also be extremely rewarding. Teamwork, discipline, and the sense of accomplishment when there's a win are the sweet rewards of a lot of hard work.

Being a competitor requires so much that sometimes athletes need this simple reminder: *sports is not life*. Your sport is one part of your life; it isn't your entire life. *Jesus* is life. He gives life; He sustains life; and He desires and deserves nothing to be placed above Him in our lives. We spend so much time with our team and in practice that our athletic endeavors can unconsciously become idols in our lives.

As a competitor, you have a constant desire to defeat the opposing team and win. As a Christian, the same is true. You must defeat the idols in your life, whatever they may be. When you conquer these idols, you become less self-centered, a better Christian, a better teammate, and a better player. God has big plans for you through your sport. Just make sure that your sport isn't replacing God in your life!

GO How can you defeat your idols and start living like God is number one in your life?

WORKOUT Acts 17:16; 1 John 5:21

OVERTIME God, I want You to be the center of my life. Help me not to put competing above my relationship with You. Amen.

Opportunity through Scrutiny

Clay Meyer

READY   "For consider Him who endured such hostility from sinners against Himself, so that you won't grow weary and lose heart."—Hebrews 12:3

SET   Does crowd noise and constant scrutiny affect your athletic performance? Imagine competing in front of tens of thousands of screaming fans who voice their immediate reactions to your every move. Add to it the nearly year-round analysis by the New York media and you have a fair picture of what Yankees first baseman Mark Teixeira deals with every day. Teixeira thrives on the pressure. "The attention means people care about the game," he says. "That kind of pressure gets you pumped up and motivated to play . . . I want to be the best player I can be every game."

As competitors, we must deal with the heavy pressure applied by those around us. But do we thrive in the face of scrutiny, seeing critiques as opportunities to excel? On a deeper level, do we also seize each moment of scrutiny to build up others, pushing them forward while sharing Christ's light through love?

In Hebrews 12, Jesus chose to pray for those who persecuted Him and endured unimaginable insults and ridicule as He carried our sin to the cross to pay the ultimate price and gain the greatest victory in history. Let each piece of scrutiny you face be a new opportunity for excellence as you compete and coach for the Lord with your all.

GO   What opportunities do you see God presenting during times of criticism?

WORKOUT   Psalm 40; Ephesians 6:10–20

OVERTIME   Father, we are constantly surrounded by the scrutiny of others. Please change our frame of mind to see those around us as people who need Your love. May we compete in ways that bring all glory and honor to You. Amen.

DAY 272

Never Quit

Wade Hopkins

READY   "While He was together with them, He commanded them not to leave Jerusalem, but to wait for the Father's promise . . . John baptized with water, but you will be baptized with the Holy Spirit not many days from now."—Acts 1:4–5

SET   If your motivation isn't greater than yourself, you will quit! As a current Master's competitor, I have times on the track when my legs are heavy and my lungs are burning and the first thought is, "go home, finish later." It seems that no matter how hard I work or how badly I want it, as soon as pain is involved or my commitment level is challenged, I waver.

It was the same for the disciples. The night Jesus was arrested they scattered like sheep. They'd left it all behind and committed to follow Him. They'd experienced miracles and swore they'd never leave. But when the chips were down, they didn't have the power within to rise to the occasion. The same can be said of us. As competitors, left to our own strength, we will give in and never realize our full potential. We need the power Jesus promised to provide through His Holy Spirit.

Those same men who fled in fear became mighty men of God who died for the cause of Christ. What made the difference? Where did the ability to stand tall and courageous in the face of death come from? Through the power of the Holy Spirit. When you face the temptation to flee from what God has called you to, dig into the power of His Spirit and don't quit.

GO   In what areas do you need God's power?

WORKOUT   Romans 8:11; Hebrews 12:2–3

OVERTIME   Father, I confess that I need Your powerful spirit living in me, giving me the resolve to finish strong. Amen.

DAY 273

Off-Season Work

Jere Johnson

READY   "The son who gathers during summer is prudent; the son who sleeps during harvest is disgraceful."—Proverbs 10:5

SET   When I was a coach, one of my biggest challenges was helping my athletes understand that improvement happened in the off-season. Each year, I got the same song and dance about how they needed time off in the summer. Yet I knew that a strong work ethic was crucial to my athletes' success.

In Proverbs 10, Solomon teaches us about a wise young person who worked hard all summer and did not waste time. Apparently, the young people in Solomon's day also needed to make the most of their opportunities, though they didn't have as many of today's distractions, like video games and cable TV. It's not easy helping young athletes understand the year-round effort required to improve their game.

Whatever our work is, we need to take it seriously. This also applies to our relationship with Christ. It takes disciplined time to get to know Him and grow closer to Him. Yet the more we do, the more we want to be with Him. Why? Because we discover in Jesus not only the standard for our work ethic but also the trustworthy God who loves us enough to sacrifice His Son's life on the cross to bring us to Him. Through His Holy Spirit, He delights in working in us that which pleases Him (Heb. 13:21), shaping our character, directing our steps, and using our gifts—professional or spiritual—for His purposes.

GO   How can you start today to work for Christ's glory?

WORKOUT   Matthew 25:14–30; Hebrews 6:10–12

OVERTIME Thank You, God, that in You I live! Help me to work today with the grace You provide in Christ! Amen.

DAY 274

Above Average

Rex Stump

READY "For we are His creation, created in Christ Jesus for good works . . ."—Ephesians 2:10a

SET As a little boy, I had all kinds of heroes, including Hank Aaron and Walter Payton. But not all my heroes were athletes. I also liked Luke Skywalker and James Bond. I didn't want to just be like the star athletes and receive applause; I wanted to make a difference by defeating the bad guy and saving the day. I didn't want to be average.

God created us each with special gifts and abilities. We were made to be above average and extraordinary—not for our glory, but to reflect our Creator. The FCA Competitors Creed states: "I am a Competitor now and forever. I am made to strive, to strain, to stretch, and to succeed in the arena of competition . . . as [a Christian Competitor], I face my challenger with the face of Christ." That doesn't sound average or mediocre.

As competitors for Christ, we understand that we have an opponent. In John 10:10 Jesus calls him (Satan) the "thief" who wants to steal, kill, and destroy us. Our spiritual opponent has deceitfully rocked us to sleep, destroying our fervency by convincing us average is okay. We need to wake up! We are competitors for Christ, created by a Holy God to do extraordinary things for His glory! As heroes for God, in order to defeat the "bad guy" we must be a spiritual threat. Mediocrity is our enemy's weapon of choice, and it's up to us to disarm him through the power of Christ.

GO What are some threats to your spiritual fervency?

WORKOUT Psalm 8; Matthew 20:24–28

OVERTIME Father, You created me to do great things for You! Revive my spirit and encourage me today to compete with greatness! Amen.

DAY 275

Commitment

Charles Gee

READY "It is a trap for anyone to dedicate something rashly and later to reconsider his vows."—Proverbs 20:25

SET Every year college coaches agonize over recruits, hoping that a star athlete will commit to signing with his or her team. But recruits can make a "soft" commitment to a school while they continue visiting other campuses. Though the definition of "commit" is "to bind" or "obligate" (which implies a definite decision), the meaning of this word has obviously been diluted in the world of college recruiting.

Commitment meant something totally different to Elisha in 1 Kings 19. He was plowing in a field when Elijah found him, threw his cloak around him, and pronounced him as his successor. Elisha responded by asking permission first to go home to prepare a farewell feast. He slaughtered the oxen, burned the plow to cook the meat, and fed his people. Then he followed Elijah and became his servant. Elisha's response was hardly a "soft" commitment; he left no doubt that he was binding himself to Elijah.

In the same way, God became man in the person of Jesus Christ, leaving no doubt of His commitment to us. Through His sacrificial blood, He now invites us to an eternal feast with Him! Because of His amazing bond of love to us, He desires that we, too, live lives of firm—not soft—commitments in all that we do.

GO How can you demonstrate commitment to God?

WORKOUT 1 Kings 19:19–21; Luke 9:57–62

OVERTIME God, thank You for sacrificing Your Son out of a committed love for me. Empower me today to show the same devoted love to others! Amen.

DAY 276

Damaging Words

Jere Johnson

READY "In the same way, the tongue is a small thing that makes grand speeches. But a tiny spark can set a great forest on fire."—James 3:5 (NLT)

SET Foul language and swearing are commonplace in athletics today. Some say these words motivate players. Others say that they are necessary to get the point across. But if this is the case, how do teachers and preachers teach lessons of life without using these words? If this type of language is used to motivate, why is over 90 percent of it used in a negative context?

In the New Testament, James shares that the tongue (our words) is a dangerous weapon. Controlling our speech is vitally important in our spiritual journey. Often we are judged not by what we do but by what comes out of our mouths. Coach John Wooden was as successful as any coach, but he did not have to use foul language in order to coach his team. Many successful coaches have done the same. To them, I am sure that controlling the tongue also meant controlling other areas in their coaching (such as anger and attitude).

Swearing can be a hard habit to break. However, just like the skills in a sport, guarding your tongue is a discipline to be practiced. If you don't swear, good for you, but let your teammates know that swearing bothers you as well. Raise the standard of your program by raising the expectations for the kind of language used by staff and athletes alike.

GO How can you tame your tongue and use words that will not offend others?

WORKOUT Matthew 5:37; James 3:1–12

OVERTIME   Jesus, my tongue needs to be controlled by You. I pray that my words will encourage others and that I will be known for using my speech to lift up those around me. Amen.

DAY 277

G-LOC

Mark Snyder

READY   "Stay alert! Watch out for your great enemy, the devil. He prowls around like a roaring lion, looking for someone to devour."
—1 Peter 5:8 (NLT)

SET   As a Navy jet pilot, I was always aware of G-LOC (pronounced "gee-lock"), an acronym for Gravity (induced) Loss of Consciousness. G-LOC occurs from excessive and sustained g-force, which drains blood away from the brain and causes cerebral hypoxia. (You pass out.) Ultimately, the keys to successfully defeating G-LOC lie with awareness, early recognition of symptoms, and timely application of prevention strategies.

As competitors we face a similar phenomenon I call C-LOC, or Culturally (induced) Loss of Consciousness, in which we allow culture to influence our character and we fall asleep to God's greater calling. As competitors for Christ it is important that we understand when C-LOC symptoms are present in ourselves. To better understand where you stand, reflect on the following questions:

- Do you honor the game? What about your opponents, your coach, your teammates, the officials, and the fans?
- Is your verbal and online communication positive and uplifting or negative and demeaning?
- Do you exhibit a "win at all cost" mentality?

This last symptom is particularly troublesome. How often have you heard the phrase, "Winning isn't the most important thing; it's the only thing"? Coach Mike Krzyzewski once said, "Winning as a goal is a disease and leads to compromise in every other area." Athletic competition doesn't just build character; it reveals character. What does your performance say about your character? Has C-LOC crept into your game? Does it have such a strong foothold that you've fallen asleep as a competitor for Christ, or do you hold strong daily to His Word?

GO   In what ways are you affected by C-LOC?

WORKOUT   Matthew 26:41; 1 Corinthians 16:13

OVERTIME   Lord, help me stay alert to Your greater calling on my life as a competitor. Amen.

DAY 278

The Ultimate Pre-Game Meal

Michael Hill

READY   "My food is to do the will of Him who sent Me and to finish His work," Jesus told them. "Don't you say, 'There are still four more months, then comes the harvest'? Listen to what I'm telling you: Open your eyes and look at the fields, for they are ready for harvest."—John 4:34–35

SET   As athletes, what we put into our bodies is very important. The pre-game meal, in particular, may be the most important meal we eat. This is our last chance to make sure we get enough energy to last through the entire competition.

In John 4:34, Jesus tells us of work that will actually *give* us energy instead of using it. Doing God's work will give us the fuel we need in order to succeed in the game of life. So what is the work that we should be doing? In Matthew 28:19–20, Jesus instructs: "Go . . . and make disciples of all nations . . . teaching them to observe everything I have commanded you."

The mission of FCA is to "Present to coaches and athletes and all whom they influence the challenge and adventure of receiving Jesus Christ as Savior and Lord and serving Him in their relationships and in the fellowship of the church." Pay attention to how doing this feeds your soul. As part of Team Jesus Christ, I challenge you to devote yourself to this kind of work.

GO   What can you do today to feed your soul so that you will have the fuel you need to succeed in the game of life?

WORKOUT   Matthew 6:11; Acts 17:11

OVERTIME   Lord, show me where You want me to work, and I will serve You. Take this life and use it to build Your kingdom. Amen.

DAY 279

Your Focus

Scott Wade

READY   "So we do not focus on what is seen, but on what is unseen. For what is seen is temporary, but what is unseen is eternal."—2 Corinthians 4:18

SET   I'll never forget the first day of football camp at the small college I attended. I'd come hoping to be a part of a winning program and perhaps even a national championship. At a team meeting, as our head coach reviewed the goals, he pulled out the video of last year's national championship, a game we'd lost. Then he threw the video to the ground, stomped it to bits, and told us that if our only dream was to win a national championship, then we'd set our goals too low!

That season, I learned what my coach was talking about. We went undefeated and reached the championship game. We lost in four overtimes, but that's not what the season had been all about. Through the influence of Christian coaches and players, twelve of my teammates made the decision to follow Christ. While most of us will forget that season's record, those decisions made during that season will have eternal significance!

As the apostle Paul wrote, rather than focusing on what is seen, our vision as Christians should be set on that which we cannot see. That is the faith we've been given through Jesus. Jesus saw beyond this world and into the next! Just as our football coach taught us, our goals, too, should be on the highest level!

GO   How do you use your sport to build the character of your teammates or players?

WORKOUT   Matthew 6:19–24; Hebrews 12:1–2

OVERTIME   Lord, enlighten the eyes of my heart that my vision may be for You and how we together can guide my team to a championship that lasts forever! Amen.

DAY 280

What Have You Done with the Son of God?

Fleceia Comeaux

READY   "After three days, they found Him in the temple complex . . . When His parents saw Him [Jesus], they were astonished, and His mother said to Him, 'Son, why have You treated us like this? Your father and I have been anxiously searching for You.'"—Luke 2:46, 48

SET   Jesus and his parents were in Jerusalem for the Passover. After they celebrated the feast, Mary and Joseph headed home. A day had passed when they realized Jesus was not with them on the road. They asked around, frantically looking for him; when they couldn't find him in their camp, they went back to the city and looked there.

I wonder if they asked themselves, "What have we done with the Son of God?" They felt an overwhelming feeling of loss and confusion because they could not remember what they had done with God's Son. For three days they asked everywhere until they heard him speaking and teaching in the synagogue. He was exactly where he should have been, in His Father's house (Luke 2:49).

Is Jesus where He should be in your life, or do you also need to ask, "What have I done with the Son of God?" It was a full day before Mary and Joseph realized He was not with them. How long have you gone before realizing He wasn't with you? When all was said and done, Mary and Joseph left no stone unturned trying to find Him. What lengths will you go to be with Jesus so He can guide you in life and sport?

GO   How long has it been since you acknowledged Christ in your sport or gave Him praise for your accomplishments?

WORKOUT   Luke 2:41–50; Luke 11:9–13

OVERTIME   Father, if should I journey away from Your side, may I leave no stone unturned until I find You. Amen.

DAY 281

P.U.S.H.

Kathy Malone

READY   "Pray in the Spirit at all times and on every occasion. Stay alert and be persistent in your prayers for all believers everywhere." —Ephesians 6:18 (NLT)

SET   I'll never forget watching Reggie Miller score eight points in the last thirty-two seconds of a 1995 Eastern Conference NBA playoff game. Miller's never-say-die heroics in the closing seconds gave the Indiana Pacers a thrilling two-point victory over the New York Knicks. Throughout his eighteen-year career with the Pacers, Miller was the picture of persistence. He didn't make every clutch shot he took, but he never stopped shooting them.

Just as Miller modeled persistence, so too do good competitors. Would a good competitor ever tell their team to give up just because they were down by ten points at halftime? Never! They would encourage their team to fight to the end, no matter how things looked at any point during the game.

Can the same be said of us when it comes to prayer? Have we prayed and persisted, even when it didn't look like victory was possible? Jesus said, "Keep searching, and you will find" (Matt. 7:7). We are to continue to come before God with our requests, even when it feels like nothing is happening.

I've seen popular bracelets with the acronym P.U.S.H. stitched on them: "Pray Until Something Happens." We should never give up when it comes to making our requests known to a God who loves us and gave His Son that we might find Him!

GO Do you have an attitude of perseverance when it comes to prayer?

WORKOUT Luke 18:1; Philippians 4:6

OVERTIME Lord, teach me to persevere in prayer as Your unseen hand works in ways I can't see or understand. Amen.

DAY 282

Seeking Treasures

Amanda Tewksbury

READY "Don't collect for yourselves treasures on earth, where moth and rust destroy and where thieves break in and steal. But collect for yourselves treasures in heaven, where neither moth nor rust destroys, and where thieves don't break in and steal. For where your treasure is, there your heart will be also . . . You cannot be slaves of God and of money."—Matthew 6:19–21, 24

SET Silence. All I could hear were the whispers of what sounded like disappointment from our coaches in the front of the bus and the sniffles of a few teammates behind me. Another loss. Another disappointment. We'd lost so many games in a row at this point it was almost as if my whole life was falling apart. Athletes and coaches know all too well the worry and anxiety that can overtake us.

In Matthew, Jesus commands us to store up for ourselves treasures in heaven, for where our treasures are found, there our hearts (and emotions) will be as well. If our treasure is our performance or the win-loss column, both of which will quickly fade, our priority and hearts are not focused on serving God.

When we allow ourselves to be so caught up in the things of this world, including sports, we lose sight of what's really important: our relationship with Christ. We cannot serve both God and the things of this world. Anxiety and worry will not rule us if we choose to seek Him first and make our relationship with Jesus our coveted treasure.

GO   How would your attitude or performance change if your focus was on your relationship with Christ first and your game second?

WORKOUT   Hebrews 13:8; 1 Peter 5:6–7

OVERTIME   Father, through Your Holy Spirit, give me a heart and mind that seeks You and Your treasures first. Amen.

DAY 283

Horsepower

Josh Carter

READY   "But you will receive power when the Holy Spirit comes on you; and you will be my witnesses in Jerusalem, and in all Judea and Samaria, and to the ends of the earth."—Acts 1:8 (NIV)

SET   There had not been an undefeated Kentucky Derby winner since Seattle Slew in 1977. Fans watching the 2004 Kentucky Derby saw a Pennsylvania-bred horse named Smarty Jones, with a trainer and a jockey who were both rookies, end the 27-year drought by winning the race, running the horse's record to 7–0.

Stewart Elliott knew it wasn't his power that was going to win the Kentucky Derby but that it was the power of his horse that would carry him across the finish line. In the same way, it is the power of the Holy Spirit that carries us to the finish line in the race of life.

Through His power, the Holy Spirit also sets us free from the law of sin and death, speaks God's words through us, convicts our hearts of sin, strengthens us in our weakness, and enables us to live the life of obedience that God desires for us.

GO   In what part of your sport do you most need the power of the Holy Spirit right now?

WORKOUT   Romans 15:13; 1 Corinthians 2:4–5

OVERTIME   Lord, thank You for the power of the Holy Spirit and for the amazing ways it moves in my life. Instruct me and show me how I can grow in my relationship with You. Amen.

Forget the Past

Chip Mehaffey

READY   "Brothers, I do not consider myself to have taken hold of it. But one thing I do: Forgetting what is behind and reaching forward to what is ahead, I pursue as my goal the prize promised by God's heavenly call in Christ Jesus."—Philippians 3:13–14

SET   As a high school basketball coach, I often notice that my players are influenced by the past—whether it be winning streaks or losing streaks. To avoid pitfalls that can follow either of these streaks, such as overconfidence or loss of confidence, many coaches remind their teams to stay focused. In our program, we remind our players to stay focused only on what lies ahead. After each game we say, "The season starts tomorrow."

As Christians, we're sometimes too hard on ourselves when we reflect upon our past sins. Satan can use this to try to make us feel unworthy of God and His kingdom. The truth is, we are unworthy! That's the good news of the gospel: we are all sinners, but we are not unlovable. Salvation is never something we earn, which is why Jesus paid the ultimate price on the cross so that we could be saved!

Paul said in Philippians to forget "what is behind" and reach "forward to what is ahead." God can still do great things with us regardless of our past. He says to each of us, "Your Christian life begins today because I love you!"

GO   What from your past do you need to let go?

WORKOUT   2 Corinthians 4:7–9; 1 John 2:12

OVERTIME   Lord, thank You that You forgive me and love me, and that You have redeemed me by Your death and resurrection so that nothing can separate me from You! Amen.

DAY 285

Identity Theft

Kerry O'Neill

READY   "Set your minds on what is above, not on what is on the earth. For you have died, and your life is hidden with the Messiah in God."—Colossians 3:2–3

SET   Each year millions of people become victims of identity theft. Another epidemic is the loss of identity in Christ. One might argue that it is also identity theft. That the enemy who comes to steal, kill, and destroy—the one who is the accuser of the brethren—is guilty of identity theft in the lives of countless Christians.

Think of the thoughts, words, and actions you had before your relationship with Christ. Perhaps your identity as a competitor was marked by anger, comparison, or a performance-based value system. Now, your identity is in Christ. He loves you regardless of your performance. There is nothing so great you could do to make Him love you more; there is nothing so awful you could do to make Him love you less. He loves you that much!

However, the loss of identity in Christ is more preventable than financial identity theft. The key is reminding yourself of who you truly are; who you are according to God, as He has described in His Word—a new creation, and a light to the world. Start reminding Satan of these truths each time he tempts you with false beliefs about yourself and your relationship with Christ. Know who you are in Christ and don't back down.

GO   Think of one Bible verse on which you can meditate to remember who you are in Christ.

WORKOUT   John 1:12; Colossians 1:13

OVERTIME   Lord, help me remember who I am in You. Give me strength to fight off the temptation to think any less of myself than what is revealed in your Word. Amen.

DAY 286

Courage

Roger Lipe

READY   "Be strong and courageous, for you are the one who will lead these people to possess all the land I swore to their ancestors I would give them. Be strong and very courageous. Be careful to obey all the instructions Moses gave you. Do not deviate from them, turning either to the right or to the left. Then you will be successful in everything you do."—Joshua 1:6–7 (NLT)

SET   When does sport demand courage? Is it when we face superior competition? What role does courage play in overcoming adversity? Today's Scripture links strength and courage in a powerful combination.

Joshua had just taken leadership of his people after Moses had died. As he assumed this most intimidating role, God told him twice to be strong and courageous, adding the second time to be very courageous. Courage would obviously be a most important quality for Joshua's leadership.

What situations in today's competitions may require us to be strong and very courageous? Some situations could be as scary to us now as replacing Moses would have been to Joshua. The Lord's words to us today would be the same as they were to Joshua. He would say, "Be strong and very courageous. Walk boldly into today's competition with strength and confidence. Take on your opponent with great courage and determination to win."

GO   When does your sport demand courage of you?

WORKOUT   Isaiah 41:1–9; John 16:28–33

OVERTIME   Father, infuse me and my team with courage. Enable us to be strong and courageous as we compete in a way that will honor You. Amen.

DAY 287

Process over Product

Toby C. Schwartz

READY   "Don't you know that the runners in a stadium all race, but only one receives the prize? Run in such a way to win the prize. Now everyone who competes exercises self-control in everything. However, they do it to receive a crown that will fade away, but we a crown that will never fade away."—1 Corinthians 9:24–25

SET   Like most high school coaches, I had a goal to someday help an athlete win a state championship. In my first season as a distance coach, achieving this goal became a possibility with one of my runners. But it was there that God taught me a valuable lesson.

I hadn't expected to be at the finals in my first year. I also didn't expect to feel the emptiness that I felt as I watched my runner compete. I remembered how much time had gone into training this one athlete as well as the time spent training my other athletes. I weighed that against how much time I'd committed to these athletes' personal and spiritual growth and realized that I'd made the goal of winning a higher priority than the process of shaping lives.

That day, I learned two things: (1) God is more concerned with *how* things are accomplished than with *what* is accomplished; and (2) God doesn't care about numbers as much as He cares about hearts. I then decided that despite the outcome, from that time forward I would be as much or more concerned with the spiritual training of my athletes as I was with their physical training!

GO   Are you more concerned with winning than with spiritual growth?

WORKOUT   Ezekiel 11:17–21; Matthew 23:23–28

OVERTIME   Thank You, Lord, for giving me the privilege of caring for my fellow competitors today. Help me to show them the imperishable crown that Jesus offers to us! Amen.

DAY 288

Change the Atmosphere

Fleceia Comeaux

READY   "I labor for this, striving with His strength that works powerfully in me."—Colossians 1:29

SET   It is not enough to know who you are; you must also know what you possess. The apostle Peter always knew who he was. Peter always understood that he had a presence about him and knew that his relationship with Jesus was different than any of the others. From the time Jesus said to him, "On this rock I will build my church" (Matt. 16:18 NIV), Peter's life would never be the same.

Though he struggled with this new reality, when Peter allowed God to unlock the potential of his presence, he began to experience God in a transformative way. Peter's very presence, or rather the thick presence of God in him, began to change the atmosphere around him. Whether he spoke or passed by, the power of God was constantly apparent.

As a competitor, there's nothing more exciting than being in a heated battle with an opponent in their home arena, stadium, or gym. You flow with every movement, seeming effortless. But just before you know it, the opponent gains the momentum and the crowd goes wild. Your coach calls a play designed just for you, you execute with success, and the crowd is silenced. You have just changed the atmosphere! If a mere play of an athlete can change the atmosphere, how much more can the power of God working through you.

GO   What can you do to change the spiritual atmosphere within your team, on the court/field or in your school?

WORKOUT   Romans 1:16; 2 Timothy 1:7

OVERTIME   God, thank You for Your desire to infiltrate my very being. Change the atmosphere in me so that through Your power, I can change the atmosphere around me. Amen.

DAY 289

Start Today

Jere Johnson

READY   "But if it doesn't please you to worship Yahweh, choose for yourselves today the one you will worship . . ."—Joshua 24:15

SET   For a goal-oriented society, we procrastinate a lot. We often forget that we are not guaranteed tomorrow. Today is the day to make necessary changes in our lives. But we are creatures of habit, and the bad habits, wrong choices, or mistakes that we make can affect every aspect of our lives—athletic, social, and spiritual.

Because Joshua understood human nature, he challenged his people to choose "today" whom they would serve. He knew that he and his family would choose to worship the Lord. He also knew that life might not always be easy. Still, Joshua understood that God was trustworthy—focusing on the Lord would be his only hope when struggles came.

Joshua's example reminds us that we need a Savior to rescue us from ourselves! Thankfully, Jesus came to Earth as God made man and proclaimed that today is the day of salvation (2 Cor. 6:2). Just as He gave all, so He wants all of us. He does not promise us tomorrow, but He does promise to be with us (Matt. 28:20). If we choose today to worship Him, we will become more like Him and see His image reflected in our own.

GO   What habits do you need to bring to the cross in order to grow closer to God?

WORKOUT   Psalm 118:24; James 4:13–17

OVERTIME   God, draw me near to You today and put a song of worship in my heart all day long! Amen.

DAY 290

Holy Hope

Sarah Rennicke

READY   "And this hope will not lead to disappointment. For we know how dearly God loves us, because he has given us the Holy Spirit to fill our hearts with his love."—Romans 5:5 (NLT)

SET   This is it—the year you earn that starting spot. You've spent all off-season sweating hard during longer workouts and watching your nutrition carefully. You put in the time and effort to step into the open spot that's waiting just for you. Come tryouts, you're flying across the field, making plays you never would have just one year ago.

When starters are announced at practice the day before the first game, there is no mention of your name. In those span of seconds, you see the months of preparation crash down around your feet. Disappointment becomes a bitterness that takes root deep inside you.

How do we pull our hearts up and keep concentrating on giving our all for the team when broken hope weighs us down? We lift our eyes to the One who holds our delicate dreams in His steady hands—the One who has seen the hours of work and sweat . . . and our broken dreams. If we trust in His purpose and character, there is an anchored assurance that He won't leave us where we are. Though we are let down by worldly circumstances, God never disappoints. He gives us a holy hope that does not diminish.

GO   In what ways can you encourage others to put their hope in Christ?

WORKOUT   Psalm 31:14; Ephesians 1:18–19

OVERTIME   Father, I ask that You comfort me in times of disappointment and shift my perspective to the eternal so I might continue to live a life that's pleasing to You and put my trust in what lasts: Your love. Amen.

DAY 291

C'mon, Blue!

John Ausmus

READY   "But the fruit of the Spirit is love, joy, peace, patience, kindness, goodness, faith, gentleness, self-control. Against such things there is no law."—Galatians 5:22–23

SET   I love baseball! It's an individual sport that relies on a team for a successful outcome. It's also the only American sport in which, during a stoppage in play, a manager or coach can approach an umpire to dispute a rule or argue a call. Unfortunately, we've all seen a manager throwing a tantrum, kicking dirt on the plate, or verbally abusing an umpire. And we've also seen the umpire retaliating in anger and, sometimes, losing control. It's hard to have someone yell at us or challenge our character in any setting, but especially in front of peers and spectators in a stadium.

In Galatians 5:22–23, the apostle Paul wrote that when the Holy Spirit dwells in us, He produces self-control in us. We can't obtain this fruit by natural means—it is produced only when we give Christ control over our lives. Granted, our sinful nature wants to yell, get angry, show off, or get the last word.

When we accept Jesus as our Savior, we begin the greatest adventure of our lives: becoming like Him! When He produces self-control in us, we see our situation clearly, control our emotions and actions, and allow Him to guide us in handling the situation correctly. Living a Spirit-filled life means living in perfect harmony with the life that God intended us to live—and bearing fruit that will last!

GO   In what areas of your life do you need more self-control?

WORKOUT   1 Corinthians 9:24–27; Galatians 6:1–5

OVERTIME   God, thank You for continuing the good work You've begun in me and for producing fruit in my life that points others to Jesus! Amen.

DAY 292

Through God's Eyes

Brittany Viola

READY   "I will praise You because I have been remarkably and wonderfully made."—Psalm 139:14

SET   It might be hard to believe, but sometimes elite athletes struggle with self-image. In 2006, two years removed from my first attempt at making the US Olympic Diving team, I found myself fighting an eating disorder. I decided enough was enough and that I needed freedom, so I attended a facility in Arizona to help me overcome my battle with bulimia.

Up until that point, I believed the lie that my physical appearance determined my self-worth. But at Remuda Ranch in Arizona, I experienced real, honest, and sincere relationships. I accepted Jesus into my heart and started a journey of self-discovery and true purpose with Him by my side. It wasn't easy. I fell back into my old struggles that next year at school, but had a teammate invest her time, wisdom, and love into my life. Transformation took root. I began to experience light where there was once darkness.

When I look in the mirror today, I am able to see myself through God's eyes. I am reminded daily that He loved me even when I did not love myself. I am reminded that His forgiveness helped me to forgive myself and that His truth has replaced the many lies that had once overtaken my mind. And best yet, I am reminded that He sees me as fearfully and wonderfully made. I am His perfect creation—chosen, holy, and dearly loved.

GO How can seeing yourself through God's eyes change how you compete?

WORKOUT Psalm 139:13–16; 1 Samuel 16:7

OVERTIME Lord, help me to see myself the way that You do. In those times when I don't feel worthy, remind me of the price You paid because of Your great love for me. Amen.

DAY 293

Confidence Building

Joel Schuldheisz

READY "Therefore encourage one another and build each other up as you are already doing."—1 Thessalonians 5:11

SET Each contest that we're involved in as competitors is filled with missed opportunities, errors, and mistakes. In some games, such as volleyball and basketball, we have only a few seconds to respond to errors. In other sports, such as football or golf, response time may be longer. Regardless of the time that ticks away, our reactions to our teammates' or players' mistakes are critical, not only for their confidence but often for the outcome of the game.

How we respond to our team's failures can empower or tear down an athlete. Throughout practices, games, and other interactions with each other, our goal should be to plant seeds of success that clearly demonstrate our belief in them. Our choice of words, the timing of those words, and the manner in which we convey them has a powerful impact on their lives.

If we are clear in our communication, constructive in our comments, and direct in our feedback, expressing both personal compassion and a passion for excellence in the process, we can help take our team to a higher level. God has demonstrated to us the ultimate response to mistakes, or sin, in the person of Jesus, and He empowers us to do the same.

GO When it comes to responding to mistakes, what situations challenge you the most?

WORKOUT John 11:1–16; 21:15–19

OVERTIME Thank You, God, for the love and compassion You show me when I fall short of Your expectations. Help me to inspire those with whom I interact to be what You know they could be. Amen.

DAY 294

Athletes and Purity

Elliot Johnson

READY "Do you not know that your bodies are temples of the Holy Spirit, who is in you, whom you have received from God?"—1 Corinthians 6:19 (NIV)

SET The question for any athlete to consider is, "What does God think about my sex life?" God is not a cosmic killjoy. He wants us to enjoy life—and have a great sex life! But the Creator knows and has told us the time and place for everything. Sexual relations with a spouse is God's plan. He tells us, "It is God's will that you should be sanctified [set apart to Him]; that you should avoid sexual immorality; that each of you should learn to control your own body in a way that is holy and honorable" (1 Thess. 4:3–4 NIV).

As athletes, most of us consider ourselves to be independent, self-sufficient, and able to handle anything. But 1 Corinthians 10:12 (NIV) says, "So, if you think you are standing firm, be careful that you don't fall!" We are really not as strong as we think!

Frankly, the majority of movies, television shows, and secular videos are trash. Spiritually, the mind that dwells on impure thoughts soon begins to rationalize, compromise, and finally lose control. As Christian athletes, we must control our minds and replace any impure thoughts with thoughts of things that are pure.

GO What will you choose to do when tempted?

WORKOUT 1 Corinthians 6:18; 1 John 1:9

OVERTIME Father, I am bombarded each day with outside influences that encourage me to do things that do not honor You. Grow in me a discernment and strength to turn away from things that cause me to stray from a standard of purity that brings You honor. Amen.

DAY 295

Jealousy

Aaron Winkle

READY "For wherever there is jealousy and selfish ambition, there you will find disorder and evil of every kind."—James 3:16 (NLT)

SET Christian coaches are called to use their gifts for the glory of God and His kingdom. When we work to set an example of faithful steward-ship, we allow our team to witness God at work in our lives. As coaches it is important that we make a point of guiding our teams away from the turmoil that comes through envy and selfish ambition.

Nothing destroys a team faster than envy and selfishness. Belonging to a team means choosing to give up our personal interests so we can commit to pursuing what is in the best interest of the group. Ignoring or knowingly allowing any attitudes, comments, or behaviors that are not contributing to the good of the team is, in fact, tearing down the team.

If we don't address envy and selfishness, jealousy will spread like an infection throughout the entire team. Trust will break down; communication will be strained; commitment will fade away. This erosion of unity, the foundation of any team, leads to chaos, as James wrote. However, if each team member seeks the shared goals of the team, jealousy will evaporate. In God's eyes a perfect game is not about the score. He delights in His children when they use the talents and gifts He has given them for His greater good.

GO How does selfishness inhibit the functioning of your team?

WORKOUT Genesis 37; Galatians 5:13–15

OVERTIME   God, thank You for giving me the opportunity to lead some of Your children. Please allow me to lead these young hearts and minds away from envy and selfishness and toward greater peace and unity. Amen.

DAY 296

Lineman Mentality

Charles Gee

READY   "Whoever wants to become great among you must be your servant, and whoever wants to be first among you must be your slave; just as the Son of Man did not come to be served, but to serve, and to give His life—a ransom for many."—Matthew 20:26–28

SET   The "lineman mentality" is a part of my DNA. A handwritten sign reflecting this philosophy flashed like neon every day I walked into my dad's office. It read, "Don't worry about the credit, just get the job done!" Coaches know that football games are won and lost in the trenches; yet to the average fan, linemen are just oversized guys that get in the way of the skilled guys. But I believe linemen are intelligent, tenacious, and relentless. With little visible reward or public recognition, they serve their team and get the job done.

A little of the "lineman mentality" would serve us well in our faith. We spend too much effort trying to be the greatest. How often are we like the receiver who, upon entering the end zone, thrusts the ball in the air and breaks into a touchdown celebration? *Look at me, look what I did for Jesus!* But Christ said that in His kingdom greatness is defined by service, not accomplishments. Are we worried about looking good and receiving credit or just getting the job done? Are we tenacious and relentless when it comes to serving and sharing our love of Christ with others or more concerned with being noticed?

GO   How can you be a leader and a servant on your team?

WORKOUT   John 13:3–7; Colossians 3:23–24

Jesus, I struggle daily with the "me first" mentality. Help me to see the ways I can serve my team. I want to be consumed to serve. Amen.

DAY 297

Forget about It

Dr. Julie Bell

READY   "We regard no one from a worldly point of view. Though we once regarded Christ in this way, we do so no longer. Therefore, if anyone is in Christ, the new creation has come: The old has gone, the new is here!"—2 Corinthians 5:16–17 (NIV)

SET   There is a great Peanuts comic strip that shows Lucy about to catch a fly ball. At the last minute, she loses sight of the ball and misses it. Lucy turns to Charlie Brown and says that she is sorry, but the "past" got in her eyes. It is easy to let past mistakes get in the way of a good performance. We remember what we have done wrong at the worst time in our lives and end up repeating the same mistakes. Then we begin the cycle of rehearsing that mishap over and over in our mind.

As a Christian, instead of letting the past get in your eyes, turn your eyes to the present and to the possibility of doing things the right way. Remember, you are a new creation in Christ and you don't have to keep making the same mistakes. Being a new creation in Christ means that you are guaranteed forgiveness for all the mistakes that you have made in the past or that you will make in the future. Instead of focusing on the past, turn your eyes to God—the audience of One—and to the present possibility of doing things right.

GO   What past mistakes do you continue to rehearse?

WORKOUT   1 John 1:9; Psalm 103:12

OVERTIME   Lord, I ask for Your forgiveness for any sin in my life. Help me to focus on the "new" to come. Amen.

Big God, Little Me

Scott Jackson

READY   "Neither is He served by human hands, as though He needed anything, since He Himself gives everyone life and breath and all things."—Acts 17:25

SET   Famous slogans are placed on T-shirts, in pictures, or painted on walls to try to motivate our athletes. One famous slogan is, "TEAM, me." "Team" is capitalized because that's where everyone's focus should be. "Me" is in lowercase to show that the individual's goals are secondary to the team's goals.

A great slogan for the Christian life could be, "GOD, me." It's easy to understand the concept of a big God because we all know that He is bigger than we are. The hard part is allowing Him to reign over all that we do. Because most coaches are competitors, they put so much pressure on themselves to have a great program that they sometimes lose perspective and forget to have fun.

As Christians we often do the same thing. We put pressure on ourselves to live a perfect life and do all these Christian "things" because we think that's what it's about. We get so busy and tired that we lose the joy of knowing Jesus. But God wants our relationship with Him to be a joy, not a burden. If we'll focus more on knowing Him and less on *doing*, we'll experience the presence of God as He walks beside us in all that we do!

GO   How can the joy of Jesus affect your performance on the field?

WORKOUT   Matthew 11:25–30; Acts 17:22–29

OVERTIME   Lord, quiet my heart and mind from the busyness of life so that I can hear Your voice today and sense Your presence. Amen.

Disappointment in Competition

Janet Turnbough

READY "We also rejoice in our afflictions, because we know that affliction produces endurance, endurance produces proven character, and proven character produces hope. This hope will not disappoint us, because God's love has been poured out in our hearts through the Holy Spirit who was given to us."—Romans 5:3–5

SET All competitors will eventually know the pain of disappointment. You put everything into preparing for the game, the competition, or tryouts. Although you poured yourself into practice and preparation, in the end, the outcome did not match your expectations. Or perhaps an unexpected event outside of your control changed the course of the success you anticipated.

Your investment seems a waste, or perhaps you question why God would allow this defeat. Disappointment is normal; however, if we focus on ourselves, disappointment leads to frustration, discouragement, and self-pity. These are all enemies to the competitor and to spiritual growth.

However, when we offer our disappointment up to God, He will use it for our good and His glory (Rom. 8:28). God wants us to rejoice in the midst of disappointment. How can we rejoice? Because we know God is using the disappointment to produce endurance. We endure by trusting God, and though disappointed, we continue to show up to practice, execute each drill with a positive attitude, and remain faithful to our coaches and teammates. God's Word promises that endurance will eventually produce a hope that does not disappoint.

GO How can you endure after experiencing defeat in competition?

WORKOUT Psalm 147:11; Romans 8:28–30

OVERTIME Lord, teach me to rejoice in defeat as well as in victory. Help me to bring them both to You, knowing You will use every outcome for my good and Your glory! Amen.

Start a Job. Finish a Job.

Rex Stump

READY "For the Son of Man came to seek and save those who are lost."—Luke 19:10 (NLT)

SET As an athlete, you condition through various seasons. You practice hard for months before your first competition. You put in endless hours of sweat and hard work to prepare your body for this one season. Now, *finish strong*!

Working hard and finishing jobs were priorities for my dad. He would work on a project and not stop until it was complete. And the job was complete when the tools were cleaned and put away in the exact place they were found, neat and orderly. The tools and shovels were not allowed to have one speck of manure or mud on them! When I worked at a lumberyard, my boss asked my dad, "Do you have more children who work like this?" It made my dad proud to know that he raised his children to work hard.

Can you imagine Jesus coming to earth, living as He did, then running away to avoid His arrest in the Garden of Gethsemane? Can you imagine Jesus never experiencing the cross? He came to earth with a mission, and He finished strong. Finish strong, and when you do, you live in a way that honors our Heavenly Father.

GO Are you finishing strong or just getting by?

WORKOUT 2 Timothy 4:7; 2 Corinthians 8:10–12

OVERTIME Father, thank You for showing me how to finish strong. Give me strength to give my best and focus on always finishing strong. May my efforts honor You and point others to You! Amen.

No Comparison

Kerry O'Neill

READY "Let us fix our eyes on Jesus."—Hebrews 12:2 (BSB)

SET I set my blocks for the 110-meter hurdles and took a couple practice starts. The starter called out, "Runners to your marks!" Nervous, I looked around to compare myself to the other runners. I noticed that the line I was using for the start was a full meter behind everyone else. I made the fateful decision to keep my feet in my blocks while moving both hands up even with the other runners. I was nearly lying flat when the gun went off. I crawled out of the blocks and hit almost every hurdle. I finished second to last!

Where did I go wrong? I took my eyes off the finish line, compared myself with others, and tried to compete the way they were competing instead of running my own race. When we focus on another person's game, it prevents us from focusing on *our* game and competing the way that God created us to compete—which means that we work to develop our own unique skills so that we can be the best that we have been created to be.

Spiritually speaking, when do we get off track? When we take our eyes off Jesus—the finish line—and begin comparing ourselves to others. Stop the comparisons and be committed to developing your skills and unique abilities so that your game is at its best and you reach the finish line having run *your* race.

GO In what areas of your sport are you comparing yourself to others rather than fixing your eyes on Christ?

WORKOUT Psalm 18:29–30; Colossians 3:23–24

OVERTIME Lord, help me to delight in my uniqueness today and to use the abilities You have given me in the way that You see fit. Amen.

Play to Your Strengths

Fleceia Comeaux

READY "Do not lack diligence; be fervent in spirit; serve the Lord. Rejoice in hope; be patient in affliction; be persistent in prayer."—Romans 12:11–12

SET As a coach or athlete, you always want to flip the game to your advantage and play to your strengths. You look for that matchup that will allow you to play your best and gain the greatest competitive advantage. Why wouldn't you do the same thing in your spiritual life? God is your X-factor, and what He provides for you are your spiritual strengths. When you use all that He gives you access to, you have the competitive advantage over any challenge you face.

In Romans 12:11–12 (NIV), the apostle Paul outlines five specifics that will give you poise, peace, and power on the sideline and the court.

1. **Never be lacking in zeal** . . . keep your passion for what you do no matter the circumstances.
2. **Keep your spiritual fervor** . . . never lose your spiritual fire or cause someone else to lose theirs.
3. **Be joyful in hope** . . . remember your hope is not in what you do but in who you do it for.
4. **Patient in affliction** . . . God is still God in the midst of difficulties and uncertainties.
5. **Faithful in prayer** . . . this is your most powerful weapon.

These five principles are a must within any believer's arsenal. Take hold of each of them and learn to play to the strengths God has provided.

GO Have you lost your spiritual fervor or zeal because you've had a series of bad plays or games?

WORKOUT Galatians 5:22; 1 Peter 5:8

Father, help me to never be lacking in zeal, to consistently keep my spiritual fervor, to be joyful in hope, patient in affliction, and, most importantly, faithful in prayer. Amen.

DAY 303

Keep the Light On

Jimmy Page

READY "Your word is a lamp for my feet and a light on my path." —Psalm 119:105

SET Once, I set out for a quick twenty-mile bike ride on very familiar roads. I *thought* I had just enough time to get back before sundown. About eight miles from home, it began getting dark fast. I decided to take an unfamiliar road that I thought would be a shortcut, but darkness came within minutes and I could not continue on. I waved down a car and called my wife to ask for a ride home. The most significant lesson I learned that night was this: Lose the light, lose your way. The same is true in our spiritual journeys.

God's Word is a lamp to our feet. A lamp provides enough light for decisions and direction. Light reveals stumbling blocks and illuminates others' hurts and needs.

God's Word is a light to our path. A light helps us see ahead so we can make decisions about our future. We need God's Word to discern our purposes and pick the paths He has for us.

God's Word shines light into our character and circumstances. It reveals what's really going on inside. It shows us what's wrong so we can get it right. God's Word convicts us, corrects us, and directs us.

When we lose the light of God's Word, we lose our way. So let's keep the light on and depend on His Word for the decisions we make today and tomorrow.

GO How can you ensure that you "keep the light on" and depend on His Word?

WORKOUT Hebrews 4:12; 2 Timothy 3:16–17

OVERTIME   Father, give me the strength to read Your Word daily and apply it as a light to all areas of my life. Amen.

DAY 304

Focus Factor

Josh Carter

READY   "But my eyes look to You, Lᴏʀᴅ God. I seek refuge in You; do not let me die. Protect me from the trap they have set for me, and from the snares of evildoers. Let the wicked fall into their own nets, while I pass by safely."—Psalm 141:8–10

SET   "I was telling myself twenty times a hole (to) keep my focus, keep my focus, keep my focus," Michael Campbell said, "and it worked." Michael Campbell began the final round of the 2005 US Open at Pinehurst four shots behind the leader. However, he was one of only four golfers who shot under par on the final day, while those atop the leaderboard crumbled, giving him a two-shot victory over Tiger Woods. Campbell's focus on the golf course paid off—to the tune of $1.17 million.

Whether it is sports or life that we are talking about, our ability to stay focused on the right things can dramatically affect the direction we go. If our desire is to compete for Christ, then our focus must be fixed squarely on Him in all aspects of competition. On the other hand, if our focus is not on Him, our competition is meaningless. Today, may you be completely focused on Christ and on accomplishing His plan for you—both in and out of competition.

GO   Is it possible to be focused both on Christ and your sport? How?

WORKOUT   Isaiah 46:8–13; Hebrews 3:1

OVERTIME   Father, so often I focus on myself and forget that everything I do should be for You alone. Help me to compete for You and have my eyes constantly set upward toward You. Amen.

Teammates of Integrity
Hal Hiatt

READY "But this is what you must do: Tell the truth to each other. Render verdicts in your courts that are just and that lead to peace. Don't scheme against each other. Stop your love of telling lies that you swear are the truth. I hate all these things, says the LORD."—Zechariah 8:16–17 (NLT)

SET Trusting others is crucial for success on and off the field. Knowing your teammate will do everything that he or she can do to help you become successful means that you have confidence in the integrity of that person. In other words, you know they will be truthful and make good decisions that affect not only themselves, but you as well.

As Christian competitors, we are accountable for what we are doing, saying, and representing with our efforts on and off the field. Continually ask yourself: "Am I doing what I'm doing (or saying what I'm saying) because it serves others or because it serves me?" The truthful answer to this question will reveal motives that are either filled with integrity or not. Also, your teammates will follow when you lead God's way.

When we are faithful to do the right thing because it helps our teammates to be the best that they can be, it creates a sense of camaraderie and opens the door for winning. Being a leader of integrity is contagious. It inspires others to follow suit and live an honest and selfless life.

GO Have you ever made a decision in practice or a game that benefited a teammate over yourself? What was the outcome?

WORKOUT 1 John 3:10–15

OVERTIME Father, I want to be a leader of integrity and inspire my teammates to follow You. Give me the courage to lead! Amen.

Perfectly Imperfect

Kristina Krogstad

READY   "Be perfect, therefore, as your heavenly Father is perfect."
—Matthew 5:48

SET   I need to coach this team to a winning season or I will lose my job. If I miss this field goal, game over. I need at least ten points tonight or coach will be mad.

Every competitor has expectations. If you fail, circumstantial consequences exist alongside discouragement, feeling like a failure, and the temptation to give up. We think, "*I need to earn my place*," or "*I need good results to feel good about myself and be accepted*." And, no matter how hard we try, we still fall short somewhere along the way.

Jesus tells us to be perfect as our heavenly Father is perfect. Have we met that expectation? Absolutely not! We have all fallen short (Rom. 3:23). Nothing we do can earn God's love and grace for us. Because of our imperfections (sins), our consequence is hell, yet because of Christ's death and resurrection, hell can be erased from our destiny.

We will continue to fall short with God and man. But rather than letting the outcomes of your pursuits drive your perspective and attitude, live constantly from God's truth of who He is and who you are in Him, trusting that His plans are best. Strive to meet the expectations upon you faithfully and obediently, but within God's grace. This releases the pressure to be perfect and gives you motivation to keep going when you do mess up. Embrace the grace; you are perfectly imperfect.

GO   Do you live in fear of always trying to be perfect in meeting certain expectations?

WORKOUT   2 Corinthians 12:7–10; Philippians 3:7–16

OVERTIME   Father, help me live out of Your love for me rather than fear of trying to earn the approval of You and men. Amen.

In Joy

Lisa Phillips

READY "Rejoice in the Lord always. I will say it again: Rejoice!"
—Philippians 4:4

SET Athletics are full of emotion. Excitement, disappointment, happiness, and joy are all part of the competitive life. Paul reminded Christians at Philippi to rejoice in the Lord always, and the message is perennial. But we live in a difficult world with real battles. As John 10:10 (ESV) tells us, "The thief comes only to steal and kill and destroy." The thief doesn't want a physical thing from us—he wants to steal the joy in our hearts.

While happiness is a direct result of what happens in our lives, joy comes as a result of trusting that God has everything under control. When we acknowledge Him and trust in Him, we'll find a peace that "surpasses all understanding" (Phil. 4:7 ESV).

Jesus came and died for us in order that we might have *abundant* life with Him! (John 10:10). That abundance is found in the joy that results from knowing that He loves us unconditionally and will use each situation in our lives to fulfill His purposes.

As competitors, we're filled with joy when we believe that God is at work in our lives, even if we might not physically see it. Because God is trustworthy and faithful, we can rejoice in the Lord always! When we do, our hearts are filled with an abundant life that no thief can ever steal!

GO How can you develop the fruit of joy more fully in your life?

WORKOUT Psalm 37:3–4; John 10:7–18

OVERTIME Lord, may Your joy spill over into all areas of my life so that others might experience that same joy! Amen.

Etc.

Dan Britton

READY "Though we live in the world, we do not wage war as the world does. The weapons we fight with . . . have divine power to demolish strongholds. We demolish arguments and every pretension that sets itself up against the knowledge of God, and we take captive every thought to make it obedient to Christ."—2 Corinthians 10:3–5 (NIV)

SET As a competitor, I constantly struggle with my thoughts. I have thoughts of doubt, confusion, pride, and more. I wrestle with doubting my athletic potential, my place on the team, and my acceptance from teammates. My mind is usually my greatest challenge, not my physical ability.

My college lacrosse coach always posted his daily practice plan before practice began. Based on where he would put my name on the practice plan, I would think better or worse of my ability. My thoughts would race as to why my coach had listed me in the order that he did. I later found out that he had no real reason for moving the names around.

As a competitor, you must take every thought captive. If you abbreviate "every thought captive," you get "etc." What a great reminder from the Lord! Surrender every thought and make it obedient to Christ. It is a daily battle not to let your mind run with incorrect thoughts. Every stray thought needs to be submitted to the Lord. Only let Christ control your mind.

GO How can you apply the "etc." principle to your competition (for example, writing "etc." on a note in your locker)?

WORKOUT Colossians 3:1–4

OVERTIME Lord, free me from thoughts that are not of You, such as doubt and pride. I desire to take every thought captive! When I compete, let Your thoughts be my thoughts. Amen.

The Wrong Way

Rex Stump

READY   "There is a way that seems right to a man, but its end is the way to death."—Proverbs 14:12

SET   The 2012 college football season kicked off with a great weekend of spectacular plays, exciting games, and even your typical miscues. Unfortunately, Kent State's linebacker Andre Parker made the highlight reel for his blunder. Kent State punted the ball to their opponent, and during the punt a Towson player touched the ball, making it live. Andre Parker quickly picked up the football and ran fifty-eight yards, in the wrong direction. He was just seven yards away from his own end zone, but got turned around and started running the other direction. Fortunately, some Towson players were just as confused and tackled him instead of allowing him to run into their end zone.

Life can present us with exciting moments: new job, new relationship, new season. In the midst of the excitement it is easy to get caught up and become confused—sometimes not realizing we're heading in the wrong direction. In Luke 15:11–32, Jesus tells the story of the prodigal son, a lesson in just how easily one can choose the wrong direction. And yet ultimately, one can return home, like the prodigal son did, and humble himself before his loving father, and find forgiveness.

Learn from history, before you make history. Become aware of the choices that lead away from God so that during times of confusion you, too, won't be tempted to go the wrong way.

GO   What "ways" have seemed right to you, but led to pain in the end?

WORKOUT   Luke 15:11–32; James 1:5–8

OVERTIME   Father, forgive me for the times I go in the wrong direction. Help me to follow Jesus, who is "the Way!" Amen.

How Big Is Your Jesus?

Ken Kladnik

READY "Before God and Christ Jesus, who is going to judge the living and the dead, and because of His appearing and His kingdom: Proclaim the message; persist in it whether convenient or not; rebuke, correct, and encourage with great patience and teaching."—2 Timothy 4:1–2

SET One day, I was leaving my office late after a challenging afternoon. Just as I was locking the door, a student whom I barely knew asked if I was on my way home. My initial thought was to ask him to come back tomorrow. But I noticed something in his eyes, so I unlocked my door and invited him in.

Then he stunned me with his question: He wanted to know why I was always kind to him and other athletes! I realized that I was being given a unique opportunity to tell a young man what motivated me to care about him. As a result of staying a few minutes late, I was able to share with him the good news of Jesus Christ, who cared so much for us that He took the punishment for our sins on Himself by going to the cross.

The opportunities that the Lord places in front of us might not always seem convenient, but they always have eternal significance. If we are to influence the people around us, we must be ready—even when we'd rather do something else—to represent Christ by our words, thoughts, and actions.

GO Think about when you have made time for another person. What was the outcome?

WORKOUT Luke 10:38–42; Ephesians 5:15–16

OVERTIME Lord, use me today to share the good news of Your kingdom. Help me to not allow the world's distractions to keep me from doing Your will. Amen.

Awestruck

Jere Johnson

READY "All of a sudden, when the whole crowd saw Him, they were amazed and ran to greet Him."—Mark 9:15

SET In 1996, I went to my first professional golf tournament at Southern Hills Country Club in Tulsa, Oklahoma. As I walked the course, I came to a hole where there was quite a buzz. People were crowding in to see a young golfer hit the ball—a young man named Tiger Woods. Tiger took it all in stride. He showed amazing composure for such a young player.

As Jesus neared the end of His public ministry, He too often drew a crowd. When people saw His disciples, they started to come together, but when they saw the Master Teacher, they would run to get close to Him. People gathered because they knew that when Jesus was around, something big was about to happen. People grew to expect great things from Christ every time they saw Him. And He never disappointed them. He continually amazed them with His goodness, His grace, and His Godness! Truly, they were awestruck!

Today people still flock to see Tiger Woods play. They expect greatness every time, every shot, every hole. But Tiger is not God. He may be able to pull an eagle out of his bag, but I've never seen him walk on water. Tiger is just a man, but Jesus is *the* Man—Son of Man and Son of God. He deserves our awe! We should be awestruck when we reflect on Him.

GO How can you become more awestruck by your Savior?

WORKOUT 1 Samuel 12:18; Psalm 2:11

OVERTIME Lord, You are the Famous One. Your name is the name above all names. Today, may I be awestruck as I reflect upon Your greatness. Amen.

Express Yourself

Rex Stump

READY "My mouth will tell about Your righteousness and Your salvation all day long, though I cannot sum them up."—Psalm 71:15

SET I don't think I've ever seen an athlete turn down an interview. Have you ever seen a coach be short of words during a press conference? Typically most athletes and coaches enjoy expressing their opinions, strategies, and explanations of game-day decisions.

We, too, have the opportunity every day to express ourselves by the way we talk. Whether you are being interviewed or not, you will eventually express yourself with words. Besides our words, our actions also reveal who we are on the inside. So my question is, "What message are you expressing?"

In Psalm 71, the author asserts that "*I will praise [God] more and more!*" (v. 14). The author also says, "*I will proclaim Your righteousness*" (v. 16) to others. He doesn't put it on his "to do" list or say "I ought to." He says "I will." That's called personal responsibility. That's called making the choice.

Too often we allow people, excuses, and possible appointments to dictate our schedules and our actions.

We need to stop allowing others to keep us silent when it comes to expressing our faith. Like the psalmist, we must make the proclamation and the choice to express our thanks to God on a regular basis!

GO How can you better express a thankful heart to God?

WORKOUT Psalm 71; Psalm 96:1–3

OVERTIME Father, thank You for all that You have done for me and given to me! Help me to be a living expression of thanksgiving to You! Amen.

A New Heart

Lisa Phillips

READY "Therefore, if anyone is in Christ, he is a new creation; old things have passed away, and look, new things have come."—2 Corinthians 5:17

SET In our pre-game talks, we tell our players to "play with heart!" and encourage them to perform their best. The more our players develop such a vision, the deeper their commitment to the sport becomes. This is exactly what Jesus wants from us. He wants to develop a heart in us that will commit to knowing Him in a deeper, more intimate way. As we develop this kind of heart, others will notice.

For years, I believed in who God was, but I did not have a relationship with Him. Then the Lord brought a friend into my life to "coach" me into wanting a relationship with Him. She cared enough about me to show me her heart. As a result, I was so drawn to Jesus that I surrendered and He became the Lord of my life. As I learned to trust Him, all of my relationships changed.

As competitors who follow Christ, we can pour out to others what He has poured into us. He'll restore and rejuvenate our relationships as He continues to change our hearts. And as we rest in Him and continue to be transformed into His likeness, the peace, hope, and joy we experience with Him will show our players what it really means to play with heart!

GO Think of those people whom God put in your life to model heart and faith. How could you now encourage them?

WORKOUT Psalm 51; Matthew 22:37–40

OVERTIME Lord, I pray as David prayed that You would create in me a clean heart for Your purposes. Amen.

Whose Side?

Dan Britton

READY "When Joshua was near Jericho, he looked up and saw a man standing in front of him with a drawn sword in His hand. Joshua approached Him and asked, 'Are You for us or for our enemies?' 'Neither,' He replied. 'I have now come as commander of the LORD's army.'"—Joshua 5:13–14

SET After playing in and coaching thousands of games, I have found that I struggle with one main issue: Whose team is God on—my team or the other team? Does God pick sides? If He does, and there are Christians on both teams, then how can God be on both teams?

Honestly, when I compete, I want God to be solely on my team and not on the other team! However, that mind-set is all wrong. In the Bible, Joshua was the commander of Israel's army and was preparing his troops for battle against Jericho when the commander of the Lord's army appeared to him. When Joshua asked him whose side he was on, the commander of the Lord's army replied, "Neither."

It's not whether the Lord is on our team or their team; it's whether or not *we* are on God's team! When we compete, we need to first recognize that we are on Team Jesus Christ, not the other way around. God wants us to be on His side only!

GO How can you apply the concept of being on God's team the next time you compete or practice?

WORKOUT Ephesians 5:1–10

OVERTIME Lord, help me to compete knowing that I am on Your team and to remember that it's not about You being on my team. Every time I step onto the field of competition, I will wear Your uniform. Amen.

Extra Hours

Sean McNamara

READY "Yet I want your will to be done, not mine."—Matthew 26:39c (NLT)

SET It was 2:20 p.m. I was late for practice. I ran into the locker room, grabbed my equipment, and headed to the training room to be taped. It was a great tape job, taking under four minutes. I ran to the field and greeted my assistant coach: "Sorry, I'm late." He chuckled. "Well, we better get moving. It's 2:35 p.m. and the rest of the team will be here in about an hour. There is much work to be done."

He worked meticulously with me for one hour before every practice so I could excel. I knew that the harder I worked, and the more I sacrificed, the more value I would be to my team. I also knew my coach wanted me to make this sacrifice to teach me and discipline me in the fundamentals and reach my full potential. My hard work paid off many times. No time was greater than when our team upset the 10th ranked team in the country! I know that being at practice early every day made that possible.

My improvement on the field gave my coach great credibility and recognition. He was glorified through my performance. If God is our great coach and instructor, what sacrifices can we make on and off the field that will glorify Him?

GO What are some disciplines that will help you off the field?

WORKOUT Matthew 26:36–46; Romans 8:18–30

OVERTIME Father, thank You for loving me and being my coach for life. Help me live a disciplined life that glorifies You. Amen.

Coming Back after Injury

Roger Lipe

READY "Therefore, since Christ suffered in the flesh, equip yourselves also with the same resolve—because the one who suffered in the flesh has finished with sin."—1 Peter 4:1

SET Who has more confidence about recovering from injury, the one who has never been hurt or the player who has come through the pain and has found renewed strength? If the answer seems obvious, you may have never been injured.

The apostle Peter makes mention of suffering and its results in the above Scripture. He's not saying that after we've suffered we're somehow exempt from making moral mistakes, but that suffering changes our mind-set and leads us to live for more than physical gratification.

Before we've suffered any significant injury, many of us play a little tentatively in dangerous situations. There is a latent fear that if we risk a possible injury, we can never recover or play the same again. However, in the player who has suffered and recovered, that indecision and fear is overcome by the assurance that even if this daring play leads to pain, he can come through it to compete even more strongly.

As you compete today, play with strength, courage, and tenacity. Don't be intimidated by the potential injury that you imagine could wreck your playing career.

GO What do you think it means to share in Christ's sufferings?

WORKOUT James 1:12; 1 Peter 1:6

OVERTIME Lord, I pray for the strength to bear the burden of Your cross with courage and assurance, knowing You are always with me. Amen.

The Playbook

Josh Carter

READY "Your word is a lamp for my feet and a light on my path."
—Psalm 119:105

SET One of the common elements in all levels of football, from pee-wee to pro, is the playbook. Without the game plan contained in the play-book, teams and players would be in a state of confusion, not knowing what to do or where to go. On the other hand, no matter how good the playbook is, it's absolutely useless if the players don't study and apply it on the field.

When it comes to life, there is no better playbook than the Word of God. It contains everything we need to defeat the opposition (the devil). Although we may recognize that God has a plan for our lives, we often do not acknowledge that the devil also has a game plan for our lives, which is in complete opposition to God's. The devil's plan is to steal and kill and destroy our lives, while God's plan is to give us a full and abundant life (John 10:10).

In order for us to consistently overcome our life's adversary, we must (1) know what God's "playbook" says by reading and studying it, and (2) apply what it says to our lives. If we don't, we are playing right into the hands of our enemy.

GO What are some specific ways in which you can apply God's Word to your life today?

WORKOUT Matthew 7:24–27; James 1:19–25

OVERTIME God, I pray that as I spend time reading Your Word, the promises in this playbook will be written on my heart. Help me apply what I read in my day-to-day life. Amen.

Time-Out

Donalyn Knight

READY   "But God proves His own love for us in that while we were still sinners, Christ died for us!"—Romans 5:8

SET   The time-out. What a great tool! When you realize that your team-mates are becoming unnerved, out of breath, and in need of a break, a time-out is a great way to stop, reenergize, refocus, reward, and reassure them. Something as simple as a water break time-out to reenergize the team is all it takes to get them going again. In the same way, our "thirst" for God requires that we take time-outs in our lives in order to be re-energized by our Coach, Jesus.

Sometimes we call a time-out to refocus because the other team threw something at us that we weren't expecting. It's like that in life too. Things happen that are out of our control. We're upset by the events of the moment and lose our focus. The way to get our focus back is to keep our eyes on Christ.

God is our Coach. We need time-outs so that we can listen to what He has to say. If we're obedient to His calling, He can set a pace for us so that we don't get run-down or lose focus or faith. We can rest in Him and know that He is God.

GO   What changes do you need to make in your own schedule to allow for a time-out with God?

WORKOUT   Romans 8:28–39; 1 Corinthians 9:24–26

OVERTIME   Dear Lord, help me to set aside time to meet with You in prayer. Remind me often that time-outs are good for the soul, not just the body. Amen.

Rubber-Band Faith

Dan Britton

READY   "When Jesus heard this, he was amazed. Turning to those who were following him, he said, 'I tell you the truth, I haven't seen faith like this in all Israel.'"—Matthew 8:10 (NLT)

SET   I always keep a rubber band around my wrist. You never know when you might need one! But my habit took on new meaning when my friend, who also wears one around his wrist, once offered me a challenge. When I asked him why he wore his rubber band, he said that it was a constant reminder that God wanted to stretch him daily.

Rubber bands are pretty useless unless they are stretched. When they are extended beyond their standard form, they can hold things together and accomplish their purpose. After hearing my friend's reasoning, I began to look at my rubber band as a reminder to have rubber-band faith.

Faith, like a rubber band, is useless unless it is stretched. Our faith needs to be tested, because when we step out of our comfort zone, it is expanded. We all need to examine our level of faith and ask ourselves if it is getting stronger or weaker. When we are willing to step out and stretch ourselves, God shows up and does what we can't do. True faith begins at the edge of your comfort zone. Be bold and courageous and step out, letting God extend you.

GO   As a competitor, how can you play with rubber-band faith? How can you live with rubber-band faith?

WORKOUT   Luke 7:2–9; Hebrews 11:6

OVERTIME   Lord, I ask for rubber-band faith—the kind of faith that depends on You to show up. Help me to be a competitor who plays and lives with faith at full-strength all the time. Amen.

Turtle on a Fence Post

Charles Gee

READY   "Let them give thanks to the Lord for his unfailing love and his wonderful deeds for mankind."—Psalm 107:31 (NIV)

SET   There is little in this world we accomplish on our own. I remember a talented running back named Steve who was reminded of this principle once. After scoring three touchdowns in the previous week's game, he felt quite full of himself. During a team scrimmage, Steve came down hard on the offensive line for poor blocking. Our line coach finally had enough and decided to teach Steve a valuable lesson. He told his linemen not to block at all on the next play, and let the defensive players know the plan too. Steve got lit up like a Christmas tree! How easy it is to forget the contributions of others. Like the old saying goes: "If you ever see a turtle on a fence post, you can be certain that he did not get there by himself."

Take a minute to reflect on those who have helped you along the way. These are the people (family, coaches, friends, etc.) who put you on the fence post when you could not get there by yourself. As easy as it is for us to take credit for ourselves, it's even easier to forget to thank God for all He's done in our lives. We call out for Him to do the impossible in our lives and when He delivers, we think we did it on our own. Take time to give thanks!

GO   How can you remember to thank God daily for His unending love?

WORKOUT   Proverbs 27:17

OVERTIME   Lord, thank You for the influencers in my life, past and present. Keep me from taking false credit and teach me to always say thank you. Amen.

From the Grandstand

Kande Speers

READY   "Therefore, since we are surrounded by such a great cloud of witnesses, let us throw off everything that hinders and the sin that so easily entangles. And let us run with perseverance the race marked out for us."—Hebrews 12:1 (NIV)

SET   Imagine this: You are on the field, the mat, the court, or the track, and the stands are full of cheering spectators. As athletes, we thrive under these circumstances. But do we remember that every day, whether competing or not, we have heavenly and earthly witnesses watching our every move? We should compete in a way that shows God's glory to those who are watching us.

Athletes know that it takes years of dedication and devotion to achieve excellence in their sport. They train every day to perfect their techniques and avoid all of those things that could hurt their performance. This is also true in our spiritual lives. Daily, we need to set aside time with God to learn His ways so that we can show others His ways. We need to pray and ask God to help us stay away from all of the things that keep us from a closer relationship with Jesus.

We are an example to others of God's greatness and love. We have a lifetime commitment to training as an athlete both physically and spiritually, and this commitment holds great rewards. Spectators are watching both in heaven and here on earth. Commit to showing them God's greatness and an athlete who loves the Lord.

GO   What ways will you show God's glory to those watching you?

WORKOUT   1 Timothy 4:7–8; Hebrews 3:13

OVERTIME   God, help me to remain spiritually disciplined. I want my actions to show others Your perfect love. Amen.

The Ring

Jimmy Page

READY "I also consider everything to be a loss in view of the surpassing value of knowing Christ Jesus my Lord . . . I pursue as my goal the prize promised by God's heavenly call in Christ Jesus."—Philippians 3:8, 14

SET In June of 2005, Tom Brady sat on top of the football world. With three Super Bowl rings on his fingers, you might think he had it all: fame, fortune, success. But Tom knew something was missing. He said, "Why do I have three Super Bowl Rings and still think . . . it's gotta be more than this?" He had fulfilled his dreams and yet was still empty.

Vince Lombardi once said, "Winning isn't everything. It's the only thing." And many coaches and athletes today agree. Wanting to win isn't a bad thing. But when the pursuit of "the ring" becomes the ultimate thing, we've got a problem.

Paul wanted to win, but Philippians shows he wanted to make sure it was the *right* prize. Paul knew that his box full of trophies was worth nothing compared with knowing Jesus. God never designed the "rings" in our life to satisfy us or give us our identity. When we put all our energy and passion into chasing rings, success, or records, we'll be disappointed and empty.

Jesus is the only prize that satisfies; He's the only thing worth pursuing with our whole heart. Stop searching for substitutes that never satisfy. Keep your eyes on the prize.

GO What things do you desire more passionately than Christ?

WORKOUT Matthew 6:19–21; Hebrews 12:1–2

OVERTIME Father, I pray that You will change my heart to love and pursue things that will last forever. Help me to refocus on Jesus, the only prize that satisfies. Amen.

The Danger of Overconfidence

P. J. Meduri

READY   "If you think you are standing strong, be careful not to fall."—1 Corinthians 10:12 (NLT)

SET   As a player, some of my worst games came on the heels of a good game, a game where I performed either up to or beyond expectations. As a coach, I was always wary of the game following a big win. Would the team still keep their edge, or would they approach the next game with a little less urgency? Confidence is good, but overconfidence can make a team vulnerable.

God warns us of becoming spiritually overconfident. We're the most vulnerable to temptation when we appear at our strongest. That's when we often let down our guard, relying on our own strength instead of on Christ. One way to guard against this letdown is by remaining in Jesus, reading His Word, talking to Him in prayer, and admitting our need for His grace on a daily basis.

If we let our guard down for a day or two and become overconfident, we can end up being vulnerable to the subtle attacks of the enemy. Peter warned: "Stay alert! Watch out for your great enemy, the devil. He prowls around like a roaring lion, looking for someone to devour" (1 Pet. 5:8 NLT).

Therefore, just as one game does not make a team's season, one day does not make our season spiritually. May we always seek God's grace and strength in order to keep us from falling, regardless of what occurred before that day.

GO   What causes overconfidence in sports?

WORKOUT   Jude 24–25; Mark 14:38

OVERTIME   Father, I need Your grace in order to stand firm. Keep me aware that I face a real enemy, and need to face each day with a renewed dependence on You. Amen.

Call Time-Out

Jimmy Page

READY   "He said to them, 'Come away by yourselves to a remote place and rest for a while.'"—Mark 6:31

SET   Have you ever been part of a game when nothing was going right? Your opponent had the momentum, and you needed to stop it before the game was lost. What a perfect time to call time-out! Sometimes we're overwhelmed by everything that needs to be accomplished; other times we're afraid to fall behind. We over coach, over train, and even push through injuries, and eventually find ourselves burned out.

God knows we need regular rest in order to be our best. He's given us two gifts so we can unplug and escape: *Sabbath* and *sleep*. The gift of Sabbath is a once-a-week opportunity for God to breathe life back into our weary souls; it's time for focusing our minds and hearts on Him so He can reset our priorities and revitalize our souls.

Also, the gift of sleep is a process that restores and rebuilds our health. A study with the Stanford University men's basketball team once showed that increased sleep dramatically improved their shooting accuracy, speed, and reaction time. They also reported better moods and less fatigue. Jesus modeled how to find rest. He practiced it and taught how to find it. If we want to operate at our highest level for Him, we need to do the same. It's time we take a time-out and let God bless us with the refreshment of rest.

GO   What prevents you from receiving the gift of the Sabbath?

WORKOUT   Matthew 11:28–30; Hebrews 4:9–10

OVERTIME   Father, give me the strength to build in proper time for You to recharge my body, mind, and soul. Amen.

Patience

Wayne Morrow

READY   "But endurance must do its complete work, so that you may be mature and complete, lacking nothing."—James 1:4

SET   In our "instant gratification" society, patience is becoming less and less common. How many times have coaches lost their temper when an athlete didn't make the right play or the right decision?

Biblical patience is a much-needed virtue these days, and it is certainly a reflection of where we are in our Christian walk. Isaiah 40:31 reads, "Those who trust in the LORD will renew their strength; they will soar on wings like eagles; they will run and not grow weary; they will walk and not faint." The key word in the truth of this promise is "trust." We should trust in the Lord by serving Him, though that's not always easy. We need to be patient as we wait for God's leading in every aspect of life.

How do we develop godly patience? By looking to Jesus, who not only exhibited great patience and kindness with His disciples but who also continues to show us the ultimate patience. Instead of giving us the punishment we deserve for our sins, He gives us forgiveness by taking our sins to the cross. Instead of condemnation, He gives us grace, repeatedly. His patience with us creates patience *in* us—patience we can then exhibit in our relationships with others!

GO   How can you demonstrate better patience with your teammates, players, friends, and family?

WORKOUT   Proverbs 16:32; 2 Timothy 4:1–5

OVERTIME   God, help me to wait on You today as You create in me an eternal perspective. Amen.

'Roids

Kyle Shultz

READY   "That is what the Son of Man has done: He came to serve, not be served—and then to give away his life in exchange for the many who are held hostage."—Matthew 20:28 (Message)

SET   Athletes at all levels these days are doing all they can to get the edge. Nutritional supplements—some legal and healthy, others not—are widely used to give athletes an extra boost, better workouts, and faster strength gain. But what are the supplements of our spiritual lives? What does the spiritual steroid (without the negative connotation) look like? How do we get a boost?

There are many answers that would work here. But from my own experiences, one thing stands out: serving. Some of the greatest boosts in my spiritual life have occurred when I served on mission trips. Back in high school, my youth group would take a mission trip every summer. There was one purpose: to serve others.

We didn't return from our mission trips exhausted, we returned energized and impassioned to live out the good news. What seemed to be an emptying of ourselves in service to others actually ended up boosting our faith and strengthening our hearts. Those service trips were like 'roids for the soul.

Jesus called His disciples by saying, "Follow Me." His life was one of complete love and service. So if you need a boost today, try serving someone.

GO   How can you serve others today through Christ's love?

WORKOUT   John 12:26; 1 Peter 4:10

OVERTIME   Lord, give me a heart of service. Show me the needs and help me to fill them. Amen.

Exit the Roller Coaster

Chanda Husser Rigby

READY   "About midnight Paul and Silas were praying and singing hymns to God, and the other prisoners were listening to them."—Acts 16:25 (NIV)

SET   Whoever said life is a roller coaster must have been involved in sports. It seems that on a daily basis, sports can send us rocketing toward glorious, adrenaline-boosted highs. But it can also throw us into a downward spiral with exasperating emotional lows.

One of our best opportunities to be witnesses to teammates is to show them that, as Christians, our emotions aren't bound to these ups and downs. If we appear to be exuberant when we are winning but seem nearly suicidal after a bad practice, we are not modeling the consistent joy of Christ. Our teammates need to see that our joy is not based on what they do or do not do, but that it is based entirely on what Christ did for us at Calvary. The reality of His death and resurrection is the source of our daily and eternal joy! That means we can honor God on good *and* bad days.

So let's exit the emotional roller coaster. Let's remember that Paul and Silas remained joyful throughout their imprisonment and sang praises to God in their jail cells *because* they knew in whom they had placed their faith! Surely, we too can remain joyful in Jesus throughout our seasons and give God the glory He deserves in our locker rooms!

GO   How can you exemplify that joy in Christ does not depend on any earthly circumstances?

WORKOUT   Psalm 51:10–13; Philippians 4:11–13

OVERTIME   God, please fill me with Your everlasting joy so that my life might be a reflection of Your constant love. Amen.

The Coaching Tree

Jere Johson

READY   "Apply yourself to discipline and listen to words of knowledge."—Proverbs 23:12

SET   A special tree grows each year in every sport. It's called the "coaching tree." Throughout the history of sport, we see a number of coaches and athletes who have been trained by other great coaches, continuing each legacy to form an incredible tree. Bob Knight, Pat Summitt, Knute Rockne, Tommy Lasorda—all have great coaching trees because at one time or another, they committed themselves to being taught and gained the knowledge they needed to give to others.

Today's verse gives us the wisdom that we need to be effective competitors as we commit ourselves to instruction and to listening to and applying the words of knowledge. What's even more exciting, though, is realizing that we can have a greater influence beyond our sport! If we follow Jesus, we can have an eternal impact. When we spread God's Word to the unbelieving world, we have the opportunity to grow branches that bear fruit for His kingdom.

Of course, this happens only as we commit to gaining godly instruction and growing deep roots in His knowledge, wisdom, and love. It comes when we are firmly planted in the truth of another tree: the tree on which Christ sacrificed His life for our sins and gave us the good news of eternal hope! As we stay anchored in Him, we can be transplanted and grow new branches for His sake.

GO   How can you start being more committed to gaining godly wisdom today?

WORKOUT   Titus 2; James 1:5–8

OVERTIME   Great is Your faithfulness, God, my Father. Knowledge of You is a Tree of Life for me today and every day! Amen.

TLINAU

Josh Carter

READY "Do nothing out of selfish ambition or vain conceit. Rather, in humility value others above yourselves, not looking to your own interests but each of you to the interests of the others."—Philippians 2:3–4 (NIV)

SET Touchdown celebrations have reached a whole new level these days. After making a touchdown catch against the Giants in week fifteen of the 2003 season, New Orleans Saints' wide receiver Joe Horn pulled out his cell phone from the goalpost and made a call from the end zone. One NFL coach responded, "This is a team game. There was a quarterback that threw the ball, and there was an offensive line that protected for him. I just think that when you draw attention to yourself, it's not necessary."

A friend of mine had "TLINAU" put on his license plates. I asked him what the letters meant. "This life is not about us," he replied. I was intrigued by the message as I thought about how often I selfishly live my life as if the world *does* revolve around me.

In athletics, it's important to remember that purposely drawing attention to yourself minimizes the efforts of the rest of the team. It's selfish, arrogant, and divisive. Jesus came to Earth to carry out the will of God for the benefit of others and to sacrifice His life so others could live. He was all about serving others through love, doing nothing out of selfish ambition. May we follow His example and remember that this life is not about us but about serving God and others.

GO What can you do today to take the focus off yourself?

WORKOUT Matthew 20:28; Romans 12:3

OVERTIME Father, please teach me how to put others' needs before my own, for this life is not about me. Amen.

The Plan

Michael Hill

READY "For I know the plans I have for you"—this is the LORD's declaration—"plans for your welfare, not for disaster, to give you a future and a hope. You will call to Me and come and pray to Me, and I will listen to you."—Jeremiah 29:11–12

SET As a football coach at both the college and high school levels, it seemed like I was always making plans. I would spend hours watching films and charting out an opposing team's offensive tendencies. When the season was over, I would start preparing to improve our team in the off-season.

The big thing with plans is that we have to trust they will work. Here's the catch: No plan of ours ever works exactly the way it did on paper! Only one plan has ever come out as it was intended, and that is God's!

The prophet Jeremiah wrote that God's declaration to us involves a plan for our welfare, to care for us and to provide for us the gift of hope each day of our earthly lives. In the person of Jesus, God's promise has been fulfilled! His plan has always been to bring us into a personal relationship with Him—not to have us fulfill a set of goals and strategies! By seeking God's presence, we can always be confident that He has a plan.

GO What steps can you take to trust in God's purposes for your life?

WORKOUT Joshua 1:9; Proverbs 16:20

OVERTIME Lord, when I'm tempted to pursue my own strategy or agenda, draw me close to You so that Your Kingdom purposes might be fulfilled in me! Amen.

In His Eyes

Danny Burns

READY   "For while we were still helpless, at the appointed moment, Christ died for the ungodly. For rarely will someone die for a just person—though for a good person perhaps someone might even dare to die. But God proves His own love for us in that while we were still sinners, Christ died for us! Much more then, since we have now been declared righteous by His blood, we will be saved through Him from wrath. For if, while we were enemies, we were reconciled to God through the death of His Son, then how much more, having been reconciled, will we be saved by His life! And not only that, but we also rejoice in God through our Lord Jesus Christ. We have now received this reconciliation through Him."— Romans 5:6–11

SET   It would be impossible to count the number of times that we disappoint someone we care about or fail to live up to our own expectations. As humans, we are mired in sin; we fail miserably all the time. Thankfully, there are promises in the Bible such as the one in Psalm 103:12: "As far as the east is from the west, so far has He removed our transgressions from us."

There is incredible power in looking at ourselves through the eyes of Christ. Even at our worst, He still loves us and died for us. When you feel inadequate, depressed, or ashamed, feel His presence. He redeems your life, rescues you from the pit, and showers you with love and compassion. He satisfies your desires with awesome and wonderful things.

No matter where you've been or what you've done, God can restore you. Take a peek at yourself through His eyes—the eyes of forgiveness and love.

GO   What causes you to be ashamed of the actions that you have done in your life?

WORKOUT   Luke 15:1–7; Psalm 103:1–5

OVERTIME   God, Your grace and mercy are unexplainable. Lord, change me. Draw me close to You, Jesus, and restore me. Amen.

Weakness Leads to Strength

Cheryl Baird

READY "So I take pleasure in weaknesses, insults, catastrophes, persecutions, and in pressures, because of Christ. For when I am weak, then I am strong."—2 Corinthians 12:10

SET Many of us learned the "Jesus Loves Me" song as children, but the last part always bothered me: "They are weak but He is strong." To me, displaying weakness seemed to contradict the very goal of competition. As I learned to compete in athletics, the idea of embracing weakness seemed ridiculous. I mean, who has ever been chosen for a team for being the weakest player? I wanted to be strong and display that power for anyone who cared to watch.

As coaches, can we display weakness of any kind and still model a competitive and driven spirit? The answer is yes. We find true freedom in Christ when we believe our weakness is an asset. When we admit our weakness to God, we rely on Him rather than on our own abilities. In fact, becoming weak is a gift that better equips us to serve Him. In the process, we become more like Christ, who became weak on the cross for our sakes, that we might be strong in Him. This is weakness that leads to strength.

To be "pleased in weaknesses" is a call to surrender to our Creator, to allow Him to reign in our beings and to take hold of our hearts. He has given us every gift we possess—even the gift of weakness—as an opportunity to honor His name, not ours.

GO How is God asking you to rely more on Him?

WORKOUT Romans 8:26; Philippians 4:13

OVERTIME Lord, teach me how to embrace my weaknesses and use every gift You've given me for Your purposes. Amen.

Focus

Bryan Wells

READY "Peter started walking on the water and came toward Jesus. But when he saw the strength of the wind, he was afraid. And beginning to sink he cried out, 'Lord, save me!' Immediately Jesus reached out His hand, caught hold of him, and said to him, 'You of little faith, why did you doubt?'"—Matthew 14:29–31

SET Homecoming week can strike fear into the heart of an athlete. There's the dance, the pep assembly, the class competitions, and *then* the game. All the festivities can distract players, presenting a challenge to stay focused for the game.

Life pulls and tugs at us, often causing us to become distracted, overconfident, or afraid. Following Jesus's invitation to go to Him on the water, the apostle Peter got out of the boat and actually walked to Him—on the water! At first he had no problem navigating his steps. Then he started sinking. His focus had changed. Instead of looking to Jesus, Peter shifted his attention to the water and the laws of gravity. But Christ did what He always does for those He calls: He reached out and saved Peter!

Most competitors I know are like Peter. We enter the game wanting to make a difference in others' lives by sharing the love of Jesus through athletics. We soon find, however, that our focus has shifted to our résumé, or the activities surrounding the game. We begin sinking because we've lost our focus on Jesus. Thankfully, Jesus always waits for us to give Him the attention He deserves. He is always ready to save us from drowning and to draw us to Himself!

GO What grabs your attention away from Christ?

WORKOUT Proverbs 17:24; Matthew 6:25–34

OVERTIME Lord, draw me so close to You today that I am not distracted by the cares of the world. Amen.

Recharging

Susan Johnson

READY   "Now faith is the reality of what is hoped for, the proof of what is not seen."—Hebrews 11:1

SET   As the head women's basketball coach at the same institution for twenty-six years, I had just completed a rewarding season. There were many magical moments during the season, and no one wanted it to be over. But all good things must come to an end.

I went through a period of letdown in which I needed to recharge for the next season. Though we'd just finished one season, a new one was around the corner. Thankfully, I had learned years before that what I enjoyed most about competition was the process of preparing for "what is not seen." So even though I didn't know what tomorrow or the next season would bring, I knew that the unknowns at the end of a season didn't have to be unnerving. Instead, they could be exciting—*if* I had faith!

That's why I'm encouraged that "faith is the reality of what is hoped for." It energizes us. As competitors, we don't have to rely on ourselves, our teammates and coaches, or our records. Instead, because Christ gave up His control by going to the cross for our sake, we can give up control and rely on Him. His peace is "the proof of what is not seen," regardless of the circumstances. Christ has filled us with His Holy Spirit, offering us hope for eternity and recharging us along the way!

GO   How do you recharge between each season?

WORKOUT   Luke 12:22–31; Romans 12:12

OVERTIME   Lord, increase my faith in You today. Thank You for the gift of peace in Jesus Christ. Amen.

Competition:
Our Mission Field

Sue Ramsey

READY "Shepherd God's flock among you, not overseeing out of compulsion but freely, according to God's will; not for the money but eagerly; not lording it over those entrusted to you, but being examples to the flock. And when the chief Shepherd appears, you will receive the unfading crown of glory."—1 Peter 5:2–4

SET Competition is an obvious part of the competitor's life, resulting in either winning or losing. But God's Word reminds us not to get so caught up in the results that we forget to take care of those who have been put under our watch. We all want to win. Yet if we forget that we're really working toward an imperishable crown (1 Cor. 9:25), then we've lost sight of why we're competing in the first place. As we compete with the goal to please the Good Shepherd, we'll also serve as examples to others.

The Lord has given us our "mission field," and He cares more about how we take care of the people He has entrusted to us than He does about our win-loss record. This is why Peter provides us with guidelines on how to serve others. We are to guide our team/teammates not by coercion or constraint, but willingly; not dishonorably, motivated by the advantages and profits, but eagerly and cheerfully; not with intimidation, but by being an example to them. And when the Chief Shepherd, Jesus Christ, appears again, we will win the unfading crown of glory!

GO In what creative ways could you care for others and thereby please Christ?

WORKOUT John 10:11–15; 1 Corinthians 9:24–27

OVERTIME Lord, may our focus, our top priority for others be based on the things above, the eternal purpose: Your glory! Amen.

Grip It and Rip It

Jimmy Page

READY "'Lord, if it's you,' Peter answered him, 'command me to come to you on the water.' 'Come,' He said. And climbing out of the boat, Peter started walking on the water and came toward Jesus." —Matthew 14:28–29

SET I love when people ask if I'm a golfer. I like playing golf, but I think it's safer to say I'm an athlete who tries to play the sport. The best round of golf I ever played came by following the advice of a friend who can really play. He told me to play to my strengths and "grip it and rip it": play with absolute freedom and confidence. I did, and it worked!

I believe the apostle Peter was the original "grip it and rip it" disciple; he was a spiritual risk-taker. Peter was the only one who took the risk to walk on water. He eventually sank, but would never forget what he was capable of when he obeyed the voice of God. Most people only remember Peter's failures, but Jesus saw his courage, passion, energy, and faith.

Peter took risks that stretched his own faith and required God to show up in miraculous ways. Peter was not afraid to fail. As a result, Peter knew great victory but also humbling defeat. We, too, can have a "grip it and rip it" spiritual mind-set and experience a life free from the fear of failure. When we boldly take risks as God fills us, we'll begin to see the miraculous done in and through us.

GO List three spiritual risks you can take to expand your faith.

WORKOUT Judges 6; Daniel 3

OVERTIME Father, take away my fear of failure and empower me to "grip it and rip it" in my spiritual life. Fill me with Your Spirit so I may walk with courage and boldness. Amen.

The No-Look Pass

Stan Smith

READY   "For I am convinced that neither death nor life . . . nor anything else in all creation, will be able to separate us from the love of God that is in Christ Jesus our Lord."—Romans 8:38–39 (NIV)

SET   One of my best friends, Mike, is a natural-born athlete, while I, on the other hand, am a natural-born glutton for punishment. During summer breaks in college and graduate school, we'd often play some basketball on one of the courts nearby. I never beat him head-to-head.

However, sometimes one of Mike's friends from college, Jeff, would stop by for a visit, and Mike would let me play on the same side with him and Jeff. Notwithstanding my participation, we were unstoppable. Mike and Jeff had an unnatural ability to find each other on the court and make the winning play. All I needed to do was to set the occasional pick and pull down the occasional rebound. They did the rest. No-look passes. Give-and-gos. You name it, they executed it. They had the ultimate in-game level of trust in one another.

When hard times come along, it can be difficult to trust God's plan for our lives. Trusting God can be a lot like those no-look passes on the basketball court. There is not a method or process for trust; we simply need to accept that God is not going to let us down when it comes to the truly important things in our lives.

GO   Why is it hard to trust that Jesus will help you win your battles?

WORKOUT   2 Kings 6:8–23; James 1:5–8

OVERTIME   Lord, thank You for Your constant protection in our lives and faithful guidance in our roles as spiritual leaders. Help us to finish the work You have laid out for each of us. Amen.

God's Fearless Warrior

Jim Shapiro

READY   "Then David said, 'The LORD who rescued me from the paw of the lion and the paw of the bear will rescue me from the hand of this Philistine.' Saul said to David, 'Go, and may the LORD be with you.'"—1 Samuel 17:37

SET   In the Bible, David was small, weaker than most his age, and by the world's standards, not prepared to play in the "big game" against the Philistines. But David was empowered by his belief in a God who could overcome any obstacle or challenge.

After a game against our league rival, as expected, our team's invitation for postgame prayer was met with rejection from the opposing team. As our team gathered, however, I saw one solitary blue jersey in our sea of white jerseys. In the middle of our huddle sat my "David"! His jersey was clean, he didn't weigh more than 150 pounds, and he looked more like a manager than a football player. But he came to pray.

What happened next was amazing. Some of "David's" teammates from the opposing side noticed that he was with us. One by one, his teammates joined our team for prayer. "David" had stepped out in faith to do what he knew God wanted him to do, and that one step impacted hundreds of people that night!

As coaches, we are challenged every day to do what is right regardless of the obstacles or costs. David could have lost his life by fighting Goliath. My "David" could have lost his reputation by praying with our team. With each individual, God was faithful and produced a great victory.

GO   How could David's example inspire you to step out for Jesus?

WORKOUT   Numbers 14:1–10; Daniel 3:8–18

OVERTIME   Thank You, Lord, that You are mightier and more powerful than any challenge I am facing. Increase my faith in Your abilities! Amen.

The Lord's Army

Jere Johnson

READY "But if it doesn't please you to worship Yahweh, choose for yourselves today the one you will worship: the gods your fathers worshiped beyond the Euphrates River or the gods of the Amorites in whose land you are living. As for me and my family, we will worship Yahweh."—Joshua 24:15

SET I was at home one morning when I heard a proclamation coming from outside of my house. It was loud and proud. It was my four-year-old son singing at the top of his voice, "I'm in the Lord's Army. *Yes, sir*!" He was sitting against the door with his lightsaber in hand, singing his praise to the General of the heavenly host.

When you play sports, you enter into battle. No matter what the sport, you choose whom you will compete for and against. This is no different from your walk with Christ. Every day you battle against the evil of the world in a war for your soul. Today, God wants you to choose whose army you will fight for.

Whether you believe it or not, you are in a spiritual army. If you are not with Christ, then you are against Him. It is that simple. Choose every day to serve Christ. Satan is out to destroy our land and everyone in it. Get with the program, and sign up for active duty! Sing loud and proud that you are in the Lord's Army!

GO How can you start your active-duty service today in the Lord's Army?

WORKOUT Deuteronomy 30:16–18; Ephesians 6:12

OVERTIME God, I want to fight on Your side. I pray that Your Holy Spirit will teach me how I can be equipped to fight the battle against evil. Amen.

Little Things

Jere Johnson

READY   "His master replied, 'Well done, good and faithful servant! You have been faithful with a few things; I will put you in charge of many things. Come and share your master's happiness!'"—Matthew 25:21 (NIV)

SET   One of my favorite things about John Wooden's coaching was that he taught his players each year to put on their socks and tie their shoes properly. He paid attention to the little things, which made the big things come more easily for his teams over the years. Of course, Coach Wooden wanted to teach his players a lesson: If they were going to play in his program, they had to put aside what they wanted to do and follow his plans for the team. That discipline in the small things gave his teams great results, as they won ten national championships.

Sometimes, in walking with the Lord, we neglect what we might perceive as "the little things" because we get too busy. We forget that setting aside daily time with God in His Word, spending time in prayer, or serving our loved ones all help us learn to be faithful. But like the parable in Matthew's Gospel teaches us, we can't assume that we'll be given many things until we're first faithful with the few.

To serve the Lord, we must put aside our own selfish desires and follow Christ in the little things. After all, as a result of His willingness to serve faithfully, God exalted His Son and gave Him the name above all names: Jesus!

GO   What little things can you do to help your team?

WORKOUT   Luke 16:10–12; Philippians 2:5–11

OVERTIME   Thank You, God, for Your faithful love towards me and for helping my attitude today be like Christ's! Amen.

Gold with God

Rex Stump

READY   "For all have sinned and fall short of the glory of God. They are justified freely by His grace through the redemption that is in Christ Jesus."—Romans 3:23–24

SET   The 2012 Summer Olympics were full of excitement and surprises! There were moments of exhilaration as athletes excelled and won in an unexpected manner, and then there were moments of disappointment when the favored team failed to win gold. Olympian gymnast Gabby Douglas was expected to win on the uneven bars. When she fell short of her goal, many avid followers were perplexed. In spite of our predictions or expectations, results can never fully be calculated.

Spiritually speaking, many of us believe that our actions are good enough to win gold with God. But as the apostle Paul says in Romans, we all have sinned and fallen short of perfection. We make mistakes. There are deductions and flaws in our lives, proving it impossible to win gold with God.

But through His love and grace, God has made a way to be right with Him. He sent His Son Jesus to this earth to live a perfect, gold-medal life and become the ultimate sacrifice for us! And Romans 3:22 tells us that by placing our faith in Jesus, our mistakes are wiped out and we "win gold" with God! It's that easy. Through His forgiveness and help, we can live a spiritually golden life!

GO   Are you trying to live a perfect life without God? How so?

WORKOUT   Romans 3; Luke 7:36–50

OVERTIME   Father, I have fallen short and made mistakes. Forgive me. Pick me up and help me live a victorious life for You! Amen.

Smack

Jere Johnson

READY   "Jesus answered, 'I am the way and the truth and the life. No one comes to the Father except through me.'"—John 14:6 (NIV)

SET   "Smack" is the vernacular talk that some players and coaches use to dramatize or publicize their performances. It is hyper-bragging mixed with trash talking. Unfortunately, in every league, game, and team, it's easy to find someone who's gifted at talking smack. Smack-talkers can talk the talk, but they rarely walk the walk.

Back in Jerusalem, there was a group of men who could talk spiritual smack with the best of them. We know them as the Pharisees—and Caiaphas was their top dog. The irony, of course, was that Caiaphas and his buddies thought Jesus and His followers were the trash-talkers. But Jesus only spoke the truth.

In John 14:6, Jesus said that the only way to His heavenly Father is through Him. Many self-righteous men thought such a claim was the ultimate smack; some called it blasphemy. After all, no sane man ever talked like this, so it's not hard to understand why the Pharisees thought Jesus could not back up His words! But they soon watched Him both talk the talk and walk the walk.

When we acknowledge Jesus as the Way, the Truth, and the Life and that His work on the cross did all the talking for us, our daily lives will reflect His. That's the one sure way that our walk can match our spiritual talk!

GO   Does your walk match your talk?

WORKOUT   Ephesians 4:17–32; 1 Timothy 4:6–9

OVERTIME   God, You alone have provided all we need in the person of Jesus, who lived, died, and rose again that we might be Your words and deeds to a world in need of both! Amen.

Personal Best

Joe Outlaw

READY "God has put the body together, giving greater honor to the less honorable, so that there would be no division in the body, but that the members would have the same concern for each other. So if one member suffers, all the members suffer with it; if one member is honored, all the members rejoice with it. Now you are the body of Christ, and individual members of it."—1 Corinthians 12:24–27

SET What position is the most important in the game of football? In volleyball? It's not the position played by the person who gets the most headlines or touches the ball the most. The answer is simple: it's the one that you have been asked to play. God's Word states that whatever you are asked to do, you should "do it with all your might" (Eccles. 9:10 NIV). If you are playing offensive guard and you don't block your assignment, the whole team pays the price. In volleyball, the hitters will never even touch the ball without a good pass from the back row.

Paul tells us in 1 Corinthians 12 that a body cannot function as it was designed to without its many parts working together. We should not consider one part of the body to be more important than another, nor should we believe that the role we have been asked to play is insignificant. Give your best each and every play. The team is depending on you!

GO According to Scripture, how should your attitude change regarding your role in life?

WORKOUT 1 Corinthians 12:12–27; Colossians 3:23–24

OVERTIME Lord, You have blessed me with gifts and talents, and I want to use them on Team Jesus Christ. Thank You for giving me the privilege to serve. Amen.

The Power of Fear

Bill Burnett

READY "If you really fulfill the royal law according to the Scripture, 'You shall love your neighbor as yourself,' you are doing well."—James 2:8 (ESV)

SET Coach Smith was aware that one of his players was smoking pot. But Coach Smith did not take any action or even talk with the player. At the end of the season, the principal called Coach Smith in for a meeting and told him that there was verifiable evidence the player had consistently violated team rules, and clear evidence that Coach Smith had known about it. Consequently, the coach was asked to resign.

Why was Coach Smith unwilling to confront his player? There may have been many reasons, but it is likely that the main reason at the core of all of this was fear. Fear can paralyze our willingness to act and do the right thing. It is certainly okay to feel afraid—that's part of being human. But when we allow fear to affect our ability to take appropriate action, we hurt others as well as ourselves.

First John 4:18 tells us, "Perfect love drives out fear." We cannot act out of fear and love at the same time. And we know from Jesus—whose obedient life and death was out of love for us—that the greatest commandment is to love! Because God loves us, we can love our players. And that means we cannot ignore their problems or pretend they don't exist. Instead, His love for us gives us the courage to do what's right!

GO How do you naturally respond when you have to confront someone?

WORKOUT Psalm 27:1–6; 1 John 4:13–21

OVERTIME Lord, thank You for Your perfect love. Help me to reflect that love to those people whom You've put in my life. Amen.

Holding On

Alvin Cheng

READY "Fight the good fight for the faith; take hold of eternal life that you were called to and have made a good confession about in the presence of many witnesses."—1 Timothy 6:12

SET Many sports watchers have probably seen the St. Louis Cardinals' "blanket" TV commercial. It begins with a man who wraps a red St. Louis Cardinals' blanket around himself. The blanket is the one constant in his life as he grows up. As a child, he uses it as a cape, and he drapes it over his bed when he studies. It's on the seat when he learns to play the drums as a teenager, in the trunk when he moves out of the house, and around his girlfriend while they watch a movie. The commercial ends with the man wrapping the blanket around his child as these words come on the screen: "Without sports, what would we hold on to?"

For avid sports fans, the commercial seems to suggest that the one thing that we can count on is our sport or team. But for Christians, there is something far more fulfilling than sports. Paul told Timothy to hold on to eternal life, because with Christ, he had been called into the most satisfying relationship that he would ever experience. The same is true for us! We hold on to Jesus Himself, acknowledging that He is the source of eternal life and the hope during every stage of life. As Christian competitors, we can show our teammates what we are holding on to by holding on first to Jesus and then wrapping His faithful love around our lives for others to witness!

GO How can you hold on to Christ as you compete today?

WORKOUT Psalm 119:30–32; Mark 7:6–8

OVERTIME Thank You, God, for surrounding me with Your love and providing me with the gift of eternal life through Jesus! Amen.

What Are You?

Jere Johnson

READY "Summoning the crowd along with His disciples, He said to them, 'If anyone wants to be My follower, he must deny himself, take up his cross, and follow Me.'"—Mark 8:34

SET When sports fans are asked, "Who do you follow?" most answer with a city, school, or mascot: "I'm a Denver fan," or, "I'm a Hoosier." No matter how you phrase it, we all follow one team or another. This applies to our lives in Christ as well.

It's not uncommon today to hear believers ask, "What are you?" Some say, "I'm a Baptist" or list a different denomination. This has always disturbed me. I am proud of my Christian upbringing and the denominational truths that I have learned over the years, but when I accepted Jesus as my Savior, I committed to Him, not some set of religious traditions or legalistic dos and don'ts.

In the Team FCA Competitor's Creed, I read, "I am a Christian first and last." So when people ask me today what I am spiritually, I simply tell them that I am a Christian who happens to attend a Bible church. Jesus is Who we are and should be. Please do not misunderstand; I am not bashing denominational preferences. But do understand that the denomination in which you have been raised is nothing without the relationship you can have—and must have—with Jesus.

If you want to get caught up in anything, get caught up in the doctrine of Jesus and His Word.

GO Are you caught up in the dos and don'ts of your faith, or are you caught up in Jesus?

WORKOUT Joshua 24:15; John 14:6

OVERTIME Father, thank You for Your Son. Help me today to find my identity solely in Him. Amen.

The Eternal Purpose

Michael Hill

READY "For the Son of Man has come to seek and to save the lost."
—Luke 19:10

SET Athletes must know their purpose on the team. For instance, an offensive lineman's purpose is to protect the quarterback and create space for the running back. A pitcher's purpose is not to allow a batter to get a hit. A goalkeeper's purpose on the soccer field is to keep the ball from getting into the net. For a team to succeed, each player must use his or her talent and experience to help the team accomplish the overall purpose: victory. If we do not have the players with the right skills or fail to place a player in the proper position, the team will have difficulty attaining its goals.

Jesus had a purpose, too. His was single-minded and simple: to seek and to save the lost. This was the reason behind His entire life on Earth and why He chose to die on the cross: to bring us to Himself! He knows His players' gifts and talents, and He knows exactly where we should be placed. As members of Team Jesus Christ, we must serve our Team Captain by doing His Father's will. Jesus came to Earth as man in order that we might be with Him for all eternity! Today, as we understand our purpose on His team, let's serve Him by spreading His message to all who will listen!

GO How are you serving Jesus in your current role?

WORKOUT John 10:9; 1 John 5:9–10

OVERTIME Father, help me today to seek Your will for my life. Thank You for uniquely creating me to help accomplish Your purposes for others! Amen.

Get Up

Clay Elliott

READY "Get up, for this matter is your responsibility, and we support you. Be strong and take action!"—Ezra 10:4

SET Former Ohio State University coach Jim Tressel cheated . . . well, at least according to the NCAA rules he did. What actually happened was that some of his players cheated, and he failed to report their misbehavior, making him guilty too.

In the Old Testament book of Ezra we read that the Israelites also cheated. God specifically told them not to marry foreign wives, but many did. So they, too, found themselves in the middle of a scandal. Both of these situations may look rather nominal to most. What's the big deal? The problem is we don't make the rules, we just suffer the consequences after breaking them.

Ezra 10:4 gives us some great advice in the midst of a controversy. First, we are to take ownership of our part in breaking the rules. Second, we need to support each other in the midst of a scandal. And third, we are to get up and take action. Don't wallow. Don't whine. Move on.

The Israelites eventually followed these instructions, and God honored them for their obedience. None of us are above scandalous behavior. And the athletic field seems to be an opportune place to sin. The question is, will we take the advice given in Scripture or will we make excuses? I say, "Get up and take action!"

GO What are the benefits to obeying God's rules?

WORKOUT Ezra 10; Exodus 20:1–17

OVERTIME Father, help me to be more obedient. When I break rules, give me the strength to get up, ask for forgiveness, and go forward. Amen.

Should Have Listened

Jere Johnson

READY "At the end of your life, you will lament when your physical body has been consumed, and you will say, 'How I hated discipline, and how my heart despised correction. I didn't obey my teachers or listen closely to my mentors.'"—Proverbs 5:11–13

SET "It will make you better, bigger, stronger."

"Don't worry, no one will ever know . . ."

These are some of the phrases that student-athletes hear when they are encouraged to take steroids. The pursuit of greatness is so powerful today that many athletes are doing things that put their lives in jeopardy.

Proverbs 5 addresses the topic of staying away from things that are bad for you. In verse 13, you hear the remorse of someone who wishes he had listened to the wise advice he received instead of choosing to follow the crowd and his own evil desires. This sad story rings true in sports and in society today. Today, athletes are getting wise counsel from coaches, parents, and pastors, but they're also getting advice from those who do not have their best interests at heart.

Whether the struggle is with steroids, drinking, pornography, or something else, athletes must choose to listen to wise advice. They often want to choose immediate gratification over long-term goals, but it is the *eternal*—not the *internal*—that really matters. Listen only to those individuals who truly want what is best for you athletically, socially, academically, and most important, spiritually. Don't be the one to say, "I should have listened."

GO How can you start today to listen to the right voices in your life?

WORKOUT Proverbs 5; James 1:19

OVERTIME Father, tune my ear to recognize when I am receiving unwise counsel so that I can make the right choices. Help me to focus on eternal things. Amen.

Running the Race

James Kirkland

READY "Let us strip off every weight that slows us down, especially the sin that so easily trips us up. And let us run with endurance the race God has set before us."—Hebrews 12:1 (NLT)

SET To persevere means to persist in an undertaking in spite of opposition or discouragement. The 2007 Boston Marathon was run under adverse weather conditions. The temperature was in the low forties, and the wind blew at thirty miles per hour, with gusts that reached up to fifty. To run in those conditions takes more than training and the desire to finish. That day, it took a will to persist in spite of opposition and extreme discouragement.

Hebrews 12:1 gives a command to develop perseverance. Satan is a formidable enemy. To overcome him takes more than training, doing the right thing, and desiring to be good; it takes perseverance. How do you develop perseverance? Second Peter 1:5–7 (NLT) tells us:

> In view of all this, make every effort to respond to God's promises. Supplement your faith with a generous provision of moral excellence, and moral excellence with knowledge, and knowledge with self-control, and self-control with patient endurance, and patient endurance with godliness, and godliness with brotherly affection, and brotherly affection with love for everyone.

Our goal is to be able to say as the apostle Paul did, "I have fought the good fight, I have finished the race, and I have remained faithful" (2 Tim. 4:7 NLT). Let us persevere in order that we might finish the race in spite of overwhelming odds.

GO Establish a spiritual training plan that will help you add to your faith each supplement listed in 2 Peter 1:5–7.

WORKOUT Romans 5:1–5; James 1:2–4

OVERTIME Lord, help me to persevere in my faith and establish a spiritual training plan to help me stand firm. Amen.

You Can't Tell a Ball by Its Cover

Ish Smith

READY "Woe to you, scribes and Pharisees, hypocrites! You clean the outside of the cup and dish, but inside they are full of greed and self-indulgence!"—Matthew 23:25

SET There are two sayings that I have heard countless times. One is "You can't tell a book by its cover"; the other is an advertising statement that assures us "It's what's up front that counts." Taking some liberty, I'll apply these statements to the sports world. Anyone who has played baseball would probably agree that "You can't tell a baseball by its cover" and "It's what's inside that counts."

At the same sporting goods store you can buy a baseball for as low as $3.00 or up to $10.00. On the outside, both of those baseballs might look exactly the same. But baseball coaches and players know that the core of these baseballs and the material used in winding the inside of each one will be very different. You won't be able to tell by looking on the outside, but once you look inside the ball, the truth will be clear.

What is true for a baseball is true for a competitor. The true test of a competitor isn't what he or she looks like, but what is inside. Those intangibles often separate the great competitors from the average ones. As an athlete or a coach, you can make an impression with how you look. But over a season, and particularly when the going gets tough, the truth of what you are made of will come out.

GO Do your teammates or players know you as one who walks the talk?

WORKOUT 1 Samuel 16:1–7; 17:41–47

OVERTIME Lord, I want to live a consistent Christian life that makes You proud, and show Your love to others. Amen.

The Flying Scotsman

Dan Britton

READY   "You did not choose Me, but I chose you. I appointed you that you should go out and produce fruit and that your fruit should remain, so that whatever you ask the Father in My name, He will give you."—John 15:16

SET   Known as the Flying Scotsman, Eric Liddell ran to victory in the 1924 Paris Olympics. He won a gold medal in the 400-meter dash and set a new world record with his time of 47.6 seconds. Liddell ran, spoke, and lived his life with incredible faithfulness. He never wavered from his commitment to Jesus Christ.

Liddell was not well-known or popular—just faithful. He was known to shake the hands of other runners before each race. At the time, the runners ran on cinder tracks, and Liddell would offer his trowel (small shovel) to fellow runners who had trouble digging their starting holes. Liddell could just as easily have been called the Serving Scotsman. God used him in a significant way because he was willing to take his eyes off of himself and focus on those around him.

As an athlete, it is hard to intentionally serve others, especially in the heat of competition. But remember that God has "appointed you that you should go out and produce fruit and that your fruit should remain." To honor God is to serve Him in all we do, and serving Him means total victory!

GO   What are some practical ways that you can serve athletes around you?

WORKOUT   John 13; Philippians 2:1–11

OVERTIME   Lord, show me practical ways to serve my fellow competitors. May my talents and abilities be used for Your service. Amen.

Fired Up

Jimmy Page

READY   "Consider it a great joy, my brothers, whenever you experience various trials, knowing that the testing of your faith produces endurance. But endurance must do its complete work, so that you may be mature and complete, lacking nothing."—James 1:2–4

SET   Cut from the team. Lost the state title. Playing time disappears. Your mistake costs the team a win. As a competitor, you may face all of these tough trials. Add to that academic pressure or conflict at home and you can feel overwhelmed.

In Daniel 3, we read the account of how Shadrach, Meshach, and Abednego refused to bow down and worship a false god, and were literally thrown into the fiery furnace as consequence. Adversity always brings opportunity. When they took their stand and were thrown into the fire, the soldiers who threw them in were killed instantly, but they were unharmed. When the king saw the unwavering faith and courage of these men and then witnessed this great miracle, he immediately recognized that "there is no other god who is able to deliver like this" (Dan. 3:29). When others see how we persevere and trust through trials, they believe.

Character is uncovered in crisis and formed in the fire. It will be *revealed and refined*. God forms our character the same way He forms diamonds—with time, pressure, and heat. The more heat and pressure we feel, the more heart and presence of God we experience. We can face trials with joy, knowing God uses pressure and pain to produce perseverance and maturity. Let your character be formed in the fire and see how lives are transformed.

GO   Have you experienced adversity that's tested your faith?

WORKOUT   1 Peter 4:12–16; 2 Corinthians 1:3–6

OVERTIME   Father, let me rejoice when I face the "fire," knowing You are refining me in the process. Amen.

Leaving a Mark

Dan Britton

READY   "I have been crucified with Christ and I no longer live, but Christ lives in me. The life I now live in the body, I live by faith in the Son of God, who loved me and gave Himself for me."—Galatians 2:19–20

SET   At eight years old, I had the opportunity to ride my older brother's motorcycle. I wanted to show him how "big" I was, so I took off recklessly. About a hundred yards down the dirt road, my front tire hit a hole. I flew through the air, landed in a ditch, and the motorcycle landed on my back. Thankfully, since I landed in the ditch, the only part of the motorcycle that touched my back was the muffler. As the muffler burned through my shirt and flesh, I experienced a world of hurt, and received a burn imprint that still resides on my back more than thirty-five years later.

An imprint is a permanent mark. Every time I compete or coach, I leave an imprint. Whether I leave a good or bad impression is up to me. The ultimate question is whether I've left an imprint of myself or of Jesus. Paul writes in Galatians 2:20 that we need to die to ourselves so that there will be no mark of us. When you are playing or coaching, be committed to leave behind the imprint of Christ!

GO   What are some practical things that you can do to make sure the imprint will be the Lord's and not yours?

WORKOUT   Ephesians 4:1; Colossians 1:10

OVERTIME   Lord, my goal is to compete in such a way as to leave behind Your mark and not mine. My prayer is that all who see me compete will know that it is all about You. Amen.

New Beginnings

Ish Smith

READY "In the beginning God created the heavens and the earth. Now the earth was formless and empty, darkness covered the surface of the watery depths, and the Spirit of God was hovering over the surface of the waters."—Genesis 1:1–2

SET I believe that we can learn an important lesson from the first five words in the Bible, "In the beginning, God created . . ."—a lesson that relates more to those of us who live on the earth than it does to the earth itself. God did not stop creating thousands of years ago when He put in His week's work and then rested on the seventh day. No, the good news of the gospel is that God wants to continue to create in our lives, and for us, today can be a new beginning.

As I reflect on my years of coaching, I can vividly remember the euphoria that was always present each year when I would go to the equipment room and bring out the bats, balls, gloves, spikes, and uniforms. For all of us who claim Christ as our Savior, we have reason to experience that same euphoria.

Yes, there is a "beginning" when we accept Christ as our Savior. But God has many more beginnings in store for our lives. He wants to re-create us for new challenges and empower us anew for responsibilities that are headed our way. When we fall, He anxiously awaits our invitation so that He might provide a new beginning in our lives.

GO What are some "new beginnings" that you would like to see in your life?

WORKOUT Ezekiel 36:26; 2 Corinthians 5:16–21

OVERTIME Lord, begin in me a new work so that I may honor You in all that I do. Amen.

Talk Is Cheap

Jere Johnson

READY   "To the pure, everything is pure, but to those who are defiled and unbelieving nothing is pure; in fact, both their mind and conscience are defiled. They profess to know God, but they deny Him by their works. They are detestable, disobedient, and disqualified for any good work."—Titus 1:15–16

SET   One of my favorite things to hear a coach say was, "Don't tell me. Show me." Today, however, some athletes have a hard time backing up what they say. They talk a good game, but they can't always live it out.

In the same way, the apostle Paul knew how easy it was for people to talk about Christ without having their lives match their words. That's why he encouraged true believers to stand strong; he did not want them to end up with empty lifestyles. Like James, who encouraged Christians to "be doers of the word and not hearers only" (James 1:22), Paul knew the importance of walking the talk. God's standard is clear for us: He does not want us to be examples of cheap talk. Rather, He desires that our lives and our words reflect the Living Word, the One who gave up all so that we might be rich in good deeds!

We all want to believe that our teammates will do what they say they will. But we also know that isn't always the case. If we can inspire them to talk less and do more, we will be leading them into success *and* integrity.

GO   How can you move beyond talk to loving actions?

WORKOUT   James 1:22–25; 1 John 3:18–20

OVERTIME   Father, may my life and all I do speak of the Living Word, the hope of all humankind! Amen.

Step Up

Rex Stump

READY "For it is God who is working in you, enabling you both to desire and to work out His good purpose."—Philippians 2:13

SET On Nov. 25, 2012, following a game between the NY Giants and the Green Bay Packers, it was reported that a middle-aged man leaned too far over the railing, lost his balance, and fell. Giants tight end, Martellus Bennett, saw the man plummeting fifteen feet toward the ground. Bennett made his fourth reception of the day, catching the man and saving him from injury!

USA Today reported Bennett as saying, "I was doing what I usually do, moseying to the locker room and meandering around. Naturally, I just wanted to step back, but I did the righteous thing and I stepped up. I caught him, I saved his life. I tapped into my inner superhero, which I do have. I'm usually a ninja, but my Spidey-senses told me he was going to take a fall, so I saved his life." Way to step up!

How many times have we stepped back, instead of stepping up? We may not have "Spidey-senses" in us to alert us to right and wrong, but we do have greater powers! As believers in Jesus, we have something better inside us—God's Holy Spirit! Thanks to God's Spirit, we have the ability and the power within us to step up. We have the power to love, to forgive, to help, to avoid sin, and to say and do the right things.

GO Where can you step up and let God's Spirit and power work through you?

WORKOUT Hebrews 13:21; Romans 8:11

OVERTIME Father, thank You for empowering me with the ability to make the right choices. Today I choose to step up and use Your power to live righteously! Amen.

The Priceless Gift of Serving

Dan Britton

READY "So if anyone purifies himself from anything dishonorable, he will be a special instrument, set apart, useful to the Master, prepared for every good work."—2 Timothy 2:21

SET There is a big difference between *service* and *serving*. Service is something we pay for, or something we might come to expect at a restaurant or gas station. But serving goes deeper. Serving deals with heart issues, involves sacrifice, and meets real needs. We don't pay for serving, though it can be costly.

Christ did not come to give good service. He came to serve. Athletes are not required to give good service to their teammates, but Christian athletes are called to serve. Christ desires that we become servants to our players, teammates, friends, families, and communities. We are His serving instruments! That might be hard to understand in a world where it seems everyone wants to be a leader, not a servant. But Jesus never told us to be leaders. Instead, He invited us to be servants, and He did so by serving us with the sacrifice of His life so that we might come into a right relationship with God!

That's the most priceless news we could ever hear. It's why leadership camps sponsored by FCA are really servant camps; their one goal is for the young people who attend to meet the most amazing servant ever to walk the earth: Jesus. If we ever hope to lead, we must learn to serve.

GO How has God gifted you to serve? How has He set you apart?

WORKOUT Ephesians 2:10

OVERTIME Thank You, Lord, for sending Jesus to love and to serve the world so that my life might become an extension of His gift of service to others! Amen.

Beyond Sight

Joe Matera

READY "For we walk by faith, not by sight."—2 Corinthians 5:7

SET Amidst the small beautiful city of Guarapari, Brazil, Derek Rabelo's father prayed that his son would become a famous professional surfer. His father named his son after the legendary Pipeline surfer Derek Ho, the embodiment of his dream. Unfortunately on May 25, 1992, his prayers seemed unanswered when Derek was born blind. Seventeen years later, Derek decided that despite his blindness he still wanted to surf and that he wanted to surf Pipeline on the North Shore of Oahu, Hawaii. Through the encouragement of his parents, best friend, and surf coach, Derek embarked on a three-year journey of grueling mental, physical, and spiritual training to accomplish his goal. Knowing it wasn't an easy feat, Derek reflected on the blessing God had granted, seeing his surfing ability as a gift directly from Him.

Being blind isn't an obstacle when you have the right attitude and a good measure of faith. Derek's story teaches us that the best journeys in life are walked out by faith and not by sight.

GO How can having blind faith move you to be more courageous?

WORKOUT Joshua 1:7; 2 Corinthians 4:18; Hebrews 11:1

OVERTIME Jesus, thank You for giving me courage and a vision beyond what my eyes can physically see. Help my life reflect complete faith in You. Amen.

*Derek and his story are the subject of the documentary *Beyond Sight*.

Leave It on the Field

David Hermes

READY "Jesus told him, 'If you want to be perfect, go and sell all your possessions and give the money to the poor, and you will have treasure in heaven. Then come, follow me.'"—Matthew 19:21 (NLT)

SET I decided to try cross-country running during my freshman year of high school. The only problems were my seven-minute miles and the thirty extra pounds that chased me. To be competitive, it was going to take everything I had. Riding my bike to and from practice only to pass out in my kitchen became my summer-long morning routine.

Two months later, two minutes faster, and thirty pounds lighter, it was time for my first race. At the first mile marker I was in the front half of the pack. By the second marker I felt sick, but I edged toward the front. By the third marker my body was ready to quit. With the finish line in sight, there was nothing that could stop me. I never saw the last fifteen yards of the race, but apparently I made it far enough to pass out over the finish line.

I placed in the top ten in that race—a race where I left it all out on the field and learned how to win. In Matthew 19:16, the young man essentially asked Jesus, "How do I win in life?" Jesus instructed him to give up all his possessions and follow Him. Jesus outlined what was and still is the cost of becoming a disciple and victor in the race of life.

GO What might Jesus be asking you to give up to live wholeheartedly for Him?

WORKOUT Mark 12:41–44

OVERTIME God, show me areas in my life that I have not yet surrendered. I want to leave it all on the field for You. Amen.

Run to Win

Sarah Roberts

READY "Don't you know that the runners in a stadium all race, but only one receives the prize? Run in such a way to win the prize. Now everyone who competes exercises self-control in everything. However, they do it to receive a crown that will fade away, but we a crown that will never fade away. Therefore I do not run like one who runs aimlessly or box like one beating the air. Instead, I discipline my body and bring it under strict control, so that after preaching to others, I myself will not be disqualified."—1 Corinthians 9:24–27

SET There are a lot of people in this world who participate in athletics, but not all of them are competitors. The difference? A competitor plays with purpose. A competitor trains, plays, and runs to win.

Paul understood the heart of a competitive athlete and knew that as Christian athletes we must train our hearts spiritually like we do our bodies physically—with purpose. As followers of Jesus, our purpose in this life is to train our hearts to love like Jesus, to serve others like Jesus, and to put our faith and hope in the Father like Jesus, in every area of our life.

Jesus said it this way in John 10:10 (NLT): "My purpose is to give them a rich and satisfying life." When we have Christ in our lives, we are not just living but we have true life; life that is rich and satisfying, life that has purpose and life that is running to win.

GO As a Christian, how do you train your heart to win?

WORKOUT Romans 12:1–2; Colossians 3:23

OVERTIME God, help me to focus my life on the purposes You have set before me as an athlete and follower of You. Amen.

H.O.T. Communication

Les Steckel

READY "Then He said to them all, 'If anyone wants to come with Me, he must deny himself, take up his cross daily, and follow Me.'"—Luke 9:23

SET When I was hired as the new offensive coordinator of the Houston/Tennessee Oilers in 1997, I knew that we had big challenges ahead. The Oilers had never made that exciting trip to the Super Bowl, so when the owners moved the team to Tennessee, it signaled a serious intention to reach new heights.

Our road to the Super Bowl was only possible through the grace of God. While at training camp that season, we discovered several effective principles for building a championship team.

One of these guiding principles was communication. Most NFL summer training camps are hot, so we decided to use the weather to guide our communication and make sure it was "hot" as well: *H*onest, *O*pen, and *T*ransparent. Since one of our main challenges that year was convincing a group of people from all walks of life to lose themselves for the sake of one cause, our communication also had to be effective.

The same is true for Christians. Every day, Christ invites us to lose ourselves for the sake of the single purpose of living for Him. When we try to hide things from Him or from our brothers and sisters in Christ, we only create broken relationships and mistrust. In order to produce unity, we must promote truth. That means honestly pursuing Him, denying ourselves for the sake of others, and transparently taking up His cross for all to see!

GO In what areas of your life do you need to be more H.O.T.?

WORKOUT Mark 8:34–37; James 3:14–18

OVERTIME Lord, may the words of my mouth and the meditations of my heart be pleasing to You today and helpful to others! Amen.

Practice, Practice!

Clay Elliott

READY   "Do what you have learned and received and heard and seen in me, and the God of peace will be with you."—Philippians 4:9

SET   We've all said it: The secret to success is practice, practice, practice. When I was in high school, I trusted my coaches completely and desired success, so I practiced whatever they told me to. Similarly, when we read that Paul urges us to "do what you have learned and received and heard and seen in me," we would be wise to heed his advice. A quick scan of the context reveals some of what Paul would want us to put into practice:

- Philippians 4:4—We should rejoice in the Lord.
- Philippians 4:5 (NIV)—Our gentleness should be evident.
- Philippians 4:6—We should pray about everything.
- Philippians 4:8—We should think about the good stuff.

As competitors, we could integrate these four ideas into our daily lives by rejoicing not just in winning but in practice or tough defeats; leading our teammates with gentleness; praying for our teammates and for every decision; and filling our minds by meditating on God's goodness and promises.

Only when we put these Christlike attributes into practice with His help will we have the reserves to see the good when difficult circumstances arise. As we do, our faith in Him will be deepened and we'll become more like the people that God has intended us to be through Jesus as we practice, practice, practice with Him!

GO   What are some things that you could put into practice with God's help?

WORKOUT   Psalm 111:1–10; 1 Timothy 4:11–16

OVERTIME   Thank You, Lord, for filling me with Your joy and gentleness. I ask for Your wisdom today as I reflect Your glory and grace to all who cross my path. Amen.

Stay Focused

Roy Helu Jr.

READY "Forgetting what is behind and reaching forward to what is ahead, I pursue as my goal the prize promised by God's heavenly call in Christ Jesus."—Philippians 3:13b–14

SET I want to be a better representative of God on the field. I want to give the same effort on the first play of the game when my body is fresh as I do on the 64th play when I'm dragging my feet and my body is telling me to give up. Accomplishing each of these goals requires constant prayer and focus throughout the game.

Jesus provided the perfect example of focus. He was single-minded about His mission on this earth and never let anything distract Him from fulfilling His calling. Even on the way to the cross, people spit on Him, whipped Him, and mocked Him. Jesus could have brought angels down to save Him and given up on His mission. But He was so focused on doing God's will that He refused to give in to His flesh.

As a Christian, my mission is to love God and love others, but it's impossible to stay focused on this purpose without an active relationship with God through daily prayer and devotion. When things get tough—on the field or in life—looking toward that ultimate prize can truly keep us focused on what's really important.

GO What are some things that you can start doing today that will help you stay focused on your mission?

WORKOUT Hebrews 12:1–2; James 1:2–4

OVERTIME Lord, help me to stay focused on the mission to which You have called me. Give me the strength to persevere and pursue the prize of eternal life while sharing the good news of Christ along the way. Amen.

The Relentless Competitor

Dan Britton

READY   "But we are not like those who turn away from God to their own destruction. We are the faithful ones, whose souls will be saved." —Hebrews 10:39 (NLT)

SET   Competitors love goals, and they pursue them with everything they have. They give their all—all the time. They are relentless.

Here's the bottom line: *Relentless* means to be strong, and *to relent* means to be weak. God wants us to move forward, be strong, and not give up. As followers of Christ, we must have relentless love, pursue relentless devotion, and be on a relentless mission to glorify God and bring others to Him.

We also need to be relentless competitors—competitors who have grit and guts and don't buckle, fade, or burn out. Relentless competitors keep their eyes on completing their missions and find creative solutions when things don't go as planned.

Busy competitors cover ground.

Most competitors cover ground but don't *take* ground. It's a matter of staying busy versus being strategic. Busy competitors are distracted by the tyranny of urgency and are often reactive, responding to the needs of the moment. They frequently play defense, maintain, and manage, but rarely advance.

Relentless competitors take ground.

Relentless, strategic competitors remain focused on the finish line. They are proactive and align their time, energies, and activities around the most important priorities. They are frequently on offense. They remove distractions and avoid interruptions. Relentless competitors move forward and take ground.

Kingdom competitors are relentless competitors who are strategic, not busy. They are decisive, not hesitant. Relentless competitors don't cover ground; they take ground.

GO   In what areas are you covering ground as a competitor? Taking ground?

WORKOUT   Psalm 31:24; Galatians 6:9

OVERTIME   Father, teach me how to be a relentless competitor. I ask for Your power and might to compete relentlessly all the time. Amen.

DEVOTIONS BY THEME

ACKNOWLEDGMENTS

Special thanks to the editorial team of Shea Vailes, Julie Martin, and Jordan Barnes. Special thanks to the Revell publishing team for their hard work and encouragement in this project; Jennifer Leep and Kelsey Bowen for making sure it became reality; and the FCA leadership: Les Steckel, Ken Williams, Shane Williamson, Dan Britton, Nancy Hedrick, Jeff Martin, and Rob Thomas.

Thank you to our devotional writers: Aaron Winkle, Adam Wainwright, Adrienne Sherwood, Al Schierbaum, Alex Hagler McCraney, Alex Harb, Alvin Cheng, Amanda Cromwell, Amanda Tewksbury, Amy Cullum, Amy Richards, Amy Walz, Bill Buckley, Bill Burnett, Blake Elder, Brad Holloway, Brad Tippins, Brian Roberts, Brittany Viola, Bryan Wells, Carl Miller, Chanda Husser Rigby, Charles Gee, Charlotte Smith, Cheryl Baird, Chip Mehaffey, Chris Kelsay, Chris Klein, Chris Rich, Christy Cabe, Clay Elliott, Clay Meyer, Dan Britton, Dan Frost, Danny Burns, David Gittings, David Hermes, David Lyons, David Vailes, Debbie Haliday, Delisha Milton-Jones, Donalyn Knight, Donna Miller, Donna Noonan, Eileen F. Sommi, Elliot Johnson, Fleceia Comeaux, Hal Hiatt, Harry Flaherty, Heather Price, Ish Smith, James Kirkland, Janet Turnbough, Jay Beard, Jean Driscoll, Jennifer Ruddell, Jenny Burgins, Jenny Johnson, Jere Johnson, Jess Hansen, Jill Lee, Jim Faulk, Jim Shapiro, Jimmy Page, Jo Kadlecek, Joe Matera, Joe Outlaw, Joel Schuldheisz, John Ausmus, John Crosby, John Register, Jonathan Byrd, Josh Carter, Judy Siegle, Dr. Julie Bell, Kallie Britton, Kande Speers, Kathie Woods, Kathy Malone, Ken Bakewell, Ken Kladnik, Kerry O'Neill, Kristina Krogstad,

Kristy Makris, Kyle Shultz, Larry Kerr, Laura Crawford, Lauren Holiday, Les Steckel, Lisa Fisher, Lisa Phillips, Loren Thornburg, Marc Agnello, Mark Snyder, Mark Wood, Matt Cullen, Matt Yeager, Michael Hill, Michael Wiggins, Mike Zatopek, Nancy Hedrick, Nate Bliss, Pat Street, Phil Jones, P.J. Meduri, Rachel Pace, Rebekah Trittipoe, Rex Stump, Rick Horton, Rob Potts, Roger Lipe, Roxanne Robbins, Roy Helu Jr., Ruth Riley, Sarah Rennicke, Sarah Roberts, Scott Ashton, Scott Jackson, Scott Wade, Sean McNamara, Sherri Coale, Stan Smith, Steve Beckerle, Steve Fitzhugh, Steve Keenum, Sue Ramsey, Susan Johnson, Tamika Catchings, Toby C. Schwartz, Tony Dungy, Victor Santa Cruz, Wade Hopkins, Ward Kinne, Wayne Morrow, and Zach Crowley.

IMPACTING THE WORLD THROUGH SPORTS

Since 1954, the Fellowship of Christian Athletes has challenged athletes and coaches to impact the world for Jesus Christ. FCA is cultivating Christian principles in local communities nationwide by encouraging, equipping, and empowering others to serve as examples and make a difference. FCA reaches more than two million people annually on the professional, college, high school, junior high, and youth levels. Through FCA's Four Cs of Ministry—Coaches, Campus, Camps, and Community—and the shared passion for athletics and faith, lives are changed for current and future generations.

FCA's Four Cs of Ministry

Coaches: FCA Coaches Ministry is the ministry method to coaches through huddles, events, training, and resources. FCA Coaches Ministry focuses on ministering to the heart of the coach first, and then supporting the coach as they engage with the Four Cs of Ministry.

Campus: The school campus is one of the most strategic mission fields with over 98 percent of all youth passing through this portal. FCA focuses on equipping, enabling, empowering, and encouraging student athletes, coaches, and adult leaders to impact and influence their campus for Christ.

Camps: Camp is a time of "inspiration and perspiration" for coaches and athletes to reach their potential by offering comprehensive athletic, spiritual, and leadership training. In FCA we offer seven types of camps: Sports Camps, Leadership Camps, Coaches Camps, Power Camps, Partnership Camps, Team Camps, and International Camps.

Community: FCA Community Ministry is the off-campus opportunities to reach coaches and athletes for Christ through the club and recreation sport environment.

Vision

To see the world impacted for Jesus Christ through the influence of coaches and athletes.

Mission

To present to coaches and athletes, and all whom they influence, the challenge and adventure of receiving Jesus Christ as Savior and Lord, serving Him in their relationships and in the fellowship of the church.

Values

Integrity · Serving · Teamwork · Excellence

Fellowship of Christian Athletes
8701 Leeds Road, Kansas City, MO 64129
www.fca.org fcs@fca.org 1-800-289-0909
COMPETITORS FOR CHRIST

COMPETITOR'S CREED

I am a Christian first and last.
I am created in the likeness of God Almighty to bring Him glory.
I am a member of Team Jesus Christ.
I wear the colors of the Cross.
I am a Competitor now and forever.
I am made to strive, to strain, to stretch,
and to succeed in the arena of competition.
I am a Christian Competitor and as such,
I face my challenger with the face of Christ.
I do not trust in myself.
I do not boast in my abilities or believe in my own strength.
I rely solely on the power of God.
I compete for the pleasure of my Heavenly Father, the honor
of Christ, and the reputation of the Holy Spirit.
My attitude on and off the field is above reproach—
my conduct beyond criticism.
Whether I am preparing, practicing, or playing,
I submit to God's authority and those He has put over me.
I respect my coaches, officials, teammates,
and competitors out of respect for the Lord.
My body is the temple of Jesus Christ.
I protect it from within and without.
Nothing enters my body that does not honor the Living God.
My sweat is an offering to my Master.
My soreness is a sacrifice to my Savior.
I give my all—all the time.
I do not give up. I do not give in. I do not give out.
I am the Lord's warrior—a competitor by conviction
and a disciple of determination.
I am confident beyond reason because my confidence lies in Christ.
The results of my effort must result in His glory.
Let the competition begin.
Let the glory be God's.

Sign the Creed: Go to www.fca.org
©2016 FCA

COACH'S CREED

Pray as though nothing of eternal value is going
to happen in my athletes' lives unless God does it.
Prepare each practice and game as giving
"my utmost for His highest."
Seek not to be served by my athletes for personal gain, but seek
to serve them as Christ served the church.
Be satisfied not with producing a good record,
but with producing good athletes.
Attend carefully to my private and public walk with God,
knowing that the
athlete will never rise to a standard higher than
that being lived by the coach.
Exalt Christ in my coaching, trusting the Lord will then
draw athletes to Himself.
Desire to have a growing hunger for God's Word, for personal
obedience, for fruit of the spirit, and for saltiness in competition.
Depend solely upon God for transformation—one athlete at a time.
Preach Christ's word in a Christ-like demeanor,
on and off the field of competition.
Recognize that it is impossible to bring glory to both myself
and Christ at the same time.
Allow my coaching to exude the fruit of the Spirit,
thus producing Christ-like athletes.
Trust God to produce in my athletes His chosen purposes,
regardless of whether the wins are readily visible.
Coach with humble gratitude, as one privileged to be God's coach.

**FELLOWSHIP OF
CHRISTIAN ATHLETES**

Impacting The World
For Christ Through Sports

Since 1954, the Fellowship of Christian Athletes has challenged athletes and coaches to impact the world for Jesus Christ. FCA is cultivating Christian principles in local communities nationwide by encouraging, equipping, and empowering others to serve as examples and make a difference. FCA reaches more than two million people annually on the professional, college, high school, junior high, and youth levels. Through FCA's Four Cs of Ministry—Coaches, Campus, Camps, and Community—and the shared passion for athletics and faith, lives are changed for current and future generations.

Fellowship of Christian Athletes

8701 Leeds Road • Kansas City, MO 64129

www. fca.org • fca@fca.org • 1-800-289-0909

DEVOTIONAL READINGS
FOR ATHLETES
AND COACHES

that offer memorable, biblical insights
for handling challenges and performing
with God's purposes in mind.

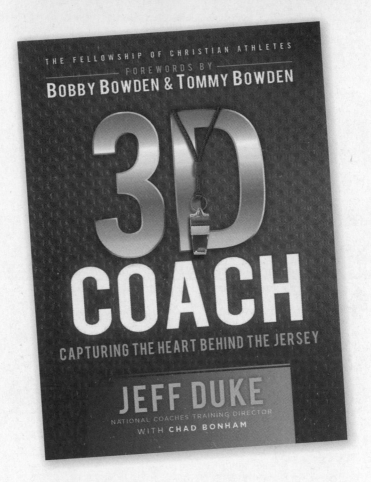

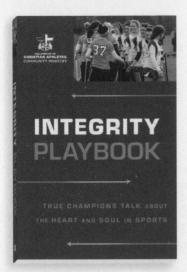
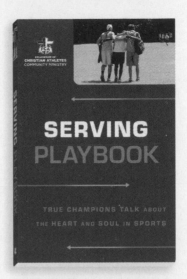
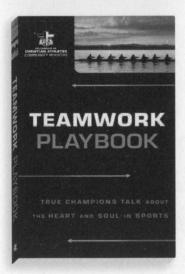
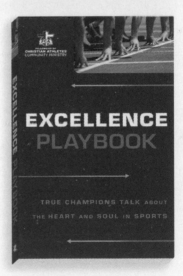